LETTERS
— OF —
SOLIDARITY
— AND —
FRIENDSHIP

LETTERS

— OF —

SOLIDARITY

— AND —

FRIENDSHIP

CZECHOSLOVAKIA
1968–71

EDITED AND INTRODUCED BY

DAVID PARKER

BACQUIER
BOOKS

ALSO BY DAVID PARKER

Ideology, Absolutism and the English Revolution.
Debates of the British Communist Historians 1940–1956 (2008)

Revolutions and the Revolutionary Tradition in the
West 1560–1991 (2000) (ed.)

First published in the UK in 2017 by
Bacquier Books
8 The Woodlands
Meltham
Holmfirth
HD9 4NN

ISBN 978-1-5262-0603-9

Cataloguing in Publication Data
A catalogue record for this publication is available
from the British Library.

Edited and brought to press by Hawkins Publishing Services (HPS)

Design, typesetting and cover design by Bobby Birchall

Printed and bound in England by T J International

CONTENTS

ACKNOWLEDGEMENTS

Without the support of Paul Zalud's son Ian, his wife Zdenka and their son David, who still live in the family home in Usti Nad Labem, it would not have been possible to publish these letters. For them they are reminders of a time of much sadness and stress. I am deeply appreciative of their agreement to allow publication of Paul's letters, including the most sensitive, as well as the lovely photograph of him with his family. Equally warm thanks go to Paul's niece, Jitka Brynjolffssen, who came to England in 1968 as a young woman. Her willingness to act as intermediary and interpreter made it possible not only to contact Paul's family, but also to communicate with them in a meaningful way. Her ready response to questions has offered reassurance that biographical errors have been avoided and enhanced my picture of the powerful personality reflected in his letters. The agreement of my brother Hilary and my sister Linda to allow me to publish letters in which they inevitably appear is also greatly appreciated.

I am also indebted to Dr Kevin McDermott of the Humanities Research Centre at Sheffield Hallam University for his answers to my numerous questions which helped to clear up many of the references to people and events in Czechoslovakia. I am grateful for his generosity in providing me with a copy of his then unpublished chapter on 'Everyday Normalisation, 1969–88', which now forms part of his book *Communist Czechoslovakia, 1945–89: A Political and Social History*. Paul Zalud's letters certainly confirm the interpretation offered in this chapter.

Others who went out of the way to respond to my request for help with significant details are Professor Karel Černý of Charles University, who resolved uncertainties over Paul Zalud's medical education, Jacob Adams at the Society of Cardiovascular Anaesthesiologists in Chicago and Judy Robins and her colleagues at the Wood Library-Museum of Anaesthesiology in Schaumburg in Illinois, USA. Thanks also go to my former colleague Professor Wendy Childs at the University of Leeds for help with Paul's passing observations about medieval history.

My indefatigable and creative editor Catherine Bradley, designer Bobby Birchall and project manager Gillian Hawkins together ensured that this venture into self-publishing has not only been stress free, but positively enjoyable. They are most warmly thanked for their care and advice; it has greatly improved the book with which they began. Finally there is no adequate way, at least in print, to thank my dear wife Margaret for her help in countless ways and for her enthusiastic support for my endeavours to bring this project to fruition.

EDITORIAL NOTE

The letters in this collection have been edited as little as possible, retaining original punctuation, spelling and the inconsistent use of both capitals and paragraph breaks. The frequently long paragraphs containing abrupt changes of content were probably not just an attempt to save paper, but also an effort to deflect the attention of the censors from certain passages. I have added a few commas here and there as my father was particularly sparing with them. Both writers were, for different reasons, prone to make up words which I have retained, and occasionally Paul, whose English was remarkable, did not find the appropriate form of the present tense. But the meaning is invariably clear. The biggest problem was that as time passed my father's failing eyesight produced some results that were almost indecipherable without looking at a keyboard to see what was meant. There were occasional blanks where his carbon paper failed and I had to work from the imprint of the typewriter keys. It was mostly possible to reconstruct what had been intended; where uncertainty remained I have used square brackets to indicate this, and similarly for words which were omitted.

At the outset I hoped to avoid imposing an overly 'academic' framework on the letters, and I hope that many readers will be able to profit from them without excessive recourse to the footnotes. However, the letters contain so many allusions to places, people and events that it became clear that, particularly for those too young to have lived through the events of 1968 or for those whose memory of them is fading, footnotes would be useful. Working on them has reminded me of how much I myself had not remembered accurately.

David Parker

January 2017

A portrait of Leslie Parker, c.1970.
Reproduced by kind permission of the artist, Alan Stones.

A photograph of Paul Zalud in 1974, with his wife Bohumila
and grandsons David (centre) and Kryštof (right).
Reproduced by kind permission of Ian Zalud.

TIMELINE

CZECHOSLOVAKIA	BRITAIN AND BEYOND

1968

	CZECHOSLOVAKIA	BRITAIN AND BEYOND
5 Jan	Alexander Dubcek replaces Antonin Novotny as Communist Party leader	
29 Jan		'Tet' military offensive by North Vietnam against the South begins
Feb	Communist Party approves extension of economic reforms	
22 Mar	Novotny resigns as President	
30 Mar	General Ludvik Svoboda elected president	
4 Apr		Martin Luther King assassinated
8 Apr	Action Programme of the CP published proposing 'a unique experiment in democratic communism' over a ten-year period, allowing other parties to stand in elections	
18 Apr	New government formed under Oldrich Cernik	
1 May	May Day celebrations show enormous popular support for reforms	
5 May	Soviet leadership expresses disapproval of developments	
10 May		Peace talks between the United States and North Vietnam begin in Paris

CZECHOSLOVAKIA	BRITAIN AND BEYOND
26 Jun Censorship officially abolished	
27 Jun 'Two Thousand Words' manifesto published by reformers calling for more radical reforms	
4 Jul Soviet military exercises in Sumava region on the Czech–West German frontier	
14 Jul	*Paul Zalud writes to* The Times
15 Jul Warsaw meeting of Communist Parties of the Soviet Union, Hungary, Poland, East Germany and Bulgaria warns Czech leaders that developments in Czechoslovakia jeopardise 'the vital interests of other socialist countries'	
29 Jul– 1 Aug Negotiations between leaders of Czech and Soviet Communist Parties. East Germany, Poland, Hungary and Soviet Union announce military exercises near Czech border	
3 Aug Leonid Brezhnev receives letter from five members of Czech Praesidium requesting military intervention to save socialism	
20 Aug Invasion of Czechoslovakia by five Warsaw Pact countries	
21 Aug	President Nicolae Ceausescu, Secretary General of the Romanian CP, condemns the invasion of Czechoslovakia

	CZECHOSLOVAKIA	BRITAIN AND BEYOND
21 Aug–25 Aug	Dubcek and other Communist Party leaders taken to Moscow and compelled to renounce parts of the reform programme and agree to presence of Soviet troops in Czechoslovakia	
22 Aug	14th Congress of the Czech Communist Party	
24 Aug		Executive of the CPGB condemns intervention in Czechoslovakia
27 Aug	Dubcek and others returned to Prague	
31 Aug	Laws abolishing censorship repealed and two new censorship offices created	
5 Oct		Civil Rights March batton charged by Royal Ulster Constabulary
31 Oct		President Johnson announces halt to bombing of North Vietnam
5 Nov		Richard Nixon wins US Presidential election

	CZECHOSLOVAKIA	BRITAIN AND BEYOND
1969		
16 Jan	Czech student Jan Palach commits suicide by setting himself on fire in protest	
20 Jan		Richard Nixon becomes President of the USA
2 Mar		Sino–Soviet border dispute leads to military clashes
21 Mar–28 Mar	Victories of Czech hockey team over the Soviet Union followed by celebrations and disturbances	
24 Mar		General Election in Northern Ireland
17 Apr	Dubcek removed from position as Party Secretary and replaced by Gustav Husak 'Normalisation' begins	
19 Apr		Riots in Bogside area of Derry following clashes between Northern Ireland Civil Rights Association marchers and Loyalists and members of the Royal Ulster Constabulary
20 Apr		British troops sent to Northern Ireland
28 Apr		General de Gaulle resigns French presidency and takes holiday in Irish Republic

	CZECHOSLOVAKIA	BRITAIN AND BEYOND
28 Apr		Resignation of N. Ireland Prime Minister O'Neil, later replaced by James Chichester Clark
8 June		Nixon announces initial withdrawal of 25,000 US troops from Vietnam
12 Jul		Riots in Derry, Belfast and Dungiven
20 Jul		American astronauts land on moon
13 Aug–15 Aug		Rioting in Belfast, culminating in 'Black Friday'
13 Aug		Further clashes on Sino–Soviet borders
24 Oct		Revolt of prisoners in Parkhurst prison, Isle of Wight
15 Nov		250,000 anti-Vietnam war protesters 'March on Washington'
15 Nov–19 Nov		33 Congress of the CPGB condemns invasion of Czechoslovakia
Dec	Dubcek made Ambassador to Turkey	

	CZECHOSLOVAKIA	BRITAIN AND BEYOND
1970		
15 Jan		End of the Nigerian (Biafran) Civil War
28 Jan	Cernik dismissed as Prime Minister and replaced by Lubomir Strougal	
2 Mar		Rhodesia declares itself a 'Republic'
28 Apr		President Nixon authorises American troops to cross the frontier from South Vietnam into Cambodia
30 Apr		President Nixon addresses the nation to explain his decision and indicates that a further 150,000 soldiers will be withdrawn
6 May	Treaty of Friendship, Cooperation and Mutual Assistance between Czeckoslavakia and the Soviet Union signed at Prague	
30 May	Dubcek recalled from Ankara	
29 May		Parliament dissolved
19 Jun		Harold Wilson loses British General Election
26 Jun	Dubcek expelled from Communist Party	
15 Jul		British dock strike
16 Jul		British Government declares State of Emergency

CZECHOSLOVAKIA	BRITAIN AND BEYOND
21 Jul	Formal negotiations begin for British entry into the Common Market
30 Jul	Dock strike ends
15 Sep	King Hussein of Jordan declares martial law after attempts to assassinate him and the hijacking of three planes by the Popular Front for the Liberation of Palestine
7 Nov	Salvador Allende becomes President of Chile
3 Dec	Burgos trial of Basque separatists begins, followed by widespread strikes in the Basque region
14 Dec	Price increases in Poland lead to five days of rioting and strikes
15 Dec	Leningrad trial of 'refusenik' would-be plane hijackers
20 Dec	Gomulka resigns as General Secretary of the Polish United Workers Party
24 Dec	Leningrad court sentences two 'refuseniks' to death (later commuted)
28 Dec	Six Basque separatists condemned to death (later commuted)

	CZECHOSLOVAKIA	BRITAIN AND BEYOND
1971		
20 Jan		British postal workers strike
1 Feb		Ford car workers strike
13 Feb		Rolls Royce nationalised
8 Mar		Postal workers strike ends
20 Mar	*Leslie and Enid move to York*	
25 Mar		Bangladesh Liberation War begins
8 Apr		Ford car workers strike ends
30 Jul		Upper Clyde Shipyard workers begin 'work in'
9 Aug		Internment without trial introduced in Northern Ireland. Twenty people die in ensuing riots
6 Sep		The Polish Communist Party publishes programme of proposed reform
6 Oct	*Leslie and Enid go to Shrewsbury*	
28 Oct		House of Commons votes to join the Common Market
9 Dec	*Leslie dies in Shrewsbury*	
16 Dec		Bangaldesh Liberation War ends

PART ONE

INTRODUCTION

On 19 July 1968, just a month before the Soviet-led invasion of Czechoslavakia brought a brutal end to the 'Prague Spring' and destroyed the dreams of 'Socialism with a Human Face',[1] the following letter, from a certain Dr Paul Zalud, appeared in *The Times*.

Sir, The "audibly rustling Times" is not yet served with breakfast in Czechoslovakia, but still we can read it two days later even in a provincial town such as Usti nad Labem.

Your thorough and fair evaluation of events in and round Czechoslovakia in your leading article, "Rumblings from Moscow" (July12), will, of course, be regarded by the diehards at Moscow and East Berlin as yet another proof of the "refined and perfidious conspiracy" of imperialists against socialism in Czechoslovakia.

The ideologists of the communist parties of the Soviet Union and of East Germany are not "prisoners of Marxist doctrine" but of what Karl R Popper calls the "conspiracy theory of society". This constitutes the basest vulgarization of Marxist doctrine. The highly ingenious attempt of Marx to explain a social event such as the present popular movement for achieving the most elementary liberties in this country quite independently of the good or bad intentions of the men who brought it about has been abandoned by the professed true Marxists of the Pravda and Neues Deutschland.

Nothing is easier and more stupid than to interpret recent developments in Czechoslovakia as the result of direct design by powerful and sinister imperialist groups. I cannot help to be reminded of the propaganda of the Nazis who explained unemployment and all social evils of

---

[1] The origin of this phrase, which was used by Alexander Dubcek and subsequently became popularised in the West, is not clear.

the thirties as the conscious design of the Learned Elders of
Zion or World Jewry

You are right in pointing out that the leaders of the Central
Committee of the Russian Communist Party have learnt little
or nothing. They are indeed using the same arguments and
threats against non-existent conspirators in Czechoslovakia as
they used against Yugoslavia and as Chinese leaders are using
against Russian and European revisionists. The hallmark of
stupidity is the failure to learn from one's mistakes.

Although no one pays heed to this kind of propaganda
here we are all acutely aware of the danger implied by
it. Whenever a conspiracy theory needs justification the
simplest tactic is to allege that it is directed against a
counter conspiracy or counter revolution.

Yours faithfully

Paul Zalud,
Usti nad Labem, Czechoslovakia, July 14

My father (hereafter Leslie), a prolific letter writer and
then 33 years a member of the British Communist Party,
evidently took great exception to this letter. He dispatched
a missive to Dr Zalud accusing him of being a counter-
revolutionary and 'fiercely upbraiding him for complaining
in *The Times* about the Communist set up'. He must have
been astounded when his 'almost gratuitous abuse', for
which he later apologised, elicited a courteous response.[2]
It turned out to be the beginning of both an extraordinary

---

[2] Letter from Leslie to his son David, 24 June 1969; see letter 6,
p.56 for Leslie's apology. Quotations without footnotes in this
introduction are taken from Leslie's correspondence with friends,
comrades and family.

epistolary saga and a deepening friendship which ended only with Leslie's death in December 1971, a month after his 73rd birthday. They became friends, as Paul Zalud so aptly said, 'by wrestling with each other'.[3] In so doing they bequeathed a remarkable set of letters which, if nothing else, are worth reading as fine examples of a dying literary form; all the more remarkable given that Paul Zalud wrote in English and Leslie's sight was so bad that he was increasingly unable to check his own prose.

This did not prevent him turning out an almost continuous stream of typewritten letters, interrupted in September 1969 – when he suffered two heart attacks – and again by the strike of postal workers from 20 January to 8 March 1971. For much of 1970 Leslie wrote once or even twice a week. Of his initial diatribe there is no trace. He might have destroyed it in a fit of embarrassment, but the fact that he followed up with at least two more letters in September and October 1968, of which there is also no trace, suggests that the decision to retain copies was not made at the outset. Subsequently Leslie assiduously filed them all. Apart from four letters, probably written by hand at moments when he was deprived of his typewriter, the 61 reproduced here almost certainly constitute the entire output, from 26 November 1968 to 19 October three years later.

Not surprisingly Paul, who had onerous work and family commitments, replied at somewhat longer intervals; but the only significant gaps occurred during the Spring of 1969 when the Soviet imposed policy of 'normalisation' began to bite'. 'As your last letter,' he wrote to Leslie on 10 May, 'was defiled by the hands of the censor I felt disinclined to continue

---

[3] Letter 26, p.122.

in our exchange of news and views. Now I am using a holiday in Yugoslavia to give some news about us and Czechoslovakia.'[4] Apart from one letter Paul did not write again until the beginning of September, when a trip to Germany, which he sensed would be his last to the West, gave him another opportunity to do so. Both men were in an almost continuous state of anxiety, frustration or anger about the surveillance of their letters and the difficulties of sending newspapers and books from England which, if selected unwisely, might well not reach their destination. In early 1970 Leslie, hearing of many arrests, feared that Paul might be among them.[5] Paul was equally on edge. On 9 July he sent a picture postcard asking whether Leslie had received his last letter, and saying that he was 'feeling tense as I haven't heard from you for more than a week'. A year later, confronted by the increasingly indecipherable results of Leslie's inability to hit the correct typewriter keys, Paul wrote that he was 'shivering at the dreading [sic] thought that some stupid nosy-poker might mistake your typing errors for a secret encoded message'.[6] At about the same time Leslie wrote to me saying that he had not received a letter from Paul for eight weeks and asking if I could use contacts in the medical world to make enquiries about his whereabouts. He stressed that it was 'most advisable for the efforts to be very discreet'.

Given the men's shared fears of interference, one might have supposed that their letters would have been cautiously mundane and trivial. At one moment Paul warns Leslie that he had to choose his words carefully

---

[4] Letter 7, p.62.

[5] Letter from Leslie to David, 17 January 1970.

[6] Letter 88, p.343.

and to avoid certain topics. At another he ostensibly declines Leslie's invitation to write a thousand words about the effects of the Soviet invasion. Yet his letters contain many thousands which do exactly that, providing an eloquent but grim insight into the process of 'normalisation' and its impact on him, his family, his colleagues and the political regime. The mood is lightened by a few anti-regime jokes that maybe even the censors enjoyed. At times both men used satire and irony, flavouring their attacks on all things Stalinist and neo-Stalinist with a bitter wit; at other times their criticisms were plain and unconcealed. Leslie did not spare the leaders of the Communist countries from his almost total contempt for the world's leading politicians, and with his letters he regularly dispatched copies of the *Morning Star*, the *Guardian* or *Weekly Guardian* and extracts from *The Times,* all resolutely opposed to the Soviet invasion. Despite his anxieties, Paul seemed surprised by the amount that got through. 'Since the beginning of May,' he wrote on 16 June 1970, 'all newspapers and weeklies my friends from abroad were sending me remained undelivered, except those letters and packets from my friend, Leslie Parker. He seems to enjoy a privileged position with our mail-robbers and I am damned glad about it.'[7]

In some ways the letters themselves require no introduction. Readers may prefer to turn straight to them, skipping over or returning later to the few paragraphs which follow as these are written with the benefit of hindsight and use supplementary information about the two men. As they never met, nor ever communicated except by their letters, reading

---

[7] Letter 45, p.183.

them blind is certainly a way of sharing the journey as Paul and Leslie made it. There is no way that my own observations can do justice to the remarkable blend of the political and the personal in their exchanges, which often move in a few lines from commentaries on the state of the world to family news. The letters may be read in different ways for different purposes: as an historical source casting a grim light on 'normalisation' in Czechoslovakia, or as a reminder of the equally depressing picture elsewhere – in Vietnam, Northern Ireland, the Middle East and Bangladesh; as a political and philosophical debate; or simply as a testimony to the power of friendship and solidarity in the most difficult times.

✦ ✦ ✦

Why Leslie was so annoyed by Paul's letter to *The Times* remains something of a mystery to me. He later, rather unconvincingly, offered an explanation based on the perfidious nature of the capitalist press and its mercenary journalists, a theme to which he warmed on more than one occasion. He would have been 'delighted', he told Paul, had he written to the *Morning Star* rather than *The Times*, 'for there you would have received both encouragement and strong criticism'.[8] But Leslie was in fact a close follower of *The Times*. On 12 August he had drawn my own attention to its prominent coverage of the progress of reform in Czechoslovakia, and of the incipient threat presented by the manoeuvres of Warsaw Pact troops on its frontiers; just a few months later he wrote to a British comrade saying that he had thought of

---

[8] Letter 6, p.56.

sending *The Times* 'some stuff ... as the Party
would not like it'.

I wonder whether Leslie ever realised that he had
completely failed to grasp the essential thrust of
Paul's letter. This could have been because it was read
out to him, and an initial intemperate reaction was
not followed by a careful consideration of its contents.
Paul's clear intention was to dispute the claim made
by *The Times* that 'The ideologists of the communist
parties of the Soviet Union and of East Germany' were
'prisoners of Marxist doctrine'. On the contrary, he
declared; it was 'the basest vulgarization of Marxist
doctrine' which led them to 'interpret recent
developments in Czechoslovakia as the result of direct
design by powerful and sinister imperialist groups'.
There was absolutely nothing in this argument with
which Leslie actually disagreed, as will become clear to
any reader of the ensuing correspondence. While Leslie
and Paul frequently clashed over the comparative virtues
and iniquities of capitalism on the one hand and the
existing socialist regimes on the other, they were at one
in their criticism of those in both the West and the East
who transformed Marxism into a closed and repressive
ideology – akin, in Leslie's view, to an arid theology.
'Marxists,' he wrote to the recently retired head of the
Communist Party's Education Department in September
1968, 'are [the] greatest producers of conceptual
language the world has ever known. We can mistake
a concept for a fact as quick as any theologian.'
Elsewhere he wrote that:

> For a long time we have been accustomed
> to think of Marx (and Lenin too) as prophets
> that do no wrong and who embrace all
> philosophical conclusions in such a way that

24

they cannot be contradicted. As I brought
myself up in a manner which has bred a certain
amount of scepticism I am glad to be relieved
of this in regard to Marx as I was deburdened
when I threw off the theological weight of the
Perfect Jesus.

This was no off the cuff remark. Before joining the
Communist Party in 1935 Leslie had been an Anglican
priest for ten years, having previously completed a four-
year training course at Kelham Theological College.
As he had left school at 14 to work first in a foundry
and then as a rent collector, this was an undoubted
achievement. Yet from the outset Leslie was never at
ease with himself or the Church. His unease deepened
in 1926 during the General Strike when he was the
curate 'attached to a tin church somewhere near the
racecourse' in Brighton; his vicar vetoed his suggestion
that they might open the church hall to the strikers
while the archdeacon 'sent a telegram of pure adoration
to Churchill who was managing the business'. Leslie
never forgave either the archdeacon or Churchill. 'Seven
years later I left the C of E, and had I known of the CP I
would have left it there and then.'[9] Elsewhere he recalled
how he 'struggled with the C of E for ten long years after
I carried with me day by day an utter sense of failure... I
came to regard the C of E as a monstrosity kept in being
by the most grossly ignorant lot of professional officials.'
Yet when Leslie left the Church he regretted the loss
of the people he had met. To some he remained very
close; at the same time that he was writing at length
to Paul he was also writing at length to long-standing

[9] Letter from Leslie to the Secretary of the Communist Party History
Group, 22 July 1968.

Christian friends.[10] While composing an essay on the
problems of communist government, he was writing an even
longer one on early Christianity. In the last months of his
life, as Leslie told Paul, he was 'reading', with the aid of his
belatedly acquired talking machine, 'a nicely scholarly and
thoughtful book on St Augustine of Hippo'.[11]

Apart from old friends Leslie brought two guiding
ideas from his Christian education. One was a belief that
history – to which he had been introduced at college – was
more important than philosophy, and that facts were to
be preferred to theory. At the end of April 1968 he happily
noted that it had been agreed to hold a Communist Party
District School on actual developments in socialist countries
rather than to use an old syllabus on the development of
socialism. 'When I turned my back on Plato,' he wrote, 'I put
away childish things like discussing general principles. ... If
Marx goes down to [sic] history he will go down primarily
as a historian and not as a writer of an elementary book on
dialectical principles.' The second legacy of his Christian
training was the belief that socialism could not be conceived
simply as 'an economic system without any recognition of
the need to meet the cultural as well as the physical needs
of the people'.[12] Without a humanist quality in communist
government, he insisted, 'we shall be a vanguard with nothing
to guard'.[13] Marx, he reminded Paul, had said that socialism
would have been impossible without the Christian ethic:

---

[10] Letter 91, pp.354–5 for his tribute to the closest of these friends
after his death in July 1971.

[11] Letter 92, p.358.

[12] Letter to *Country Standard*, 30 April 1968. *Country Standard* was
the CPGB-led journal for rural affairs published from 1935, mainly
from Norfolk. It is still available online.

[13] Letter to Jack Cohen, recently head of the Communist Party
Education Department, 16 September 1968.

Marx and Lenin largely thought much about
gaining power, Lenin to some extent how to
keep power. But neither gave any thought as
to how to govern in a socialist country. If
future communist governments think they can
do this and ignore the long tradition of moral
teaching that has always been woven into the
political cloth of socialism they could not be
more wrong.[14]

Long before the Soviet-led invasion of Czechoslovakia
created yet another crisis for the international communist
movement, Leslie was deeply concerned about the damage
done by what he described as a 'primitive' communism.[15]
He grasped in a way that eluded many of his comrades
how Stalin had 'bloodied the image of the Communist
Party', making it difficult to turn the Party's considerable
influence in the workplace into political growth. He was
fond of quoting comrade Ivor Montagu's view that it would
take the British party 20 to 30 years to recover from the
1956 invasion of Hungary.[16] In November 1963 Leslie took
issue with the Executive Committee's view that 'temporary
setbacks' in the USSR had been overcome both there and
in Britain. 'Had Russia not suffered from Stalinism the
forces which its cessation released in such power might
never have been frustrated.'[17] In May 1968, writing to a
member of his own party branch, he declared that:

[14] Letter 6, p.62.

[15] Letter 96, p.375.

[16] Ivor Goldsmid Samuel Montagu (1904–84), distinguished
filmmaker, producer and critic.

[17] Letter to the National Executive Committee of the CPGB,
14 November 1963.

All intelligently read people will need positive assurance that there is a real core of humanism and human idealism resident in Marxism–Leninism. They won't want England to be like Cuba, or C-Slovakia, or Russia or China; they want a dependable leadership and to a certain extent an answerable one, not an oligarchy and certainly not [a] Father Figure, either Santa Klaus or Santa Stalin.

On 18 July Leslie wrote to the General Secretary, John Gollan, expressing alarm about the deteriorating relations between the Soviet Union and Czechoslovakia. 'It would be pretty calamitous for the growth of our Party if USSR armed forces rearranged the government in Czechoslovakia,' he observed.

In the longer run this proved to be the case. While a majority of members and branches supported the Executive Committee's rapid and unequivocal condemnation of the Soviet-led intervention, a substantial minority continued to oppose it. At the 31st Congress in November 1969 the opposition mustered 118 votes, nearly 29 per cent of the delegates. Increasingly bitter divisions reflecting fundamentally divergent conceptions of socialism resurfaced over revisions to the Party programme and then in a battle for control of the *Morning Star*, which the Party lost in 1985. Four years later the collapse of the communist regimes served only to hasten the latter's demise.[18]

Yet in 1968 nobody, in either the West or the East, foresaw such an outcome. In the few years still left to

---

[18] The present Communist Party of Britain was founded in 1988, in opposition to the legally distinct Communist Party of Great Britain which was dissolved in 1991.

Leslie the Communist Party might even have received a slight boost from its stance on Czechoslovakia. New recruits were made; some who had left the party came back to it. These were years of increasing labour militancy and industrial strife. Communists led the work of the Liaison Committee for the Defence of Trade Unions. Jimmy Reed and his comrades became national heroes for their leadership of the famous 'work in' to save shipbuilding on the Upper Clyde. Communist 'universities' offered lively and open discussion to increasing numbers of students. These were also the years of rising opposition to the Vietnam war, of a successful international campaign to free the black American communist Angela Davis, and in November 1970 a Marxist President was elected in Chile.

Leslie, for all his scepticism and independence of mind, had no doubts that his membership of the Communist Party had a purpose. 'We ourselves did not join the C.P. because we loved the Party,' he wrote to Paul. 'We joined it because we realised that in Britain it was the only possible instrument for organising any movement towards socialism.'[19] While he was equally dismissive of those who clung to ideas 'of dramatic upheaval and chaos' which 'we could well do without'[20] and of those who waited for socialism to arrive 'by accident' or 'through the USSR navy sailing up the Thames',[21] he never doubted that ending capitalism was the indispensable condition for the full flowering of human potential, both collectively and individually.

[19] Letter 6, p.57.

[20] Letter to John Gollan, General Secretary of the CPGB, 21 August 1968.

[21] Letter 59, p.231.

'The fact that you are on the other side of the Revolution,' he told Paul in December 1968, 'is of absolute importance. While I am quite, quite convinced that the absence of exploitation of man by man is by no means anything but the basis of socialism, without that basis ... life is just uncertainty and anxiety.'[22]

At this point Leslie's convictions confronted Paul's personal and deeply unhappy experience of socialism. 'You are saying,' Paul countered, 'we are on the other side of the socialist revolution and that is of great importance. Alright! But the chief lesson of the Czechoslovakian crisis is that the social revolution is a necessary but not a sufficient condition for abolishing the exploitation of man by man.'[23] Returning to the same question in August 1971, he appreciated that Leslie understood that:

> We are far from this happy state of affairs, but you still maintain that through a change in property relations the SU and the other socialist states have gained a momentous leverage point which puts them in a moral rank order highly above all western industrial countries. To think so is a very big error and contrary to all known facts.

While Paul was happy to agree that it was a moral duty 'to work for a just, democratic and egalitarian society', he demurred at the idea there were 'iron laws of history 'and that 'the desirable state of society or mankind must necessarily become a reality'. This was

---

[22] Letter 2, p.40.

[23] Letter 3, p.44.

to try and 'prove too much'. How justified Paul was in seeing in Leslie's approach an almost religious faith in the unfolding of 'iron laws of history' the reader may judge, but he was more than able to challenge Leslie on Marxist terrain. 'All we can say with Marx and Engels,' he insisted, 'is that "We make our own history".'[24]

What Leslie clearly did not expect when he first sallied forth to berate Paul for writing to *The Times* was to discover that he and his two brothers had been members of the Czech Communist Party from their youth. Indeed, it seems that Paul had spent two spells in jail as a result of this in the late 1920s or early 1930s. His parents owned the village store in the remote Bohemian village of Kvilda, less than two miles from the German frontier – part of the Sudetenland annexed by Germany in October 1938. Fortunately by then Paul, the eldest son whose high ambitions would have received the family blessing, had completed six years of medical training at the Germany University of Prague. Just before the Nazi invasion of March 1939 he fled with his wife and infant son to England, where they were welcomed into the Oxford family home of well-known British communists. In 1941 it became possible for refugee doctors to acquire temporary registration in England, and Paul became resident surgeon and trainee neurosurgeon at Southmeads Hospital in Bristol. The same year he left the Communist Party because, as he told Leslie, 'The facts in 1941 were in striking contrast to the expected consequences and the standards of behaviour entailed by the theory. That is why I left the theory and the C.P. Then I was condemned

---

[24] Letter 97, p.380. See the opening of Marx's *The Eighteenth Brumaire of Louis Bonaparte* (1852) for his statement that 'Men make their own history'.

by Dr. Goldstucker,[25] by my two brothers and by my friends at the local group of our Czech party organization at Oxford.'[26]

As soon as the war ended, despite an affection for England which he never lost, Paul returned to Prague with a group of health workers to look after concentration camp victims. He was allocated a place in a hospital in Usti nad Labem and stayed there for the rest of his career (choosing not to join the flood of doctors, or his brothers, who emigrated during the Prague Spring). Dissatisfied by the absence of a team of specialised anaesthetists with whom to work, he immersed himself in the theory and practice of anaesthesiology. 'His single-minded goal,' he later recorded, was 'building a unit of intensive care which puts an anaesthesiologist right back into general medicine'.[27] By the time he was writing to Leslie he was head of a sizeable Department of Anaesthetics (and Intensive Care), while the hospital had become a regional centre with a postgraduate training unit. Paul retired as head of department in February 1978 but continued to teach, passing on his expertise to future generations of anaesthesiologists. He died in 1988, aged 76. From 1991 his pioneering role was honoured and reflected in an annual conference of anaesthetists

---

[25] Eduard Goldstucker (1913–2000). A member of the Czech government in exile during the Second World War, who in 1948 became Ambassador to Israel. Although jailed for five years under the Novotny regime, Goldstucker remained in the Communist Party. In 1968 he was both an MP and President of the Union of Writers, which was to the forefront of the Prague Spring. Goldstucker fled to Britain in 1969, where he became Professor of Comparative Literature at Sussex University. After returning to Czechoslovakia in 1991, he retained his communist beliefs.

[26] Letter 45, p.182.

[27] Letter to Enid Parker, 7 November 1974.

and intensivists called Zalud's Days ('*zaludovy dny*').
Paul's professional stature was such that it may partly
explain why he got away with expressing himself so
freely in many of his letters to Leslie, although he was
often shabbily treated.

The satisfaction Paul gained from his professional
achievements compensated barely, if at all, for the
terrible personal tragedies he endured. The first, of which
there is no mention in his letters, was the loss of his
Jewish parents, two uncles, four aunts and three cousins
in the holocaust. The second was the death of his sister-
in-law and niece in a plane crash as they left London
for Prague in 1945. The third, and hardest to bear, was
the suicide of his elder son Peter at the age of 33 in
November 1969. Paul's letter bearing the news to Leslie
a few weeks later is the most poignant of all. Sadly the
mental disabilities to which Peter succumbed reproduced
themselves in the next generation, and the strain of
coping with a disturbed grandchild weighed heavily on
all the family in Paul's last years. Paul himself, as his
letters reveal, went through bouts of depression and
morbidity – on occasion sufficiently acute to cause Leslie
to write in real alarm. He also smoked heavily.

There were indeed reasons enough to explain this:
isolation from the outside world, lack of reading
material, lack of resources at the hospital, lack of
consumer goods, overwork and insufficient pay – not
to mention highly intrusive bureaucratic-cum-political
surveillance. Through all of this Leslie strove to maintain
Paul's morale, supplying him not only with reading
material, but also with other things either unavailable
or unaffordable as Czechoslovakia turned inwards:
some quality knitting wool for Paul's wife Bohumila,
a saxophone reed for his son Ian, a little cash to spend
in the foreign currency shop on their grandson and even

a suit length of good Yorkshire cloth for Paul himself. Above all, despite his own poor health and frustrating battles with his typewriter, Leslie wrote as often as he could.

The sadness which descended over the Zalud household when they learned of Leslie's death was palpable. Although Paul continued for a while to exchange occasional letters with my mother Enid, and in 1972 she fulfilled a promise to visit the Zalud family, by 1979 the correspondence had petered out. Paul lived for longer after that than he expected, but the smoking eventually caught up with him, as he knew it would. Already in February 1978, aged only 66, he told Enid that he could no longer go skiing with his grandson 'as the bus journey and walking uphill is too much for me'.[28] Nonetheless he was spared a few more years than had been allowed to Leslie. On April 2 1988 Paul wrote to his brother blaming his own 'idiotic stupidity' for his chronic bronchitis, emphysema and ischemic heart disease. 'But it is futile to increase my misery by self accusation. The severe limitation of my exercise capacity, sleeplessness and early awakening, endless boredom, all the wretchedness of old age and the 'niceties' of life in a socialist country are enough of a punishment.'[29] He went on to say that he was nonetheless attempting to break new ground by studying molecular biology and genetics. Six days later Paul collapsed in the garden. He died in hospital without ever regaining consciousness.

---

[28] Letter to Enid Parker, 26 February 1978.

[29] I am grateful to Paul's niece, Mrs Jitka Brynjolffsen, for a copy of this letter and permission to reproduce it.

PART TWO

THE LETTERS

1968

OCTOBER TO DECEMBER

The first letter which survives is that from Paul to Leslie on 28 October. But it is clear that after Leslie's initial broadside to Paul, probably written in late July, there was at least one exchange of letters between the two men before Leslie began to store them. Paul almost certainly spent part of his annual leave at a conference in London during September. His decision to return to his home country after the Soviet invasion had ended the democratic reforms of the brief 'Prague Spring' while his two brothers joined the stream of exiles was a momentous one for him and his family.

At the end of October Paul appeared to retain some hope that the 'brave rearguard action' of the Czech Communist Party in defence of its 'right to manage its own affairs' might have a positive outcome. But just a few weeks later, in his letter of 5 December, he reported that the Czech party had been reduced to seeking the approval of their Soviet comrades for its public statements. He also disabused Leslie of the latter's hope that the Czech economy would improve for 'the Russians have completely wrecked the carefully worked out programme of economic reforms...'. This exchange also brings to the fore the divergent historico–political perspectives of the two men which colour much of the later correspondence.

1

28th October 1968.

Dear Mr. Parker,

Thank you very much for your kind letters and the newspaper you forwarded to me. While I spent my annual leave abroad 30 000 Czechs and Slovaks, among them many doctors, left the country. I decided to return home to pull in the same yoke with other men.[30] So far my family and I are alright. It is comforting to see that the CPGB is rebuking the double mindedness of the Russians who identify proletarian internationalism with the reckless promotion of their own imperial policy. The battle is by no means all finished. The CP of Czechoslovakia is fighting a brave rearguard action. The question at stake is, of course, whether the Communist Party of any country has the right to manage its own affairs and to safeguard the rights and interests of its own people. You in the UK ought to know that Russian officers are busy to foment disunion and sedition against the cherished leaders of the Czech and Slovak Communist Party who are still wholeheartedly supported by the workers and all other section of the two nations. While proclaiming non-interference in our internal affairs the Russians and East-Germans do everything to reshape the affairs of this country according to their own unexceptional, and unchallengeable Stalinist line.

With best wishes to you and your wife
Yours sincerely

Paul Zalud

---

[30] It is almost certain that Paul attended the Congress of The World Federation of Societies of Anaesthesiologists, which was held in London in September 1968.

2

Shoreham-by-Sea, Sussex, England
26 November 1968.

Dear Doctor Zulad,

Forgive me if my promises have not been fulfilled.
Perhaps I ponder imaginary difficulties. Not only do I
not know how much you know of what is going in the
capitalist world, but I am unable to think what you
would like to know about it. It is a gloomy November
for everyone I think. Mr. Wilson, our Prime Minister,
who when first elected with a large majority was going
to lead the country into a new world of technological
splendour and economic rewards, started off his new
world by increasing the unemployed by 100,000 and
[they] gradually increased from about 300,000 to nearly
600,000. In 1949 the then Labour Government devalued
the £ 30% since when the £ has misbehaved itself with
startling intransigence. The present Labour Party full
of capitalist rectitude has devalued the wretched thing
several times since. Now it dances a defenceless jig
before King D-Mark and Gauleiter de Gaulle refuses to
devalue his holy franc and bow out of the competitive
picture. When De Gaulle refused to let Britain enter the
E.E.C. he was derided and sneered at by all reputable
journalists in the USA and the UK but now this peculiar
phenomenon is gloomily regarded with a mixture of
suspicion and respect. Suspicion because he is not doing
the right thing don't cher know old boy, and respect
because he is going to keep the workers in order. Added
to this fracas is Mr Wilson's recent increase in the price
of petrol, purchase tax on many goods, a whopping
increase on whisky and some increases on other alcoholic

beverages – all presumably designed by a dialectical providence not only for the purpose of slaking our thirsts but of producing a state happily devoid of any mundane considerations.

Meanwhile the Tories have really set upon Mr. Wilson but only succeeded in putting the whole of the Labour MPs behind him. They have also startled the country with their proposals (Tory proposals) to cancel all free school meals, to reduce still further school milk, to make people pay for a visit to the doctor, to reduce expenditure on hospital building (little enough already) and maintenance and above all to produce a value tax on all consumer goods, reduce tax on stock exchange profits, on the corporation profits and on the higher incomes. The Tories feel they are riding swiftly towards political power when the next election comes. They may be counting their chickens well before they are hatched for their recommendations for the 'stabilising of the economy' will weigh more heavily on the lower income groups than anything the present Labour Government has yet done.

One thing is quite definite in my mind. Difficult and cramped as the position of people is in other parts of the world the fact that you are on the other side of the Revolution is of absolute importance. While I am quite, quite convinced that the absence of exploitation of man by man is by no means anything but the basis of socialism, without that basis ... life is just uncertainty and anxiety, the probability of world devastation and the necessity of social revolution. The furore in the capitalist papers about the invasion of C-S has died down here. Nevertheless many anxious eyes scan the papers for real news of your country. We realise the pressure to be great but I myself am pretty well convinced that though you may be taking two steps backwards you actually took three or even more steps forward. If the Czech economy begins to thrive on a reanimated agriculture and industry in which people are deriving satisfaction from accepting responsibility and displaying initiative then a still greater basis is laid, which must result in cultural benefits that we communists here long for you to possess.

Our own Party here conducted a great number of discussions on the invasion. Every Branch voted on it, every member wrote and said what he liked and finally every District Congress treated it with grave concern. The results were varied. Some voted for the Executive Committee's declared opposition to the invasion simply [because] they wished to be loyal, some voted on behalf of the invasion, but I think the general majority against the Russian move was about 3 or 4 to 1. The majority at our (Sussex) District Congress was 19 to 4. In my own Branch 14 for 2 dubious. Our Party has many members over 50 and quite a lot over 60 and many have been taught to regard the Russian govt as both miraculous and infallible. I have never been a lover of infallibility except my own when I have a disagreement with my wife. At the present time the C.P.G.B. is standing out against joining the proposed anti-imperialist conference of all fraternal parties etc. in May. We are in a difficult position. While we are not in love with imperialism we do not feel inclined to wipe the USSR slate clean. The Moscow PRAVDA accused us of 'following the dictates of Washington during the Hungary crisis and the precepts of Bonn during the invasion C-S'. We are not exactly ravished by this opinion. Another question also arises – does being anti-imperialist mean always agreeing with the foreign policy of the USSR? Many Communists in the West say R's foreign policy is concerned with stabilising the status quo internationally. We cannot remember when the USSR particularly went out of its way to help the Western Parties. What we have accomplished we have accomplished by sheer tenacity in the British Isles and in France and Italy by work based on the heroism of the partisans, freedom fighters etc. In all the long history of Stalin I can never remember him pursuing any policy that positively helped the cause of the western parties. Nor do I see any evidence that the USSR govt is doing that. Of course we may be wrong in our estimation. On the other hand we are forced to try in our own ways to defend the existence of the Communist countries. If they were to go the salvation of humanity would be put back possibly centuries. The communist countries are of infinite trouble to the capitalists whose principal vocation appears to lie in making the poor poorer and the rich exceedingly rich. I am daily more astonished at the gulf that exists and widens between the have and the have nots. Nothing you have read in your papers about this gulf, say in the USA, could be an exaggeration. So our choice of attendance at this Conference is one likely to produce a headache.

It would give us great pleasure to send you a Christmas gift. We understand you like English textiles. If you and your wife would be willing to accept our gifts perhaps you would send your shirt collar size and your wife's bust size. If however you would prefer something else – books? I'm afraid I can't think beyond clothes and books but I'm tolerably convinced our shops do sell other things.

With every good wish, yours sincerely,

Leslie Parker

3

Usti Nad Labem, Czechoslovakia
5 December 1968.

Dear Mr. and Mrs. Parker,

Thank you very much for your very kind letter, Morning
Star and the cuttings from The Times. We very much
appreciate your kindness in offering to send us a Christmas
gift but we really do not want anything in particular. If you
are determined to express your sympathy in this way you
may send something for our 2 years old grandson David
whom we both love very much.

You are saying that many readers are scanning the papers
for real news from this country but apparently in vain. This
is hardly surprising. All our newsmen and reporters who are
the most experienced in finding out what people think and
say are prevented by fear from presenting the truth. I am
enclosing the caricature which has led to the banning of the
weekly organ of the Czechoslovak journalists. This picture
has been originally published by a Russian newspaper,
refers to state visits in Washington and is an allusion to the
outcome of the Moscow negotiations.

There is an interesting bit of news which you may have
missed. On November 15th or 16th while the Central
Committee of the CP was still in session Mr Dubcek and
other party leaders paid a surprise visit to Brezhnev who was
attending the Congress of the Polish party at Warsaw. The
purpose of the visit was to ask Mr. Brezhnev for his approval
of the resolution adopted and permission to publish it! This
dependency of the Czech CP had a most damaging effect. If
not even the supreme body of the CP is free to decide what
it regards best for the people of this country, how much
freedom, people are arguing, is left for the rest of the people!

You are saying we are on the other side of the socialist revolution and that is of great importance. Alright! But the chief lesson of the Czechoslovakian crisis is that the social revolution is a necessary but not a sufficient condition for abolishing the exploitation of man by man. Without democratic control of the office-holders and freedom to criticize them oppression and exploitation of the majority of the people by a small gang of power lusty bureaucrats continues. We have learned this lesson throughout 23 years. The expropriation of the means of production and the verbal declaration that the proletariat has been raised to the position of the ruling class is by no means a foolproof device to do away with exploitation.

Palme Dutt[31] in his ideological justification and apology of the invasion of Czechoslovakia accuses the party leadership of having given away too many vantage points and key positions in the press and radio. The party is certainly controlling now the means of communication and has curbed the freedom of the press. But this is not good enough for the USSR. They are issuing and distributing a newspaper called 'Zpravy' and are operating a wireless station broadcasting in Czech and Slovakian. These means of opinion formation are neither owned by the CP nor controlled by it, on the contrary, their continuous use is against our laws and constitution. The kind of information spread by those illegal means shows clearly to everybody to what ends the Russians want the Czech CP to use means of mass-communications.

You say 'If the Czech economy begins to thrive...', but the facts are that the Russians have completely wrecked the carefully worked out programme of economic reforms which could have saved this country from bankruptcy.

---

[31] Rajani Palme Dutt, editor of *Labour Monthly* and leading opponent in the British Communist Party of the Executive's condemnation of the Soviet invasion of Czechoslovakia.

Why should the workers now work harder, why the managers accept responsibility and display initiative if this country has been forced to accept economic policies contrary to our interests? There are already now some sinister symptoms of still worse things to come. Prices are rising, people are frantically shaping and hoarding goods. There are special stores at Prague where the holder of convertible foreign currency, respective for tokens from relatives from abroad can buy Western goods. Goods were stocked for Christmas. These goods are now sold to Russian officers and their wives although the Rouble is not convertible. I am told that Russia on her part will not accept payment in roubles but only in currency for goods they are selling to us. I am asking you, Mr. Parker, why do you affix the label 'imperialism' only to the highly developed industrial countries of the West if we hear of business transactions such as I have just described to you? The result of all this is that a thousand doctors, highly skilled technicians, engineers and scientists are daily leaving the country with a large number of party members among them and that in spite of some travel restrictions, recently imposed.

I am very sorry that I cannot report any good news in a more cheerful tone. I have also to concede that I myself feel already uncomfortable to discuss politics with you as I am not a party member. I really would much rather do what most people are doing now, turning away from public affairs. I shall soon submerge myself in medical and scientific literature as I did before January 1968.

You did certainly your best to give us some hope and cheer us up. My wife and myself never doubted the extreme kindness of the British people and we also believe in the inherent goodness of our own people.

With best wishes and a 'Merry Christmas' to you

Yours sincerely

Paul Zalud

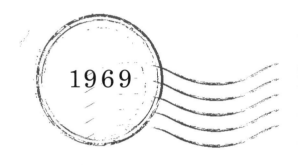

1969

JANUARY TO DECEMBER

During this year, ushered in by the self-immolation of Czech student Jan Palach, the process of 'normalisation' rapidly gathered pace. Paul's letter of 21 January was mildly but surprisingly optimistic. He noted that 'we are still enjoying a large measure of personal freedom' which 'we owe to the courage and tenacity of purpose of President Svobada and men like A. Dubcek, Smrkovsky and Cernik. As long as they are holding positions of power we can feel fairly safe'. Although Dubcek clung on to his post as general secretary of the Communist Party for another three months, Paul's optimism evaporated almost immediately. Intimidated by the censors' interference with Leslie's lengthy and highly political reply, Paul wrote to him on only three occasions between 21 January and 21 September – two of these when briefly permitted to travel abroad, once for an uplifting holiday in Yugoslavia and once for a conference at Saarbrucken. From the safety of Germany he observed that 'after a year of relentless blackmail, shameless meddling in our affairs, often appalling distortions and falsifications of history and the true state of affairs, the Russians have finally achieved what they call normalisation: a nasty and brutish police state'. Returning to the 'dreary land of socialism', he was well aware that this may have been his 'last journey to the West for many years to come', but evidently resolved to take up the epistolary cudgels again, filling out in some wonderfully terse prose a graphic picture of the stresses of daily life in a 'normalised' world. More or less at the same time Leslie's own flow of letters was interrupted when he suffered two heart attacks. Communications had barely been re-established before they brought devastating news of the suicide of Paul's eldest son.

Apart from some discussion of the reasons for East Germany's superior economic performance, Leslie did not return to the problems of the socialist countries after the early violation of his correspondence. No doubt the censors would have found less to object to in his disquisitions on the double standards of the Western press, the misdeeds of the Labour government, the explosive situation in Ireland and the growing opposition to the American onslaught on Vietnam. They may even have shared Paul's appreciation of the descriptions of the Parker family and its doings which were so much part of Leslie's endeavour to sustain the morale of his Czech friend.

4

Shoreham-by-Sea, Sussex, England
20 January 1969.

Dear Doctor Zalud,

The nicest present I think I had at Christmas was the
photograph of your David. I suppose it was taken last
summer. He is therefore very satisfactory I am sure as
the grandson of a medical man – good physique, almost
too good looking (?) and obviously being so concentrated
of unusual intelligence. I suppose one day he will be a
grandfather, so we must therefore do our best to lay the
foundations of a liberal socialism. This is no mean task
but one that simply has to be accomplished.

We too have a David but a son for we have as yet
no grandchild. Our David is 28 in March, has just had
his thesis accepted for a D. Phil at Liverpool University
where he took his first degree. He is an assistant lecturer
in French History of the 17th and 18th CC in Leeds
University. Leeds is one of our largest cities, as possibly
you will remember; it is situated in Yorkshire, where the
people work hard, the factories make a lot of soot, the
men go to see football matches in almost unprecedented
crowds and afterwards drink beer in vast enough
quantities to bring joy to the hearts of those who have
shares in breweries. David is much devoted to his work,
his wife and his political work. He was [so] successful in
speaking on the c-slovak question at his District Congress
that 90% voted [against] the Russian govt's defence of the
invasion. Most of these were working men who are quite
a bit sceptical of 'the intellectuals'.

While we know to our cost the misuses that capitalist
newspapers put their freedom, exaggerating the sins of

the socialist countries, hiding the wickedness of the capitalist countries and indeed praising people like Johnson for upholding freedom in Vietnam etc, etc, we are very much convinced that publication of the truth is a very necessary part of a journalist's debt to his fellows. The more I hear of the smooth gents on our BBC television pasting over the cracks, to mix a metaphor, the more I know how very necessary it is that people should judge for themselves. Except in cases like C-Slovakia, where the truth is well on the side of the anti-socialists, all sorts of difficulties are dressed up so that the minds of the people will skid over them. Like people everywhere perhaps we glean the news by reading between the lines, searching for periodicals not too widely read and so forth.

We have however certain freedoms that we do not underrate and that we intend to fight for though the exigencies of capitalism appear to demand not only the general lowering of the standard of living, the inordinate increase of profits but also the gradual elimination of some freedoms. Mr Enoch Powell is busy quite definitely working up nothing less than race hatred because we have 3 million coloured British citizens here. Most of these are poor and tend to get into the slummiest parts of *our* cities. Many, like our unemployed of whom they form part, are underfed and appallingly housed. Mr Powell thinks they should swim back to Jamaica, Pakistan, Guyana and Ghana. Many Conservatives are openly supporting Mr. Powell and despite students' demonstrations [he] has now managed to wheedle his way into a number of universities. As the present Labour Govt has covered itself with ignominy it is quite likely that Mr Powell and his lot will be returned as a Govt in about 18 months time. Then the class conflict will most assuredly begin; the Labour Govt by handicapping the great mass of organised workers by restrictive laws will have nicely prepared the way for the Conservatives.

As a surgeon you may be surprised to hear that if Mr Powell had his way and all the coloured people were sent packing three quarters of hospitals would almost close down. There is no hospital except one or two of the snobbiest that has not a large number of coloured doctors and nurses on its staff. Many casualty departments for instance are entirely staffed by Indian and Pakistani doctors simply because white doctors will not work 24 hours a day. If we did not receive 250 doctors per year from abroad our output of 400 of which at least 200 elect to practice outside the UK would be woefully more inadequate than it actually is. For this shortage of surgeons and doctors the people, of course, pay. Most doctors do their best but the manners of some are insupportable. Doctors politely or impolitely are in a hurry. Very often surgeons work 10 or 12 hours in the op. theatre.

Yet Harley Street where the consultants of the rich live is packed with the money takers.

Of course our doctors are underpaid but their emoluments are handsome compared with the millions of people they serve. Nevertheless a senior doctor in multiple general practice can get £4000 or slightly more a year, a junior not less than £2000 and fairly quickly going up to £3000. Consultants, who grumble a good deal, can be full-time private and once they are known get £10,000 or £40,000, part-time National Health Service and part-time private and so generally do well; full-time N.H.S. consultants get four or five thousand a year, sometimes more. All doctors are crying out that the National Health Service is dead and can they have more money now!

You may be glad to hear two things: I have a charming doctor but one far too busy. Two, my younger son Hilary is now in his fourth year in the medical school of Birmingham University. He is very lucky and loves his work. He is tough too physically; he plays squash and climbs mountains and drinks too much beer, has a massive appetite, a big mouth and – when he is not filling it – an engaging smile.

To all of you and to all indeed in Czechoslovakia my wife and I send our sincere greetings that the New Year will bring increasing love and comradeship.

Yours sincerely

Leslie Parker

5

Usti nad Labem Czechoslovakia
21 January 1969.

Dear Mr Parker

Thank you for sending me the newspaper and the cutting. I am glad to see that the Morning Star is still covering developments in this country and supporting the cause of democratic socialism. The Russian 'Pravda' holds that this adjective is not only redundant but also bad and a sign of revisionism! The article about Russia from the Sunday Times I found particularly interesting and shocking. But from what I can see here and learn by hearsay I am ready to believe every word of it. Fortunately we are still enjoying a large measure of personal freedom and everyone knows that we owe it to the courage and tenacity of purpose of president Svoboda and men like A. Dubcek, Smrkovsky and Cernik. As long as they are holding positions of power we can feel fairly safe. Particularly now after the supreme sacrifice of young Palach, party, government and the people of the Czech socialist Republic are firmly united once more. Not so in the Slovak state where there is a certain alienation between the leaders and the people. How long we can withstand the pressure and the dirty work of a superpower will depend also on the support our cause is receiving from the CP abroad and from men like you!

Sincerely Yours

Paul Zalud

6

Shoreham-by-Sea, Sussex, England
27 January 1969.

Dear Doctor Zalud

When the Russians invaded your country we were deeply angered not only by the cruel stupidity itself but also by the political and philosophical chicanery that went along with it. We expected personal tragedy and pain to be the outcome, as well of course as political weaknesses developing along the whole Communist front.

We were seared by the death of Jan Palach. This was something very personal to both of us. It might have been one of our own boys; it might even have been my daughter. Ever since my birth in 1898 the world has been in turmoil. Wickedness is not always perceivable. I thought the first world war was just but when my young and vigorous friends went down in the mud dead I knew war was what had to be striven against.

Some deaths like Jan Palach's are more than doubly painful. In 1937 I said goodbye to a young man we loved – strong, self-reliant, a scholar, cheerfully committed – he went to Spain. He died. Others spring to easily to mind: Karl Liebnecht and Rosa Luxembourg, the Rosenbergs, those killed at Sparkville, South Africa, those in Russian labour camps, those in Greek islands, those in Spanish prisons.

The capitalist press has done very nobly by Jan Palach. Every periodical that has never heard of Vietnam or oppression in the south Americas has suddenly blossomed into virtue and hushed voices and great indignation with the Russians. While I have no doubt that many [good?] journalists [are] working for the capitalist papers I have also no doubt that the principal aim in this outburst of commiseration was to make the whole conception of socialism and particularly Communist Socialism stink in the nostrils of all those who [are] striving to seek a way through the inhuman morass that human beings have made for themselves. It has for instance been notable that at the time of the invasion of C-S [by Hitler?] the whole of the American press remained largely silent in the same way as the English press remains silent over the massive demonstrations for peace in Vietnam that took place in President Johnson's time. When two years ago a young American burned himself alive on the steps of UNO to bring to people's minds the great sin of Vietnam the American and Western press very signally failed to give this heroic sacrifice any space at all. Apart from the natural sorrow of any decent man who even writes indecent stuff for his newspaper the enormous avalanche of words that has flowed from the capitalist press all over the world still leaves us who are in the centre of this Russian–capitalist pincer with

the question on our lips what shall, what can,
we do?

I am sending you two extracts from our newspapers.
In one of these there is a self-portrait of a black man
who is vigorously searching for a way out to some sort
of freedom for himself and his son. In the other there is
a cosy description of Moscow intellectuals. There, vigour
once exercised in satire and sarcasm about the Russian
political and social set-up now takes two forms. Historical
retrogression, interest in the Russian past including
icons and church music and writing orthodox stuff in
the soviet press. If this is a true picture of intellectuals
in revolt we have little to hope from them. Satire never
provided the basis of a new philosophy whether it be
that of Voltaire or Swift. To crawl back into the wash of
the Russian revolution is certainly to become something
less than infantile. To lard this with vodka, icons and
(indiscriminate) lovemaking is only to gild the stinking
lily. The Psalmist says: 'I would rather be a doorkeeper in
the house of the Lord than to dwell in the palaces of the
ungodly.' No one keeps his integrity by writing so-called
Marxist Leninist balderdash and realises better than many
who read it exactly what slush it is.

There are, of course, in all countries men and women
who spend their time denigrating Russian achievements
and the Communist Party in general. But the denigration
of a certain system while it may provide some sort of
living does not provide the basis of a new life for many.

This is the great need of the greatest number of
people. Capitalism or imperialism or whatever you
care to call it while still producing gracious livings for
many thousands refuses to do the same for the multi
millions. There is no doubt of this. All writers including
the potboilers of the daily columns are well aware of
this. For there are no more cynical people than those

55

who live by writing for the capitalist periodicals. They write anything to order and believe nothing. Every national newspaper, except the Morning Star, is in the hands of a multi-millionaire who knows vis-a-vis communism or capitalism where he stands. So far as liberal or democratic movements force themselves into the columns so will they print them. Nothing more. But in every case every effort is made to deprecate and depreciate the movements made by the people in efforts to improve their condition. This was the basis of the activity to discredit the democratic movement in Chicago not so long ago. In Britain the Labour Movement is beginning strongly to resist the impositions that the Labour Government is determined to heap upon them. At one and the same time the Conservatives leap to the aid of the people, attack the black immigrants and take pot shots at the government carrying out their own policy.

For all these reasons I was incensed when you first wrote to The Times who doubtless printed your letter with glee. Those who run The Times care more for profit than they care for either the truth or the wellbeing of the people. Had you written to the Morning Star I should have been delighted for there you would have received both encouragement and strong criticism. I am now very sorry that I was rude to you. Then I did not know you were a man of integrity. I thought you only cared so long as you were comfortable. Of course I most stupidly jumped to wrong conclusions. I had no right to be arrogant and was, most unusually, vulgar. I honour you for the stand you made before the party came to power and I deeply sympathise with you when you consider whether what you did was worth it. Not until you wrote did I have any real idea of the pressure that you and your family were under. Theoretically I had but of course one holds a lot of feelings and ideas theoretically.

We ourselves did not join the C.P. because we loved the Party. We joined it because we realised that in Britain it was the only possible instrument for organising any movement towards socialism. If there were, in my opinion, any better movement I would join it, any better Party I would join that. There isn't in England.

Our Party is different from the strictly regimented Parties abroad. We have great freedom in discussion, we have great freedom to approach any leadership on any level. We can make ourselves felt. We embrace rigid-minded, old-fashioned ones who think everything Russia does is OK. People who are delving and thinking are not restricted to the top leadership. For one thing our Party embraces many scholars and commercial people who are accustomed to making decisions in their daily lives. Secondly and perhaps the more important, is that the British working class is much more intelligent than it was before the war. Work demands ... a rather better standard of education and the general turmoil of contemporary history from international events to demanding houses to live in and sometimes when achieved demanding lower rents, have all contributed to the general quickening of the mind. Possibly television too, though God and Marx know television standards are not high by any means. In fact many factors which never existed in Russia contribute to create a Party in this country very different from the highly regimented Parties of those countries that have been devastated and fought over and reduced to the last degree of poverty, economically and culturally.

Tough opposition is never wanting in this country to any political or economic enterprise that would benefit the people. And this can come from the Labour Party itself. In face of this opposition and the long history of collaboration that the Labour Party has with the capitalists, the CP has had a chequered career; many wilt under the strain; many depart. In fact we are witnessing a great uneven development of the Party at the moment for it is very active in some parts of the country and sluggish in others. Even where our members are recognised for their integrity and where their devotion to the working class is accepted, indeed very freely, the CPGB is not an attractive proposition to the workers of Britain generally. Their loyalty to the Labour Party is often absolute and they will vote for no other.

Our difficulties, however, do not entirely spring from internal affairs but from our connection with the CP of the USSR. When the USSR was winning the War which Chamberlain and others had prepared for it nothing was too handsome a tribute. But as soon as peace broke out so did the continued opposition to Russia and Communism. The Politbureau, whatever their faults, did not invent or create the Cold War. Everything was done to undermine the Communist countries' positions. For instance not only did Germany leave eleven thousand secret agents in the USSR but one of the first things the USA did was to vote 14 million dollars specially for anti-Russian espionage. Compared with this Russian espionage was play acting. Nevertheless the Russian methods of government reverted to the ways of the Stalinist era before the war. Stalin was always a frightened man and his country was devastated again. Many of us are of the opinion that had it been psychologically possible for the Russian govt to adopt a less regimenting policy they would have got more [done] in a shorter time. There was not a problem they had [not] to tackle. Basic protection, food and agriculture, education and schools on all levels, millions of houses were needed. 10,000 villages and small towns had to be rebuilt and many cities. The external and internal pressures caused Hungary.[32] The Hungary affair occurred when Khrushchev was deliberately easing the pressure on the communist populations. But Rakosi[33] was Stalin in a new person and perpetrated evil. Of course the people paid and Communism, all Communism, was declared evil too. No wonder.

All the same, despite its mistakes in foreign policy and its iniquitous internal policies, the USSR is providing 220 million with a much better life and because of that with a much better future than any Czarist government could have done; or Hitler or Johnson. To Churchill the Russians were the barbaric hosts for whom he had much contempt. The condition of the Russian people is almost daily improving which is more than 40 million in the USA and three million in our own country can say (we have a million little children suffering from malnutrition). No young person wishes to be a manual worker in the USSR. On this general increase in knowledge over a vast area of the population rather than on the withdrawn intellectual rebels must we place our trust for the future internal development of Russian society, I think. It will not be a quick process; it will go in jumps and zigzag back and forth. There is however no need to be patient with it. But where we condemn the government we should remember the past and seldom perhaps condemn the people.

Without the USSR the world would be in greater turmoil than it is now and war would be spread far and wide with a dozen Vietnams. With the massive power of Russia leaning on them the imperialists are hardly likely

---

[32] This is a reference to the Hungarian uprising of 1956.

[33] Musty Rakosi, General Secretary of the Hungarian Communist Party 1945–48 and then of the Hungarian Working Peoples Party 1948–56; intermittently also Prime Minister.

to allow their economic and political wars [to] develop into military wars. Military expenditure weighs heavily on the USSR but on West Germany, the UK and the USA it daily drags them down so that their people are offered no respite from the cry for exports and burden of taxation, very high profits and rents that aim [at] only the highest peaks. Our property companies have made thousands of millions of pounds. The marks of the beast are slums, high prices, lowered standards of living and the urge to war.

I do not wish to see my country like Russia but I know its stupid politicians are stopped from crazy military mistakes by the fear of Russia. Fear is not a good basis for peace anywhere. But while there is peace we can struggle, we are at least not dead.

So far as we are concerned we have a struggle on both hands. We fight to enlighten our own government as to what are the needs of the people. We struggle to curb the growing oligarchical rule of the Cabinet, or Mr Wilson and two or three more. We fight for work, food, houses, leisure. On the other hand we join with the democrats in the communist countries who wish to enlighten their governments, remembering this is not the end of history but the beginning.

Our gravest problem in Communism is to keep alive under the pressure from the West. Our next greatest is to study methods of more democratic ways of government that will suit the traditional ways of each country. Some Russians spit when they hear the word democracy as I remember a young German doing in 1937 when I was breakfasting with him. The problem of democratic government in a new kind of non-exploiting society is one that must be studied, discussed and brought into the minds of men and women. It is not a simple problem, particularly in Russia. Many Communists and certainly no Russians (except those who have witnessed some capitalist democracy at work) can have an idea what it means. Nor in many ways do we know. I cannot see Communist democracy developing in my own country from anything but capitalist democracy but I am sure that communist democracy will be quite, quite different. So we must start from where we are with what we have got in the way of customs, laws and more important, men and women. Men and women are not grown on trees who like the fruitless fig tree in the gospels can be cut down and thrown in the fire. Men and women are moulded by the places and people that give them birth and succour. Men and women are difficult but I believe that they respond more when urged with love than with a whip.

While Marx and Lenin may have worked [out] some ways of nurturing and carrying out a revolution, while they certainly spoke of certain necessities like the Dictatorship of the Proletariat and breaking up the old capitalist machinery of State, conditions have so changed that new ways in addition to these must be worked out.

In his early writings Marx was powerfully aware of war between good and evil. He always regarded socialism as Good Triumphant much as Milton regarded the God as the Power of Good over the Satan who is evil personified. Marx said that it would have been impossible to conceive of Socialism without the Christian ethic. This saying is not often quoted. The one thing that has been noticeable about capitalist government is its absence in practice of the Christian ethic. We have Bishops blessing nuclear warheads in Polaris submarines. Blessing regimental colours is [not] far from a la mode nowadays. Nevertheless the Christian ethic of Love Thy Neighbour has lived beyond the confines of money making, of wars of aggrandizement and class rule. It is still alive and very much kicking in society at present. But it is

only recently become part of the discussion on What is
Socialism. Marx and Lenin largely thought much about
gaining power, Lenin to some extent how to keep power.
But neither gave any thought as to how to govern in
a socialist country. If future Communist governments
think they can do this and ignore the long tradition of
moral teaching that has always been woven into the
political cloth of socialism they could not be more wrong.
Socialism is not essentially a dictatorship; it is only
incidentally and temporarily...

[Remainder of letter missing]

7

Betici, Yugoslavia (by hand)
10 May 1969.

Dear Mr Parker

As your last letter was defiled by the hands of the censor
I felt disinclined to continue in our exchange of news
and views. Now I am using a holiday in Yugoslavia to
give some news about us and Czechoslovakia. Most
people are convinced that agents-provocateurs turned the
manifestation of joy over the victory of our hockey team
at Stockholm into violent anti-Russian demonstrations.
Here at Usti n.l. Russian tanks were overturned and set
on fire. After the arrival of Marshal Prechko Russian
armoured cars patrolled our street every two hours while
most people were digging their gardens during April.
Resolutions in support of Mr Dubcek were suppressed.
The Communist Party organ Rudé Pravo released only
resolutions supporting the new line and leadership. These

resolutions were declared as interference in the internal affairs. But the Pro-Russian conservatives did not think it an interference that Soviet jets were blazing through the sky during the deliberations of the Central Committee on April 17th. I regard as an offence of common sense to state, as the new leaders did, that Anti-Sovietism is Anti-Socialism.

After the dismissal of Mr Dubcek ten thousands of party members resigned, many themselves supporters of Dubcek and his concepts are being purged from their positions in the party and in the mass media. The people is knocked back into apathy to public and political affairs as any claim as regards the policy of the CP is rejected as 'interference' or as an attack against the leading role of the party. People are also turning away from the communication media. TV has become very boring and most people receive their political information from the broadcasts in Czech of the Radio Free Europe, Deutsche Welle or the BBC. Only the back pages of the newspapers are read, while the front pages are ignored.

I am having a wonderful time in the Recreation Centre of the Czechoslovakian trade unions at Betici near Budva. There are 300 workers and a few white collar workers and a few bureaucrats. We are getting on well with each other and with the Yugoslav Communists who are visiting us. Only here we can talk freely – while at home political discussions are once more inhibited by fear of giving ourselves away.

With best regards
Sincerely yours

Paul Zalud

PS Leaving here on May 23rd 1969.

8

Shoreham-by-Sea, Sussex, England
2 June 1969.

My dear Doctor Zalud,

A photograph of a very young gentleman taking his bath
in the garden quite unperturbed despite possible publicity
has been shining down upon me for several months now
and finally impels me to ask how all the other adorers
of this same young gentleman are doing. It is a long
time since you heard from me and a much longer [one]
since we heard from you.[34] My wife, having presumably
nothing much to do on a Monday morning, said 'Write to
Doctor Zalud and tell him at least that the sun has shone
two days in succession'. So I do and it shines upon both
the unjust and the just. Nevertheless it has taken about 7
dreary winter months to manage this initial splendour.

Now maybe we can depend on four months to prepare
us for the next lot of dismal months. If we were rich we
[would] take ourselves off to the shores of Florida or
the black sea where, as Tennyson said, 'every prospect
pleases and only man is vile'. As it is we shall be inviting
a mild disaster by going north very soon. We are first of
all going to Derbyshire which is my home county and a
very pleasing one at that, embracing as it does several
kinds of scenery from a wild and rugged peak area to a
rich and rolling landscape towards the south. I shall, as
far as my depleted eyesight allows me, look on fondly
at trees that when I was young were little more than
saplings and perhaps on gentle old ladies that I knew as

---

[34] An untruth, intended no doubt for the censor.

sprightly and evocative young women. There will also I trust be bees, burbling brooks, buttercups and beer and all other sights, sounds and tastes suitable to the palate of the most refined Marxists. From Derbyshire we shall take [the] train to the not so noble manufacturing city of Birmingham. We shall not go there to sing hymns of praise or even of hate to Neville Chamberlain who first invented the betrayal of Czechoslovakia. We care neither for its fat and treacherous business men nor for the truly awful brand of English that is spoken there nor even for the gathering storm over the colour problem that is arising in Birmingham and nearby towns. We are going primarily to look around the medical school attached to the university to ascertain whether it is adequate in size, profound enough in learning and humanitarian enough in outlook to continue teaching our youngest child who has been there almost a year now. Having been reassured on all these points we shall then inspect his latest female attachment, consider how temporary or permanent this is likely to be, persuade him to change his lodging from a rather damp room with an inadequate electric fire and a window with a pane out to a rather more accommodating domestic environment. I dare say we shall go the cinema, eat too much too expensively and talk about patients and all the surprises they have been holding [in] store for youngsters unwary enough to dedicate themselves to healing.

After this we proceed a little more northwards to York where my daughter is married to a lecturer. They are a very cheerful conversational couple and the only way sometimes to get a word in is to say Shut UP it's my turn to speak. To which they will probably reply You had your turn yesterday. They inhabit a century old house that would tumble down were it not assisted to stand up by a house on each side. Thank heaven they have

recently had central heating put in for before its advent
the house was, as the Americans say 'like a morgue'.
My daughter ... went to London University to study
the Classical languages and even had an Exhibition,
but failed to get a degree [at] all. Even now we cannot
tell why this was. Sometimes we put it down to the
arid learning that classics entails. Sometimes to a too
intimate knowledge of London's cafes and cinemas and
sometimes to her being far from well during her last
year. She is now taking a two year course at a college for
training teachers for junior schools. They took her rather
against their better judgement on the strength of a very
strong recommendation from the head of a school where
she taught for a year. She should make a versatile teacher
for she gets along in French and Italian, Latin and Greek,
cookery, needlework and repartee. I should like to have
two daughters; their differences would be absorbing.

Quite possibly as absorbing as the politics we are
surrounded by, De Gaulle has gone and is even now in
one of our colonies, Ireland, where innumerable
reporters dog his footsteps. Meanwhile Pompidou carries
his flag leaving Poher in the hands of the Communist
Party.[35] The Social Democrats have at least got their
deserts for they, like all bourgeois liberals, cannot make
up their minds what they want.[36] All our newspapers are

---

[35] The first round of the French presidential election was held the
day before Leslie wrote this letter, leaving Georges Pompidou and
Alain Poher as the two candidates to go forward to the second
round. The latter, as President of the French Senate, had been the
interim Acting President since the resignation of De Gaulle on 29
April. The communists, whose candidate, the popular Georges
Duclos, came a very respectable third in the first round, refused to
choose between the two men. Georges Pompidou was duly elected
President on 15 June.

[36] The three socialist candidates took less than 10 per cent of the
vote between them, less than half the communist vote.

waiting almost breathlessly for the result of the French
election because all their proprietors are intensely
interested in pushing us into the Common Market.
This, I am afraid, will only increase British government
restrictions upon the freedom of the British working
man and woman. A very keen fight is going on between
the leaders of the Unions and the Government over the
Government's insistence that acts of Parliament must
be passed so that trade unions and trade unionists can
be fined if they withdraw their labour. All our seven
national dailies are against the unions and only the
CP paper the Morning Star maintains the workers'
rights. While capitalism shows an enormous capacity
for producing goods in enormous quantities and every
splendid variety the exigencies of capitalism demand
an ever increasing restriction upon the buying capacity
of workers. Our living standards vary throughout the
classes and sections of the population. We have many at
subsistence or below subsistence level while at the same
time we can, along with America and West Germany,
produce millionaires galore. Money is tied up in banks
and armaments and men and women in idleness while
we need hospitals, schools, doctors, teachers, houses (at
least three million) and so forth. Working people in every
country are compelled against restrictive governments
to fight for their living standards. Many of us look over
the garden hedge of socialism and hope that Communist
Governments will continue to uphold the rights of the
proletariat and the people generally so that in liberty and
culture as well as in material satisfactions the communist
countries will be a beacon showing the way to all the
peoples. If in the past I have appeared to speak in any
way harshly about political affairs in your country and
have perhaps inadvertently hurt your feelings. I wish to
assure you that [I] hold your countrymen and women in

the very highest regard and you yourself in the highest esteem. I feel sure we shall not quarrel over the true way in which your country can fulfil her aspirations.

With every good wish
Yours sincerely

Leslie Parker

9

Usti nad Labem, Czechoslovakia
9 June 1969.

Dear Mr and Mrs Parker,

Thank you for your gracious letter of June 2nd. I appreciate each of your letters, apart from the news it contains, also as an outstanding example of the now somewhat forgotten and neglected art of letter writing. By the characteristic style of your writing my vocabulary of English is greatly enriched.

In the true English tradition I too shall begin by commenting on the weather. Ever since I arrived back from my holiday in Yugoslavia a fortnight ago I am feeling cold and shivery. The average temperature has indeed been between 4–10 degrees Celsius and the occasional eruptions of pimples on my tanned skin were caused by insufficient acclimatisation and not by the fact that socialism with the human face has now turned into socialism with goose flesh. Please do not think that I am the author of this brilliant jocular saying. It is only one of the numerous jokes with which our people is trying to ease its plight. In this particular saying the

gay and resourceful humour of the Czechs is alluding to
the name of the new party leader Doctor Husak. Husak
means 'goosling', 'gander' and I am reminded of a famous
saying of Martin Luther who said: 'Vor hundert Jahren
briet man eine Gans' [A hundred years ago they roasted a
goose], referring to the condemnation of Jan Hus at the
Council of Constance in 1415.

I am aware that you are not rich and that you could
not afford to take off to Florida. I am the last to make
a case against you going to Derbyshire which is 'Home
sweet home' to you. But I dare say that you are rich
enough as to [go] next spring to Yugoslavia [or] to go
to the shores of the Black Sea of Romania. Those are
certainly the only two Socialist countries in the world
which command the respect and support of anyone who
claims as you do to be a refined Marxist. One man's
beauty is another man's missed opportunity. For several
years nostalgia carried me back to my home village,
hidden deeply in the Bohemian forest, in the borderland
between Bohemia and Germany. I usually went there
during my annual leave instead of going to Yugoslavia as
I did this year. I could never expect to find this purpose in
the eternal onslaughts of the Turks, the imperial armies
of the Hapsburg monarchy, of the Fascists of Mussolini
and Hitler. As long as they lived and worked in these
houses they were never subdued by anyone. But now
they are voluntarily leaving their archaic households and
going down to build the highway along the Dalmatian
coast and the hotels and auto-campings [sic] and all
the rest of the tourist industry which is providing a
large number of people with incomes and Yugoslavia
with foreign currency. Then Svaty Stefan or Saint
Stephen appeared. A village on an island was evacuated
and the village resettled on the coast. Their huts were
rebuilt as a block of houses, having preserved the

essential architectural features of plain, unpretentious houses of white stone with red roofs. But these stern walls contain the most luxurious apartments, bars, restaurants, clubs, cafes, terraces etc., accessible only to German and American millionaires. On we went to our place: a nice clean, modern dining hall, kitchens, reception and offices with a flat roof on ground level. In front of it there was an open veranda and a dancing terrace. Between the deckchairs and tables I noticed 6–8 flowering oleanders. We all were housed in clean 2 or 3 bed-containing rooms with a bathroom and a shower corner attached. I stayed with a very shrewd and intelligent glass-worker and a petty official from Pilsen. We soon found out that we were all sharing the same views and got on very well with each other. Following a social evening with music, dancing and wine, an atmosphere of mutual trust, free and uninhibited discussion was established and we felt as though forming one large family. This unity became quite obvious when we had the good fortune to cheer and greet President Tito in his own country while passing by the centre to make speeches at the celebration of the anniversary of the rising against fascism in 1941 in Montenegro. The weather was fine and only on one day of our excursion to Dubrovnik the sky was overcast. We could make a choice out of 4 different meals of excellent quality and great variety. A ¼ of a litre of red wine was served with each meal. I got up several times at 6 o'clock to have a swim before breakfast. After several hours of swimming and sunbathing I could read German and English papers which I received from tourists after they had read them. As we only had 175 dinars pocket money I could not afford to buy newspapers at the kiosk. In the evenings everybody was free to view either the Italian or the Yugoslavian TV. No one is afraid of censorship of the mail and Yugoslavs we met knew a good deal about our country and asked many pertinent questions. They were extremely friendly towards us, offered free drinks and sold us souvenirs for half the price they charged the Germans. Of course there was a little bit of black marketeering [sic] going on all the time. While our people were very interested in buying coffee, tea, cocoa, chocolate, olive oil, wine and spirits and shorts. Beautiful black and red, handwoven carpets and the most delicate filigree is available only to tourists with hard currency, most of which are Germans. English, Swiss, Dutch and Scandinavian cars take the second place. Building is going on day and night and even on Sundays. Although the wages of the workers are lower than ours and we have a higher standard of mechanisation, we were amazed at the rate the building progressed. There seems to be a larger gap between the working class and the incomes of white collar workers, particularly the state and party bureaucracy and administration, than we are observing in this country. How exciting to see an oriental market and the shops of independent shoemakers, watchmakers, barbers etc., all of which have disappeared to the detriment of the consumer in this country.

These were 14 days of serene happiness and bliss. Only a 'Marxist' with sore eyes, deaf ears, with his sense of smell dulled or obliterated, could go for tourism to any other country than Yugoslavia or for that purpose to Romania.[37] Only men with a failing memory for recent events and a total inability to think and judge

---

[37] Romania refused to participate in the invasion of Czechoslovakia; its President and Communist Party secretary, Nicolae Ceausescu, whose popularity had not yet waned, was widely regarded as a reformer.

for themselves will not see that those who most loudly proclaim the fight for the principles of true Marxism do not live up to them.

David was most pleased with the pebbles I collected for him, less so with the oriental slippers I bought for him. Everyone was very excited with the presents I brought as they did not expect any. While I was away my wife with the help of her sister and other members of my family made a remarkably good study out of the bathroom in which I was compelled to work and smoke through the horrible winter months.

Kind regards and best wishes
Yours sincerely

Paul Zalud

10

Shoreham-by-Sea, Sussex, England
17 June 1969.

Dear Dr Zalud,

We are so glad you had a good holiday. Our hearts lifted with jubilation as we enjoyed the countryside, the sunshine and the bathing and the tremendous invigoration that you spread so generously through the pages of your letter. Whatever comes we must keep our joy and belief in life. I shall go on my holiday with renewed eyes and renewed convictions that no stupid politicians, no greedy moneymakers, no motley crowd of servile and sensational writers can separate the men and women of goodwill that people the earth. I have sent your letter to our David in Leeds and we shall all read it in time.

I must say that your English is startlingly good and a great pleasure to read. The only unusual thing about my English is the possibly unusual spelling which I do not correct because I have difficulty in reading. If I should mislead you I am sorry but no matter as long as it elicits a reply. I envy you your languages, You must have a laudable knowledge of at least three. I'm afraid I am reduced to English but my wife has fairly fluent French. We English people have been taught languages very badly, even our own, but at last many schools can claim language laboratories which deal adequately with French, German, Russian and Spanish. A few years ago Russia had a vogue and is, I believe, still widely taught in our better secondary schools. My daughter learned Italian ... when she refused to read any more Latin and Greek. So they gave her Italian to keep her occupied. Then later she spent three months in Italy with a very wealthy family who were 'in ceramics'. These people had five different houses in Italy, five or six cars and a private aeroplane. When Linda was with them the domestics went on strike and spent time indulging not in a 'sit-in' but a sort of hurling out. They just hurled through the windows all the brushes, pans, domestic utensils and whatever through the windows as added decorations to an expensively laid out garden.

If you will forgive me and if they will let us in I think there is only one country at the moment we should like to visit and that is your own. Many of our friends have been in Yugo-S and we should like to go there and there are some parts of the GDR I should like to go to also, but at the moment of crisis Czechoslovakia calls us. We are not really well off though we live in a charming little house that many people in C-S (and indeed in

England) would be glad of – but we might manage to get abroad next year. This house shortage, considering the enormous capacity in materials, labour and technology, that all countries in Western Europe possess, is shocking. We have nearly 3 million slum dwellings alone. Many hundreds of thousands are living in houses already condemned as unfit for human beings. We also have the anomaly of many houses 'scheduled for demolition in order to facilitate redevelopment' remaining untouched and unoccupied for numbers of years. In Brighton (about 4 miles from here, a town dedicated to pleasure seekers and very cosmopolitan) there are 3,200 quite good houses that have not been occupied for three or four years and which will probably not be demolished for another three or four, standing empty and useless. Meanwhile there are about 4,000 families of low or lowish income groups waiting for municipal houses that are built in fewer and fewer quantities every year. In the UK we do not build more than 400,000 houses per year and about half of these, or perhaps more, are only for those lucky enough to buy them. Perhaps I am wrong to call these 'buyers' lucky, for since the rate of interest from the moneylenders who sell money specially for the purchase of houses has gone up to 8.5% many of these 'buyers' will not live to call their houses their own. Capitalism is producing a society of people who have no worry about possessions – they are quite beyond the dreams of avarice because such dreams would be quite useless. Meanwhile even though the stock exchange is rolling in the depths of a murky depression we make one or two new millionaires each week. These alas go unheralded which is a pity for they represent the acme of our moral striving. Although West Germany has a massive housing project in hand and is doing well with it I think in the course of time the Socialist countries will head the list in creating dwellings despite the setbacks and the enormous expense of armaments. It is said that the cost of armaments plus that of space exploration take half the national product of the USSR. Though NATO is frayed at the edges the German Fed Republic military and industrial complex is doing its evil best to keep NATO alive and venomous. We had Strauss hobnobbing with our defence minister Healey only last week and that was both frightening and utterly sickening. Nevertheless I could think of ways that would reduce the USSR's military costs.

I don't think my Marxism is always refined but I do make efforts to be concise and analytical. When I consider the numberless generalities of some Marxist politicians from whose mouths tumble words of gigantic proportions frothing over into cascades [of] meaninglessness I wonder whether it would not be better if the Hegelians deflated their verbal balloons with a little look at Aristotle. My old history tutor used to squeal (perhaps with indignation, perhaps with enthusiasm) 'Let's have change for phrases; small coin for long words'. All the same I am all for Proletarian Internationalism – it's a long phrase and it will take us a long time to get to it. Marx and Engels didn't say 'You have nothing to lose but your brains'; [they] said 'chains'. By the way is it true that factories in Romania are turning out bottles of ink for export to the USSR so that Russian children can throw them at the Chinese embassy? Oh dear! I do hope not.

Regards to you all

Leslie Parker

11

Shoreham-by-Sea, Sussex, England
4 August 1969.

Dear Doctor Zalud,

Despite dastardly attempts by vicious elements
emanating either from the Arctic or the Atlantic,
Summer at last enfolds us. The sun shines on us as
well as Moscow, Prague and Bucharest; it shines with
gentle insistence that grey wet clouds will never again
threaten and that even our minds will be no more
than breezes specially designed to blow small boats over
glazy seas. You will gather that we are now back among
my wife's gladioli, red roses and white roses and all
shades in between with dahlias and lots of other
flowers I understand have secret code names in some
dead language.

I endured Derbyshire and started a lovely spasm
of asthma that neither grew worse nor better for a
fortnight. Notwithstanding after leaving the wet dismay
of Derbyshire my wife, our younger son and I met in
Birmingham where we [were] acquainted with a too
large campus, a too detailed medical museum and a too
decrepit house where it please my son to spend his few
sleeping moments.

We ate and drank so much that we had no time for
other cultural experiences. Rather reluctantly we made
our way to the ancient city of York which the Romans
called Eboracum. It is still semi-walled and the Cathedral
Church, called the Minster, is a fine gothic building
started in the late 13th century, well worth seeing. We
found our energetic daughter and very hospitable son-
in-law snowed under with unexpected guests who slept

somewhere or other and swept in and out like gentle
locusts seeing what they could, with politeness, devour.
I promptly went to bed for five days until I was full of
a range of antispasmodics that would have stopped
Hitler in his oracular tracts. Antibiotics of pain bearing
qualities completed my quiescence. Meanwhile while
I was on a tame diet of Radio and raw carrots they
all went to sundry efforts of the York Festival. They
heard much modern poetry proclaimed by the poets
themselves, a good 'Figaro'; they braved the cold winds
from 7.30 to midnight and enjoyed a mystery play, they
heard four massed brass bands from Yorkshire collieries
blowing their silver harmonies in the Minster. During the
second week, jealousy having eaten into my miserable
soul, I arrayed myself and heard some modern poetry
myself, gazed with intense enjoyment on a series of
ballets by the Nederlands Ballet Company. Their dances
were utterly vigorous and utterly human and were saved
from crudeness by their form and grace. They were far
removed from classical ballet both in choreography and
conception. Our final delight was listening to the organist
at the Minster. I am very suspicious of organ music
because either it is thin or sentimental or rapacious
and rowdy like nineteen hands all over four manuals
13 feet lashing out at every base note they can lay their
marauding toes to. A varied selection of short pieces
in which the playing seemed to increase in vigour and
understanding gave way to a Bach fugue and prelude.
In England these (may they be given to others) are
generally played like an army scampering through a
bed of violets, utterly barbarian; but that evening I
heard Bach played as I have never heard Bach before.
It was gentle, it was vibrant, it was tender, it was robust,
of great stature. It was indeed worth having 8769 doses
of antispasmodics for.

During our last three days the sun shone all over us, just and unjust, cultured and uncultured, and we travelled back in a too rapid train to a too hot London and then in a still hotter train to home. Where we are amidst the roses typing and cutting the grass of the lawns.

Things have been happening since I last wrote though I have forgotten when that was. The Labour Government which with the help of all the national and provincial papers (save the Morning Star) had made numerous efforts to deprive our Trade Unions of all rights to withdraw their labour from their workplaces, succeeded by a unity unparalleled since 1926, [which] compelled the Govt. to withdraw.[38] This has done the workers a tremendous lot of good. Ever since Mr. Harold MacMillan, Prime Minister in the 1950s, began to make it more and more impossible for the workers to improve their standard of living the profit making has gone on very happily and without hindrance. Taxes have descended upon the lower incomes while tax avoidance by the rich has been scandalous. In the course of the last two or three years shares have trebled in value and the speculators on the stock exchange together with the bankers have been having a lovely fat time. Now the workers are getting quite uppish though the threat of unemployment in some branches of industry is very considerable.

As Mr Wilson and his miserable cabinet are seeking ways of turning the wrath of the lower orders they have recently declared there is to be a wealth tax that will start at either £50,000 or £75,000. It is estimated that this will bring in £500 million.

---

[38] The White Paper 'In Place of Strife', published in January, proposed to introduce pre-strike ballots and a 28-day cooling-off period. The government, itself divided and faced with opposition from the TUC, had backed down by May.

The movements towards peace in Vietnam are prevented from developing largely by the Americans promising to withdraw 100,000 troops (not combat) 'by the end of this year' which as we say 'is the sweet by and by'.[39] In fact the bombing in south Vietnam has increased devastatingly and we have news today that the USA air force is using poisonous gases and 'nerve' gases.

On the other hand movements by the USSR towards some sort of agreement to a European Peace Agreement sponsored by Finland and Belgium is beginning to attract some attention in England and America.

Meanwhile Tricky Nicky[40] (President of the USA) has gone careering off to the Philippines thence to Vietnam (to say how brave they are and to explain 'why you are doing this' and not succeeding) and thence to Thailand to say that the USA will always 'back you up whether against internal or external foe'. The Thai ruling class dream of hordes of communists pink, yellow, brown, white sweeping down and washing the whole exploiting lot into the sea. Then Nicky went on to Romania not of course to make remarks about the Chinese/Russian imbroglio but [to] assure everybody that everybody was everybody else's gentle little brother and proclaim in very vague terms the USA's love of peace, friendship and whatnot. The Romanian people met Nicky with enthusiastic abandon; the crowd of welcome were enormous; their gladness at the sound of the word Peace unalloyed.

Mr. Harold Wilson suffered at the hands of the President more ignominy than had Mr Harold MacMillan [sic]

---

[39] *The Times* as early as 14 April reported unconfirmed rumours of intention to withdraw 50 to 100,000 troops of the 549,000 in Vietnam. On 8 June Nixon announced the withdrawal of 25,000. Over 100,000 were withdrawn by the end of the year.

[40] More usually referred to as 'Tricky Dicky'.

when he went over to the West Indies to meet John Kennedy to receive his orders. This subservience set up a 'special relationship' between the USA and British governments. This was finally exemplified when the President's plane after leaving a communist country dropped down in England (now a bit of America with a military colony of 5,000) and allowed Mr Wilson to hear what the President thought might be good for him. Our most conservative papers are by no means enamoured of this treatment. Now the President has flown home there to decide exactly what year he will not withdraw his fighting forces from Vietnam.

The Vietcong (National Liberation Front) will not agree to elections while the present govt is propped up only by USA military forces. I do not doubt the Saigon govt would vanish almost completely if the mass of the Vietnamese had their way. The USA have been successful in murdering two or three millions of Vietnamese whether in the north or south; they have brought immense increases of venereal disease; more and more corruption among the already corrupt government and have increased too the lust for money that brings girls of very tender years out on the streets as prostitutes. If this fight for the Vietnamese were to fail it would be a very bad thing not only for the whole of S.E. Asia but also for the Southern Americas where the drain on the wealth by the USA is increasing poverty daily.

So far as your own country is concerned we have heard very little. We read a sad article by Mr Dubcek who for the time being seems to be defeated. We heard that it is difficult for the periodicals to find competent journalists so great is the reluctance of the best journalists to submit to a censorship that cannot state its principles beyond vague talks of unity, normalisation, solidarity. We are told, but I do not know how true this is, that the workers and many professional people are very dispirited, that workers' councils have been disbanded or made innocuous and that your radio and television services have become quite wooden and lifeless. The heads of your Govt and Mr Brezhnev and Mr Kosygin are I understand both holidaying [in] the Crimea where 'if they meet' they might well have talks about the weather. We in England may hope that your weather does improve and we have no doubt that there are meteorological specialists who will do their best. A Socialist land without sunshine is as depressing as Socialism without Brotherhood.

Finally we must make mention of the American Moon Men. We sat up until the grey dawn watching them walk on the moon, talking quite composedly unlike 'film' Americans, picking up moon dust, shoving up the American flag, making footprints in the volcanic dust of the ages. Some hours later we heard them lift off. Which was the more tense – the landing by manipulation or the ascent from the Moon – I cannot say. I have many thoughts, some antagonistic and some almost hopeful as to the meaning of this event but I will keep them until I write again. I seldom forget your country even when full of antibiotics and Bach. You should have two postcards from me. Did they reach you?

My wife and I send you our very best wishes

Leslie Parker

12

Shoreham-by-Sea, Sussex, England
20 August 1969.

Dear Doctor Zalud,

Since I last wrote to you one or two things have
happened each important in its own way.

As you know our Government for nearly a year by
its own utterances, threats and through the media of
newspapers, television and radio told the nation how
necessary it was to cut wages, have some unemployed
and behave with decorum to the international bankers.
So much were the workers in the end outraged against
the intention of the Government to reduce the Trade
Unions to a part of the Government itself that strikes
became pretty well threatened everywhere. The intention
to legislate [against] the industrial power of the workers
and TUs to negotiate their wages and conditions of
living ... had to be dropped in the face of the antagonism
not only of the productive workers but also of the
professional ones. The Govt was glad when Parliament
went into the summer 'recess'.

During this time however a storm blew up of violent
and significant proportions in Northern Ireland (called
the Six counties sometimes and often called Ulster).
This northern part of Ireland owes its existence to
the massacres of Elizabeth I (about 1590) and Oliver
Cromwell ('The Protector' of the short lived early
bourgeois republic) after the beheading of Charles I
in 1649.

From Cromwell on Northern Ireland received
large numbers of Protestant (ie Church of England)
entrepreneurs. This sort of colonisation was often

called The Plantations. These entrepreneurs brought with them the largest accumulations of capital then known in the whole of Ireland. They also brought the soldiery, taxation and exploitation.

From earliest times migrations from England, Scotland, Brittany had made Ireland their home. From the 11th century a line of English and Welsh settlements occupied the east coast mostly defended by a ditch or ramparts of some kind. This defence was called the Pale. Even now we have a saying of a man or woman who is 'not quite the thing', outré, don't you know that he is 'beyond the Pale'. Just as the Greeks called all foreigners Barbarians or stammerers.

From the time of Cromwell there the whole of Ireland came under the domination of the British Parliament, soldiery, magistrates. The British founded great estates, the Church of England, a government at Dublin and invented rack-renting, famine. In return the population obliged with arson, outbursts of civil war and dying by the million or emigrating to America.

The northern Six Counties or Ulster refused to be part of this republic. Ulster was not only richer having more manufactures and capital than the rest of Ireland but engendered a fierce Protestant religion. The differences of the Roman Catholics and Protestants have been turned to good account by the Ulster capitalists. For fifty years the RCs have been at a disadvantage in civil rights (often not allowed to vote), in police protection and magisterial justice (for all the police and magistrates were Protestant), [and] in jobs and housing.

Year by year the Protestants have 'baited' the RCs, flaunting their police protection by making demonstrations in the RC areas. This disparity has been most marked during times of relative prosperity and in the two principal towns of Londonderry (in the north) and Belfast in the north east. But times have been uneven of late and getting worse for the RCs. Yet neither prosperity, [nor] religious rancour, [or] unscrupulousness by the Government has prevented the rise of joint associations of RCs and Prots. In addition development has made it essential that in some areas Prots and RCs have had to live in mixed communities.

Nevertheless the old hatred is still fanned by gross injustice in jobs, civil rights and in the courts; it is also fanned by unscrupulous leaders, largely Protestant and sometimes clergy.

After the election of the last Government some months ago – of course the Prots romped home – the British Govt brought a little pressure on the then Ulster Prime Minister. This pressure was resisted, the Ulster Govt was reconstituted with a Nobody as Prime Minister. The Prots to make their case clear increased their demonstrations, the police often broke all the windows and threatened the tenants of many streets of RC houses. In the end because they were simply getting no protection and their minds were enraged the RC areas barricaded their streets and defied the police in Londonderry. Molotov cocktails, stones and curses were hurled from barricades to police and back. The newspapers had a glorious time.

The British Government which is the creator of the Ulster Government did nothing but suggest in private. Then just as Londonderry was quietening down Belfast went with a bang. Many factories were set ablaze, many broken heads went to hospital, snipers were on the roofs and one young man and one boy of 13 years were shot.[41]

600 British troops are now settling the affair in a kindly way for mostly the Ulster people were glad to see

---

[41] A nine-year-old boy was shot as he lay in bed.

them. At first only 300 went to Londonderry and they thought that would do. But when Belfast started the rest of the division moved in.

This is an enormous disgrace to the British Govt because they are ultimately responsible. The Protestant and ultra capitalist Ulster Government with all its chicanery, gerrymandering and corruption has proved to be what it is. The police with its secret agents, the agent-provocateurs and its horrible semi-fascist contingent of special 'B' police has not only demonstrated its cruelty but also its uselessness in time of civil tension.

I have no doubt that our Labour (social democrat) government knew what was likely to happen. Yet it preferred to attack wages rates at home, reduce production efficiency, demoralise many workers, slow down the production of people's housing rather than tackle this festering sore in Northern Ireland. We may rest assured that in civilised society where justice and fair treatment are trodden underground there will the people be forced to win back their rights and make sure that corruption and inefficiency (which always go hand in hand) will give place to brotherhood, efficiency in production and a government that heeds the people. We have not yet heard the last of Northern Ireland, for the Irish whether RC or Prot, when not inflamed by outdated myths of enmity, will rise and take their future into their own hands. I say long live Proletarian solidarity and the Unity of ALL workers. For nothing in the long run can daunt them.

My deepest respects to you and your family. There is not a day comes and goes but I think of you all. Be quite sure of that.

Leslie Parker

13

Shoreham-by-Sea, Sussex England
23 August 1969.

My dear Doctor Zulad,

The weather in England is now sunny but windy and the
new wind now coming from the north threatens a cold
autumn with coughs and colds and wintry chilblains to
follow. The politicians now on holiday will be turning
their thoughts to cold and wintry problems. The
proletariat are by no means the legally dominated angels
they were to be transformed into; firms, particularly
shipbuilders on the River Clyde, are losing millions
of pounds (sterling) of orders even for ships for our
own country. The Times business news is full of polite
lamentation. Meanwhile, or should I say, in addition
to all the ills which a government in recess is supposed
to get over without reference to the more democratic
criticism of the House of Commons, [it] is no more
distinguishing itself than it has done in the last four
years. Happily, however, save for one short harangue we
have been saved from Mr. Wilson's long-winded periods
by means of which he glosses over every difficulty
without explaining a thing.

Northern Ireland continues to vie in the papers and on
television with Czechoslovakia. Not of course that anyone
who has been immersed in the scientific, proper scientific
attitude towards history in general and socialist history
in particular would draw a parallel between Northern
Ireland and Czechoslovakia.

After the trouble in Ireland [...] (where 300 Irish
had been massacred by the British troops) all Ireland
save Ulster was accorded a sort of freedom under the

title of the Republic of Ireland. From this time, 1920, the British Govt did its best to thwart the Republic's economic development; refused to buy its dairy produce, refused to invest etc etc. Therefore quite a number of Roman Catholics from the Republic migrated to Ulster and joined the Roman Caths there. Altogether they constituted one third of the population of Ulster. From 1920 however the reins of Govt have been in the hands of the Protestants, the Orange men or Men of Ulster as they are called. The RCs endured such brutality, shame, unemployment, deprivation of welfare, housing and so forth and were often forcibly prevented from voting at local or national elections.

As you know the anger and frustration lately burst into flames. It is impossible to keep a minority down for ever unless the tyrant wants the whole country to fall back into barbarism. The attempt to solve the economic ills of Ulster at the expense of the minority has failed utterly. For a long time the Govt has not only acceded to the brutality of [a] specially chosen police force and encouraged private citizens of its own kind to carry arms but it has developed a neurotic inability to look steadily at any question. Someone has truly said that any government that determines on the subjugation of a minority develops a neurosis that predetermines it to further stupidity. One also remembers what Lenin said, 'A country that is determined to enslave another country can itself never be free'. Many governments would do well to ponder the earlier writings of Lenin which largely deal with the misdoings of capitalists. Of course Lenin wrote very little about the manner of socialist society but a good deal is being written bit by bit. One or two interesting books have come from the Communist Party. Marek on The Philosophy of Revolution is well read by all sections of the Party; so is Adam Schaff, Some

Problems of Marxist Philosophy (published in Moscow, Warsaw and London). Gramsci, an Italian, now alas dead, who suffered at the hands of Mussolini and wrote some reflections on the moral nature of Socialism is well worth having a look at. He is well known in the USA and British Communist Parties and his work is undoubtedly a new way of looking at the nature of Socialism.[42] Another book, rather a long [one] which has recently been published in Moscow, is Alexander Werth's History of the Great Patriotic War. Werth lived in Leningrad until he was 17, emigrated with his people to France with which country he was well acquainted, then lived in England when he was not travelling. He stayed with the Russians throughout the War and his work in English will long be regarded as the most excellent account of Russia during the war. It is technical, human and quite free from emotional involvement though he has no great regard for Stalin. Werth's other books are well worth reading, particularly on France before the War and on Russia after the War. Alas he is now dead. He was well regarded by the Russian Govt who cut some pieces from his greatest book.

My plums which load down my little tree are turned red and ripe and we wish you were here to admire and even eat them. We have almonds too but they are very bitter to the taste. In fact the tree is quite useless but I am very reluctant to cut it down. It is so firm and solid and its leafy arms turn themselves enchantingly to the sky rather like a lovely woman braiding her hair.

---

[42] Interesting comments since apart from Louis Marks – *The Modern Prince*, published in 1957 – the major translations of Gramsci (1891–1937) were yet to come.

My son is at present in France and he says that while the papers have much to say about Ireland they are reticent about C-S.

We trust your affairs go well and that you are all in good health. Up to now we have not heard that you have successfully sent a man on the moon to undergo a heart transplant? Perhaps you have more pressing needs.

We all send you our affectionate greetings

Leslie Parker

14

Shoreham-by-Sea, Sussex, England
30th August 1969.

Dear Doctor Zalud,

My wife has reminded [me] to tell you that the cause of my typewriting errors is not a chance acquaintance with [a] cow over the hedge nor an attempt on my part to hit the keys with my fist but a certain or uncertain temperamental disinclination of my machine to present the right key at the right time as well as an inability to read my script after I have smashed it out. You may think perchance that English spelling has changed since you bought your last dictionary. Rest assured that except for schoolboys and my typewriter English remains substantially the same. Of course the Americans are changing our pronunciation and I think much for the worse. They also do this with the French language. They call café caffay and beret berray with a heavy accent on the last syllable. But the Americans dare to do anything.

They go to the moon where they find as many craters as they make in South Vietnam; they have the finest record for rape, murder, arson, larceny, spiv bankruptcies, housebreaking, hooliganism, drug taking, robbery with violence and other forms of human pleasure that any country could boast. Until this last year or two they easily had the highest incidence of divorce but now the USSR has caught up with them. The USSR has, I also understand, taken the lead in abortions. Indeed according to an article by a USSR specialist the birthrate shows a steep decline in some cities and a stagnancy in Western Russia that is alarming the authorities. On the other hand in China, a country with which the USSR has frank and comradely relations, the authorities there attempt to persuade, or is it force, the population not to make love until they are 28 years no months. If in their infinite wisdom this law should be adopted here we shall have to expurgate the books of our national poets by taking away all love lyrics, romantic songs (and even comic songs) from the delight of adolescents. I rather fancy that in both capitalist and communist countries the law will be difficult to enforce because in many areas dwellings are neither plentiful nor large. Over the lintels of these will have to be written 'abandon hope all ye who enter here' or 'remember proximity makes the heart beat stronger'.

Our legislators are still engaged in sorting out the Northern Island fracas. Some few hundreds of people have either had their summons to court dismissed or they have been let out of prison where only [...] remain. Oppression, it is declared, is quite useless so in future there are to be equal rights for all, efforts made to keep the police civil and impartial, free speech, without guns, molotov cocktails and rifles, will be allowed; there is no question of domination of the Northern Ireland Government by the GB Government and money will be supplied from England for rehabilitation. 500 dwellings, mostly Catholic, were burnt down, some factories (mostly Protestant) and barricades still decorate many streets where refuse and even sewage has not been collected for three or four weeks. The lesson of this is quite clear. When another nation sets out to destroy the liberties of a smaller nation it makes for itself so enormous a number of problems that relations become impossible. In the case of Northern Ireland the British Government has depended on dividing the Irish by bribing and suborning a section of the Irish population to do their governing for them. The British have learned only too well divide et imperium. They were however not the only learners; even contemporary history demonstrates that they have quite earnest pupils.

I have sent you some Morning Stars in which there are three articles on the development of the economy of the G. D. R, (East Germany). The speed with which this largely agricultural area has developed industrially is very surprising. Of course it has been essential to produce an economy that ranks well with that of West Germany which at the present time is the most flourishing capitalist country in Europe. In this (helping the GDR) the USSR has been extremely liberal with gifts of money and equipment ... even agriculture is in advance of most agriculture in the USSR where 50% of agric. costs are still taken up with labour. The GDR shows a significant advance on any other country but Czechoslovakia. East Germany and C-S had two advantages over other countries in the Communist bloc. They had a highly educated people and a highly developed intelligentsia and technology. Perhaps the GDR had one advantage over C-S and [this] lay and still lies in its keeping nearly 4,000 privately owned enterprises; some, plastics for instance, of quite significant importance. It is a heartbreaking shame that C-S has not been allowed to use its manpower, human goodwill and technology in the same way that the GDR has. You already [know] much about the YS difficulties and their consequent experiments. Considering that three parts of the country have been for several centuries enemies and that only one part could ever have called itself reasonably well off YS has accomplished much. Hungary still has many enterprises of a capitalist or semi-cap nature and provided we have peace will forge ahead. But possibly the greatest strides will be made in Romania. The harshness of the late 1950s is disappearing, people can talk politics and religion once more. I have been told on good authority that three million bibles are to be printed by the State Printing House whereas four or three years ago anyone who gathered for religious discussion with two others or for prayer was hauled to prison wherein to meditate on the divine or human will for as long as they cared to. The Chinese-Russian affair blows hot blows cold while the Americans with claws well concealed look eagerly for some tasty morsel. The USA has far more men under arms than the USSR and it is costing a pretty penny too. We rejoiced to learn that the President has tossed the poverty stricken of America another million dollars. Meanwhile the Americans are buying up every conceivable concern in England and Europe they can lay their hands on. All shares are a long way down the hill; they plummeted like a falling star, but profits keep on steadily going up week by week while men and women are out of work or striking for wages to keep level with prices.

My wife and I send you all our respectful affection. We ask you to remember that there are many real friends of C-S in this country. Real friends who do not wish to make money or capital out of your perplexities and who certainly do not wish to undermine the will of the people determined on a humane socialism.

Leslie Parker

15

Saarbrucken
5th September 1969.

Dear Mr and Mrs Parker,

Isn't it a shame that I am daring to reply to your kind letters only while being on German soil? Ever since returning from Yugoslavia I have been living in a state of disgust and fear. It is silly and futile to explain away what millions of our people have seen, heard and perceived by direct sense perception. The events of 21 August last year and everything that has happened since is being etched in to the memory of Czechs and Slovaks with the deepest grief and cannot be erased. Our children and children's children will still speak about the humiliation and the suffering the Russians have inflicted on us. How after a year of relentless blackmail, shameless meddling in our affairs, often appalling distortions and falsifications of history and the true state of affairs, the Russians have finally achieved what they call normalisation: a nasty and brutish police state. On the anniversary of the invasion all buses at Usti were nearly empty. So were the shops, the pubs and the cinemas. After noon a few youngsters and teenagers gathered as usually in the main square. They were at once attacked by heavily armed secret police, arrests were made and even people who left their houses on the main square were beaten up with truncheons. There were no demonstrations at this town although the police tried hard to provoke them. Somebody remarked to the soldiers and militia men lining the streets, 'Where [were] you last year on August 21? We did not see you then.' He was immediately taken away. To save the police embarrassment and prevent any inhibitions they were sent to different towns and we had the police force from Most at Usti while the masked policeman from Pilsen 'treated' the people of Liberec. Everything was done to furnish a belated proof that there was a counter-revolution last year and to convince the Russians that the Party and state had sufficient power to cope with it. These 'brilliant Marxists' are apparently forgetting that in the course of one year the situation has profoundly changed. While there was no counter-revolution, but only a reform movement last year – now there is a universal opposition against the pro-Russian regime. I left very nervously and with anxiety about being turned back from the frontier. Contrary to expectation the custom officials were very polite and did not even look into our luggage. I received 30 D.Marks for a fortnight's stay in Germany!!! Twenty Czech anaesthetists are attending the congress at Saarbrucken and again several of them are not willing to return. I am going without a proper breakfast to the lectures and can afford only the cheapest meal: a sausage and chips. Fortunately coffee is served without charge in the foyer of the lecture hall. Observing all the affluence without any means to share in it makes one feel pretty awfully. This is another world, Mr Parker, and socialism has for ever failed to catch up with it. While I am enjoying to be able to see this new and rich world I am horrified when I am

thinking that in a few days all will be over and I shall
have to return into the dreary land of socialism.

Many thanks for your kind letters and sympathy.

With best wishes to you and your family
Yours sincerely

Paul Zalud

16

Usti nad Labem, Czecheslovakia
21 September 1969.

Dear Mr. and Mrs Parker,

It was a benediction to have your letter after returning
from Germany to my tranquil and pitiful home. During
a fortnight most private conversations I had nilly willy
to listen to turned round the subject how to make money
and where and how to get still more money out of the
art of healing. Thanks Goodness there are still a few
men concerned with the fate of humanity at large and
not preoccupied with self-centred interests. My visit
to Germany coincided with the election campaign and
with the outbreak of a wave of wild strikes[43] which took
German politicians of all parties and shades by surprise.
Strikes are called in Germany 'an English disease'. I
had to smile when I heard Herr Kissinger on the TV
suggesting that these wild strikes were fomented by

---

[43] Presumably a reference to so-called 'wildcat' strikes, conducted
by members of Trade Unions in defiance of or without the support
of their Union.

foreign influences, an argument which was ad nauseam oversold in this country in a different context. I have so far never seen such well clad and well feeding people and shops abounding with such a tremendous variety of goods – from the most useful consumer goods to the most superfluous luxury fur coats, carpets and jewelleries. I could not help but admire the streets of Düsseldorf, Koln and Frankfurt where I spent a day or so. The comfortable homes and mechanized kitchens of' my friends who offered me hospitality, the extremely efficient communications, colour television, the impressive buildings ranging from medieval cathedrals to the magnificent business premises of concrete and glass of Thyssen, Bosch and Banks, that all made a deep impression upon me.

At the congress at Saarbrocken I was looking out for meeting someone from England. I had the good fortune of meeting Professor Epstein from the department of Anaesthesia of the University of Oxford. At breakfast at the Catholic students' hostel where I and about 20 Czech anaesthetists were staying I met two English girls from the British Council. I had a good chat with them but they were rather conspicuous by their plain dresses at the gala dance amidst the German splendour and elegance. For me, at least, brains matter not dresses. After the congress I visited hospitals and university departments, stayed over the weekend with a working-class family from Usti which emigrated last year to Solingen, then with an old friend of mine at Düsseldorf and at last I spent a day with my former brother-in-law who is a general practitioner near Frankfurt.[44] His sister was the former wife of my brother and died with her small daughter in 1945 on

---

[44] Paul mistakenly describes his sister-in-law's brother as his own brother-in-law.

the airport at London when the plane, scheduled for
Prague, crashed and came down in flames. I slept very
little throughout my holiday in Germany as I managed
to read through 2 books which I would not be allowed
to take back with me to Czechoslovakia: 1. Yewgenija
Ginzburg: The harsh route of my life. 2. Milovan Djillas:
The imperfect society. From 2 to 6 pm I spent in public
libraries and reading rooms, searching through the
papers and magazines. All the Czech refugee-doctors I
met are doing very well and I was glad to hear that their
work is highly appreciated in Germany and Holland.
Some of them are receiving a fair share from the cake of
affluency [sic] but do not feel happy and secure. Others
have turned within the span of one year from Socialists
into money grabbing egoists and have lost all interests
and connections with their homeland. One of these
fellows told me a malicious story: 'Do you know how a
clever Czech communicates with a stupid one? Answer:
Over the telephone at Munich.'

As I am not clever I returned on September 2nd[45] to
my beloved ones being well aware that this may have
been my last journey to the West for many years to
come. I was only looking forward to the moment I could
present to my family all the gifts I received for them
from friends. Although I left with only 40 DM currency
there was something for everyone in my suitcase. David
showed me the lovely children's books you kindly sent
him and he can name a good many animals and objects
but, so far, in Czech only. To teach him English is the
most noble task for a grandfather I can imagine. To this

---

[45] This date is clearly a mistake. The 11th Central European Meeting
of the German-speaking Societies (Anaesthesiology) was held from
4 to 6 September, and Paul records that he stayed in Germany for a
fortnight.

end the books will come in handy enough. You don't know, Mr. Parker, how much I appreciate your friendship and persistent attention. I read with great interest the leader and the readers' letters in [the] Morning Star. To cut us off from the West and to shut us in behind the curtain would be the worst tragedy. A son of Dr. Husak and a brother of the hard-liner Lubomir Strougal chose to go to Switzerland and England respectively. They too are Czechs wherever they are. The son of Dr. Husak is, of course, a Slovak.

With best wishes and kind regards
Yours

Paul Zalud

17

Shoreham-by-Sea, Sussex, England
Tuesday [28th] October 1969.[46]

Dear Doctor Zalud,

If you have two heart attacks in six days they have a deleterious effect on your energy. While they enable you with good excuse to lie in bed and think magnificent thoughts, bless whatever gods there be for friends who send you Get Well cards, some sentimental, some of dubious propriety but all of sound wellbeing and affection. Despite the world's injustices, its squalid slums and greed I am quite convinced there is enough goodwill

---

[46] Dated from internal evidence.

and love and men and women that they have no need of
moral political or theologic [*sic*] protection.

We are ourselves sufficient reason for being alive.
When the Papalists and other authoritarians have
exhausted themselves in bashing their stupid skulls
against the resilient wall of human aspirations then those
aspirations will flower. As you know we came down from
the North to enjoy what we hoped would be a lovely
end of summer and autumn. The sun did in fact shine
every day. There were days when the clouds completely
disappeared. The plums ripened in prolific abundance
on our single little plum tree. My wife gave them away
to refuse collectors, postmen, children and even to me.
I lay on my back listening to smooth voices recounting
the world's more polite happenings or those happenings
that our government approved of.

The Italians contracted the English disease, even
the RC Bishops with them, the Russians remained
unmoveable over this and that, so did the Americans,
so did the Arabs, so did the Israelis. There's a lot of oil
in North America and a British firm tried to get into
the retail gasoline market in the USA (really!); fighting
still went on in Northern Ireland and everywhere there
are naughty extremists who just don't understand the
point of view of the other extremists. The price of cocoa
is manipulated by British and American monopolists
and it is all blamed on the Ghanaian government; the D
mark goes almost up to heaven. A chess master is thrown
out of some party and put into jail because he wrote an
article in a Dutch newspaper and loved liberty.[47] And
Husak stalls and stalls and manages for the time being

---

[47] Presumably a reference to the recent arrest – not for the first
time – of Czech grandmaster Ludek Pachman. He was charged with
defaming a representative of the Republic and supporting Dubcek.

to keep away from secret trials. And many are dying in dreadful imprisonment on Greek islands.[48] And in labour camps elsewhere. There are riots in British prisons because many men received a sentence of 30 years for stealing discarded money from a train. And all the time the world's work continues. In Shoreham and Usti the sun shines. And even in Moscow, where snow has already come down from grey skies, men and women make love and babies are born who grow up and look into each other's eyes and much of the true meaning of life. While, as the Psalmist says, the heathen so furiously rage together we can rise from our beds, our operating tables, our sinks, our workbenches and rejoice that while there's life there's more than hope.

En avanti

Leslie Parker

18

Usti nad Labem, Czechoslovakia
6th November 1969.

Dear Mr. Parker,

During the past fortnight I attempted twice to write to you, chiefly to wish you a speedy recovery and to thank you for supplying me occasionally with bits and pieces of information which are very welcome indeed. I am particularly grateful to you for the thoughtful article

---

[48] A reference to those imprisoned by the Greek Junta, in power since 1967.

by W. Lippman. I think he is right with his diagnosis
that Western societies are in a process of revolutionary
change and that we are living in the age of inventiveness.
In spite of all misgivings, conflicts and complaints 'there
can be no contentment but in proceeding' (Thomas
Hobbes, 'Leviathan'). The more depressing to me is
to see that our East-European societies are moving
like determinate machines in regular and inevitable
circles, reproducing all the evils we all have at one time
condemned. In the quiescence, assured by the Emergency
Regulations and Censorship, our lives are running down
and we have become once more an isolated society with
no external trade in tourists, scientific and technological
hardware and information and ideas. I just learned that
the whole party of Czech biologists who were scheduled
to read papers at an international scientific meeting in
West Germany has been prevented from leaving. The
underprivileged in intelligence and imagination, those
who have been found wanting in personal and moral
responsibility and were therefore gently turned out of
office, they all are back again in leading positions. With
great ado we are being offered the same old remedies
which have failed in the past and produced omnipresent
stagnation. The odds against overcoming the general
sense of gloom and decay with the measures proposed
are fantastic indeed. Common sense has hitherto
accepted the meaning of national sovereignty as just
that and neither in the case of the Dominican republic
or, to quote a more recent example, Lebanon, arose the
need for a new definition. The need to redefine the term
National Sovereignty in the case of our country is not
obvious to me unless it was violated. On a pure logical
basis adding a conjunction entails a self-contradiction.
All this nonsense we had to learn just on October 28th,
since 1918 Czechoslovakia's independence day! (Sic!)

It happened more than once in Europe that the victors showed some magnanimity and grace at the conclusion of peace to the vanquished. Mr. Palme Dutt in his essay on Czechoslovakia in the Labour Monthly had something to say about underestimating national feelings.[49] He ought to decide for himself whether a note of cynicism and humiliation is not discernible and whether men on the wrong side of their fifties are not likely to lose their human dignity if made to change their minds within the span of one year. The large majority of our people simply cannot abdicate to think and judge for themselves what they have seen and heard. They remember the starting position and recollect all the stages in the developments. There can't be an obliteration of the past and as regards loss of self-identity, they will not follow the precepts of the leaders.

You are quite right. The sun is shining and it is remarkably warm. David can still play on the sand and twaddling about in the garden. The leaves are down and so are the apples and pears. I hope you will take care of yourself and will not go to the congress of the CP-GB.

Remember me to Mrs. Parker and your children!

Yours sincerely

Paul

---

[49] Rajani Palme Dutt, *Labour Monthly*, October 1969.

19

Shoreham-by-Sea, Sussex, England
8th November 1969.

Dear Paul,

Your letter was very welcome: we both gave forth sounds
of relief when your handwriting appeared. Your letters
are always valuable for the reports in our papers about
CS are not too frequent; nor can they always be relied on.
We like to have the truth and let it be known.

Now there are one or two practical things.

In case I become too ill in the future or incontinently
die. Or you wonder where I am – Heaven, Hell or Europe.
And what a choice! Will you please write to my elder son,
Doctor David Parker. He is a Party member upon whom
you may rely. The address of my daughter which might
be useful for any of your friends who need a meal or a
bed for a night or two is [...]

Of course David and his wife Margaret will always
help any of your compatriots.

Quite recently Professor Galbraith of America wrote
a book called the Industrial State which has been
translated into Russian. I am going to send you a copy in
English and hope you will get it. It is a faithful picture of
the interrelationships of politics, the Industrial lords, the
military interests and Security forces. The central theme
that the advancement in technology in the USSR and
USA will produce the same sort of social economy in the
end is, I think, mistaken. Social revs. are not produced
by gadgetry. Besides there will almost certainly be a civil
war in the USA.

Last year I was generally incompetent in the matter
of Christmas presents. Will you please ask your ladies if

I may send wool for knitting. Or do you have plenty? If wool what colour(s). If not wool will you please, encore please let us know what we can reasonably send from a top-heavy capitalism?

Although the sun shines it is quite cold so we are putting up the gas consumption. Mr. Dubcek, they say, never did anything ideological. The evil that men do lives after them but the good should be enshrined in print. What a lovely job you have putting people to sleep. I could have done with a whiff in the middle of the night when my stupid mind began to define Freedom. Now that's [a] mind and body shaker if you like.

Leslie

20

Shoreham-by-Sea, Sussex, England
Undated [*c*.20–25 November 1969].

My dear Doctor

I am enclosing two items depicting the charms first of a money harassed monarchy that all told has something like an expenditure of three million pounds sterling. Most of this is seldom discussed by our newspapers let alone accounted for. The second item is about a problem of colour prejudice that is being rapidly exacerbated by a company of sadists called the national front. We have about 3 million coloured immigrants, most of whom are poor and most are gathered together in villainous overcrowded houses without proper sanitation, enough running water (no hot of course) and often with the worst paid jobs. Of course we have very large numbers of whites living under the same conditions. These are daily being told by an MP named Powell that their situation will become worse because of the coloured people living here and will soon be told by the National Front that the cause of their evil conditions is that the blacks are taking away their jobs and best houses.

Meanwhile our highest achievement to date is a small imitation of the peace demonstrations that are now rocking the American government. The capitalist papers report that just [about] 250,000 people coming from all over the USA assembled in Washington. At the end of the day the more radical elements engaged the police in a variety of scuffles and numbers were arrested. I rather fancy the USA govt. wanted more trouble so that the whole movement could be disgraced and disgraceful. But nothing very much occurred. Yet the time may come when the radical elements may well become much more revolutionary than they are now. President Nixon appears to be favouring the anti-black reactionaries of the Southern states by slowing the integration of white and coloured education which even Johnson had tried to speed up. Nor has there been in the USA any attempt made to increase the number of jobs available for the poorest whites and blacks. Incidentally CPGB Congress 295 agst invasion; 118 for. There is certainly much feeling in the USA agst the war in Vietnam and by and large I should say constitutes the most obvious test for, or rather of, the validity of the USA govt as a humane agency. An enormous amount of pressure for peace is coming from people in the USA who have never thought of demonstrating ever before. Nothing should or can withstand the people in the end. As Lenin said, once the people have grasped the theory of becoming free that theory in their hands will become concrete and unassailable. All the world is joyful that Lenin's works are now translated into 45 volumes. I shall certainly leave these for my grandchildren to read. Or their children anyway.

Laus Deo.

LP

21

Usti nad Labem, Czechoslovakia
26 November 1969 [by hand].

Dear Mr and Mrs Parker,

I find it difficult to control my thoughts and my pen. On Saturday November 2nd I suddenly and unexpectedly lost my son Peter, aged 33. He finished his unhappy life by hanging himself. He left the house silently while we all were asleep. Then he rushed to a little wood and committed himself to Eternity. While most human beings are crying out for help when in danger, he planned, witnessed and carried through the act of self-destruction without flinching. When my wife noted the empty bed, his wristwatch on the table and his farewell note, it was too late. We all are grieved and shocked by this bereavement. Peter has been suffering from mental depression on and off for the past few years. Three years ago he had to give up work in a chemical laboratory. He received a fair sickness benefit and led a still, withdrawn life beside us, without hurting or offending anyone. He used to help me in the household and liked to look after David while his mother went shopping. We were pleased to see him taking more interest in the social life of the town lately. He went to town nearly every day last week to search for Christmas presents. At the same time, however, he more often complained of not working and of being good for nothing. He did not want to be a burden to others – and his life became an unbearable burden to himself. Poor Peter! We shall not forget your clean and over sensitive soul!

I am very grateful to you for sending me J.K. Galbraith's book. I saw it in the bookshops in Germany but did not have the Dms to buy it. I arranged with a local bookshop to send you an album of Hradcany castle in pictures. There was no better choice available. You really should not bother to send us anything for Christmas. We don't want anything for us, although goods are short and people are going to the GDR for shopping. I overheard my daughter-in-law complaining the other day that she cannot get any underwear for David, not even boots. If you are insisting on a Christmas present, please send some underwear – vests and pants for a boy aged 4.

With best wishes,

Yours sincerely

Paul

22

Shoreham-by-Sea, Sussex, England
1st December 1969.

My very dear Friends,

Your letter has come and we are deeply grieved to learn
of death of your Son. What can we say to comfort you
first in in the ... months of his illness and at last in his
death? You will find your house very empty, I'm afraid,
for we miss those for whom we have to care day by day
rather more than those who are self-reliant and vigorous.
To you both and to your daughter-in-law, strangers in the
flesh though we be, we send you our deepest sympathy
and love. If this message comes to you over the many
miles that divide us with any comfort we shall indeed
be blessed.

We did receive the book with the most beautiful
photographs and intend to give it our full consideration
very soon. But you must not try to repay what little we
can do [for] you in kind. We do what we can and rejoice
in it. I may say that I part with a book with a little less
pain now than I used to and with even less pain when
I know what I send will be appreciated by a more able
mind than my own.

Within a week or so we shall send you the underwear
for David. As we have no grandchild of our own we shall
be pretending that we have at least a god-child or should
I say a Marx-child?? If you will please stand the young
gentleman on a white sheet of paper in his stockings or
socks and draw round his feet with a vertical pencil I
will procure him some walking-out shoes. Please let me
do this. By the way if you wish to read a particular book
please let me know. I have the very vaguest ideas of what

you are allowed to read from the West and indeed of what you wish to read.

One of the great surprises in the modern world is the rise of production in the GDR. They are now claiming that they are 9th in world production. This success is due I think to the proximity of West Germany and the necessity of creating a standard of living that will be satisfactory to Germans. Secondly to their care of technologists and managers, particularly those of 4000 capitalist or 'mixed' firms. And thirdly to the GDR's close relationship with Moscow. So far as I know there is no suggestion of Novotny[50] or (worse still) Rakosi methods in the GDR. Poland on the other hand seems to be in a sorry plight. [Several illegible lines relating to Harold Wilson and President Nixon's visit to Romania are omitted here.]

Meanwhile we get along here with promises of taxation, an array of strikes that would smite dismay even into the heart of Brezhnev and a rapid transformation of marvellous summer and autumn into an era of north winds and snow. I am allowed to go out, the garden looks darkly sorry for itself and my wife (I am told by my admiring sister) puts up with me very well. The prospect of developing a saint in the family had not hitherto occurred to me.

Yours most sincerely

Leslie P

---

[50] Antonin Novotny, General Secretary of the Czech Communist Party 1953–68 and President of Czechoslovakia 1957–68.

23

Usti nad Labem, Czechoslovakia
18 December 1969.

Dear Mr. and Mrs. Parker,

We received the parcel with underwear, stockings and
the 2 Penguin books and we thank you very much
indeed for this kind Christmas present. At the same
time I wish to correct your erroneous assumption
that my deceased son Peter is David's father. I had
two sons, Peter and Ian. Ian was born at Southmead
Hospital in Bristol in 1943 where I was working as
a medical officer during the war. We lived in a small
house in Delvin Road, quite near the Filton aircraft
works. The owner of this house was in the army,
letting his house to us for the duration, as one used
to say. Although we experienced two or three air-raids
there, we were very happy. Ian is a schoolteacher of
Russian and the musical arts. Apart from measles
he got soon after Peter's funeral, he is alright and
fortunately he never suffered any depressions. His
wife Zdenka, 23 years, is working in a publicity
department. My wife, Bohumila, has the rather tiring
job of looking after David, keeping him warm, clean
and happy, while at the same time she has to do most
of the shopping and housework. Zdenka is leaving at
6 a.m. and coming home from work at 4–5 p.m.

My wife has still a broken heart and cannot
get over the bereavement. I myself can find some
consolation in my work, where sometimes we are
able to save someone [...], help some disabled and

best of all to relieve the pangs of pain of childbirth. After many months of great despondency, there is now a glimmer of hope in the climate of opinion in this country. While Christmas is coming fast and the year is fleeting, we still are feeling weary. But when the lights will go on and we shall listen to the Christmas carols from England and our own country, we certainly shall feel united with all men of sense and good will wherever they may be.

So let me wish you once more a very HAPPY NEW YEAR to you all!

Yours

Paul, Bohumila, David, Ian and Zdenka Zalud

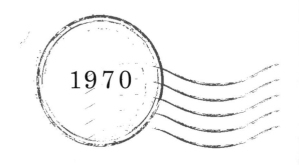

1970

JANUARY TO DECEMBER

During the course of this year, despite an unexplained gap in March, the frequency of the exchanges increased. Leslie wrote no fewer than 36 letters and Paul reciprocated with 21. The terms in which they addressed each other became more intimate; photographs and family news were exchanged, together with an invitation to the Parkers to visit the Zalud family. Paul became increasingly concerned by Leslie's poor health while Leslie strove to alleviate Paul's 'isolation' and 'extreme solitude and boredom'. Occasionally the depression eased – partially in July, when he went to Prague for a medical exhibition, but could only admire equipment that his hospital could not afford, and more completely in September, when his spirits were raised by the congress of anaesthetists also held in Prague. Domestically the year ended on a happier note when the Zalud household, after much hassle and disappointment, acquired central heating and Paul no longer felt cold at home as well as work. Otherwise it was, he recorded, a year of 'gloom and hard work' in inadequate conditions not helped by 'stupid bureaucrats ... lacking in foresight and sensibility'.

Despite certainty that their letters were interfered with, both men seemed much less concerned than previously about offending the censors by their often explicit attacks on Soviet-style socialism and its leaders; Paul even threw in some popular jokes for good measure. In December Leslie asked Paul to write a summary of the consequences of the Soviet invasion. Paul responded by saying that it was far too risky to say to do so, and then preceded to provide a passionate denunciation of the impact of the purge of 'followers of the reform movement' in the party, industry, civil service, universities and educational establishments, the judiciary, trade unions, cultural associations and the press.

24

Shoreham-by-Sea, Sussex, England
7th January 1970.

Dear Paul,

I read your beautiful greetings letter to the whole of
our family, and today to my sister and brother in law
who lunched with us. I feel sure you could not begin to
calculate the warmth of their feelings towards you and
your family. They are not all socialists by any means,
indeed my sister is an avowed, if lazy, conservative
but the contemporary history is so well known arid
appreciated by them that they symbolised the goodwill
that all good Britons feel for your country and your
countrymen and women.

Of course they were particularly interested in how
our friendly communications began [and] they were
vastly amused at my eventual discomfiture. My sister
and b.in law were particularly interested in your being
in Bristol during the war because at that time they were
both members of the Doyly Carte Opera Company – the
people who play the famous Gilbert and Sullivan Comic
Operas you know – and they were pursued right up
the west coast of England, having been bombed out of
Hammersmith Theatre, London, by the Nazi bombers.
The bombers were so assiduous in Manchester that the
whole company went to live some 30 miles off. 'Oh yes,'
they exclaimed, 'we know Filton very well.' My sister also
wishes me to say that she too has a son named Ian. He is
a large chap with a lovely wife and three children and he
earns his living by being a Major in Her Majesty's army.

You were indeed often in our thoughts because we
are so much aware what a very sad year this has been

for you. My wife particularly sends heartfelt sympathy to your wife. We both hope that the very great loss she as a mother has suffered will be made up in some measure by the love her family and friends bear her. We are quite sure that the parents of the boy you have lost have no cause for blaming themselves. The world is very oppressive these days and gives little help very often to those who are particularly oppressed by it. In our own country we are just being made aware of the ever increasing number of men and women who are in need of spiritual and psychiatric help. Our techniques are almost primitive because of our ignorance and our mental hospitals are nothing less than a disgrace. Our present epoch is one of great turmoil and inhumane irresponsibility in high places – St. Paul called it spiritual wickedness yet it is more than that. In some sections of our people and indeed among our young people there is a tendency towards cynicism and hopelessness but we who have visions of what men and women can do must go steadily on laying some little part of the foundations of the happier future.

To all your family therefore and to all women and men of goodwill I will make an old toast 'I look towards you'. For we have great need of each other.

We started quietly at Christmas with only one son but they came along in quick time and here they are. David and Margaret; Linda and her husband, Hilary and his fiancée to whom he got engaged on Jan 1st and of course Leslie and his Enid.

Leslie

25

Shoreham-by-Sea, Sussex, England
Undated [probably c.15th January 1970].

My dear Paul,

A very hurried note conveying our hopes and best wishes
for you.

Herewith the Weekly Guardian which for the time
being we can send regularly if you wish it.

The article by Zorza is interesting. Z has taken the
place of Deutscher who died and who was much more
objective about the Communist countries.[51] I do not think
that Stalin was aggressive at all on the international
front. He was if anything very reluctant either to prepare
for war or go to war. He signed the Russo-German
Pact, even after the Germans were rapidly advancing
into Russian he ordered no shooting, he had quite old-
fashioned generals like Budenny and Voroshilov and in
the end he let Greece go in a pact with Churchill and
Roosevelt. That he was a bully there is no doubt and also
the negation of socialist government everyone knows. But
aggressive no. No more than Brezhnev is now.

If you find the paper useful or not let me know.

Our sincerest regards to you all.

Leslie

---

[51] This allusion may mislead. Isaac Deutscher had been dead for
three years and seems not to have written for *The Guardian* since
1960. Both he and Victor Zorza wrote for the paper in the 1950s,
but Zorza was far more prolific. Between 10 December 1969 and 17
January 1970 Zorza wrote a series of articles about the possibility of
hostilities breaking out between China and the Soviet Union.

26

Usti nad Labem, Czechoslovakia
19 January 1970.

Dear Mr. and Mrs Parker and family!

Thank you very much for your kind and comforting
letter and for the two copies of the Guardian-Weekly. It
is a tremendous pleasure to read a decent newspaper
from time to time. Like many of my compatriots I am
boycotting all domestic news media since the end of
May 1969 – thus making use of the last remnant of
liberty: the liberty of the consumer to leave what he
does not want. You should be aware that the Morning
Star is like Humanité, Unita, Borba[52] etc. available at
the city library where one can read all the organs of
the CP but nothing else. For Czechs who understand
German it is easy to keep informed by listening to the
newscasts of the powerful radio stations of Germany
which through geographical proximity can be distinctly
heard in this country. I have been a regular listener to
the BBC for 20 years and I don't want to give up my
allegiance to this unique and fair broadcasting station
which is relatively free from strict government control
and unlike the American news media less subject to
commercial interests of the big corporations. Because of
the wild jamming carried out on our side and the poor
selectivity of our radio sets it is at times a tiring and
time consuming task to get the gist of some excellent
news-comments from the BBC. In the British merchant
navy the sailor has, so I was told, to repeat the order

[52] Newspapers of the French, Italian and Yugoslav Communist
Parties respectively.

of the captain or commanding officer to make sure
that he understood it well, word for word. So I too am
sometimes compelled to listen to the same broadcast a
second time to get it completely. While you are sitting
in an armchair and spreading the Morning Star, The
Times or the Guardian on your knees we have to do
news hunting. On New Years Eve we had a party and
an irreclaimable illusionist remarked that an eventual
European Security Conference might place our country
in a nuclear-free zone. I said that a frequency band, free
of jamming, would for the time being be a more desirable
result. On January 7th I had to attend a meeting at
the institute for postgraduate education at Prague.
Because of the epidemic of influenza and the shortage of
electricity only a very few tram street cars were running
and I had to walk several miles through the centre of
Prague to reach the place of the meeting. Shivering with
cold and all my toes numb from the bitter frost I noted a
huge red banner: On Lenin's Road towards Communism.
The men who put up this slogan didn't probably take into
account that some old chaps like myself still remember
that it's now 50 years ago that Lenin said Communism
is Soviet power + electrification. But after the meeting,
not minding the cold, I walked through Wenceslaus to
feel the pulse of Prague. I was astonished to see plenty
of nice goods, many of foreign origin, behind the shop-
windows. The women in their fur coats and high boots,
students with their long hair protruding below their fur
caps, looked pretty, strong and healthy to me. The social
life of Prague is pulsating and convulsing, undisturbed
by purges and arrests under the Emergency and Secrecy
Acts, I thought, and I boarded my unheated train and
took a seat in complete darkness. A few minutes before
departure the lights were turned on and I saw myself
confronted by two young, well clad and intelligent

looking men. We were soon engaged in a critical dialogue about conditions here and elsewhere, carried on in a fearless and frank manner. The discussion proceeded in such a frank style that I began to wonder whether we are really in the year 1970 or still in the year 1968. I thought that through my knowledge of English and German I am in a privileged position as regards news from the outside world but these two fellows knew everything I learned. After returning home and warming up with several cups of tea, I related my astonishment about the goods I saw at Prague (about the pretty women I kept, of course, silent). My wife explained to me that these goods were ordered for the Christmas shopping with the currency reserves the right-wing opportunists had accumulated but were belatedly unloaded because of the dismal state of affairs at the railways.

Some years ago some American psychologists fiddled about with an instrument, called a tachistoscope. With this instrument two neutral and two vulgar words were exposed to students within the fraction of a second. The subjects were required to recognize all four exposed words but when they reported only the two clean and decent words, the psychologists thought that they have discovered and proved what they call 'PERCEPTUIAL DEFENCE'. It only later turned out that the obliging students withheld the pair of obscene words being strongly motivated by the wish to present a most favourable image of themselves, an image of complete conformity with their professors. Fortunately students have profoundly changed since and are in an open rebellion against all authoritarian creeds and establishments. The talk we had in the cold railway car convinced me that the Czech people also has profoundly changed. They perceived very well that our president did not even mention the educational and scientific estate in

his new year's message while the west-German government
is going to spend 3 billions DM for reforming the
higher education and that in the Rhineland alone 9 new
universities, 13 colleges, will be opened already during this
year and thousands more students will be admitted.

It is alleged that the goal of the deplorable events of
August 1968 was the restoration of the leading role of
the Czech CP. But we are perceiving that a proposal was
made and apparently seriously considered to refuse the
new membership cards to all those party members who
have a bad record and a university education. It is argued
– with some justification, I admit – that an intellectual
with a university degree cannot be regarded as having
been misled, misguided or disorientated by the right
wing opportunists. Only blockheads, dupes and reckless
bumpers for sinecures are eligible for the leading role.
Most sane persons seem to perceive that an inner ring of
politicians who identified with Russian bureaucracy are
controlling the party with the sole aim to manipulate the
working class towards friendship and cooperation with
the occupying power. We are perceiving that the most
vocal party officials are either publicity or secret service
agents of Russia, posing as international Marxists. Our
overt behaviour is, however, disappointing as no one
demonstrates and no one stands up for those who are
being fired. We are perceiving alright that our Western
neighbours are just about to safeguard the constitutional
right of demonstrating in public and to put this right
into practice and make it effective. The right to peaceful
demonstrations is, of course, taken by the British judges
as something as natural as are income-taxes or bedbugs
in the hotels of East European countries. Persons whose
inner life is not reflected in overt behaviour tend to be
regarded as idiots or lunatics by Western standards. But
in this country the witch-hunting is just being followed up

by the notorious spy-hunting and people are indeed being dragged away from their homes. I should like to plead that we are not really idiotic or lunatics but that we are suffering from PERCEPTUAL DEFENCE.

I know no better reply to your lovely old English toast: 'I look towards you' but to write about topics of mutual interest in the hope to catch your ear while you are looking. Thousand thanks for your pleasant letters and for all the many kindnesses you have rendered us since we became friends by wrestling with each other!

Yours sincerely

Paul

27

Shoreham-by-Sea, Sussex, England
24th January 1970.

My dear Doctor,

l have no doubt that the S. Govt are to a large extent taken in by their own revanchist propaganda but events and proximity are forcing both the Soc. and capt. powers to at least make some show of peace talks and this problem seems to us to be the greatest problem we can tackle. What can be done from your end I have little idea of but the peace lovers of all kinds and denominations are girding up their loins to many different demonstrations this coming Easter. The capitalists of various countries are not only full both of suspicion of the socialist countries but they are torn with the ineffable desire to make money out of each other. Grappling for or before the Common Market is now an irresistible occupation of all British and German newspapers and politicians. Though mostly all the people in these islands realise that our going into the C. Mkt. will only put up prices and particularly of foodstuffs our politicians of every colour but red are ready to sell whatever souls they lay claim to for the honour of weighing us down with bigger prices, greater unemployment and outpouring of capital. So in the face of this stupid endeavour I have no doubt that the S. Govt. is fearful. The weakness of the Soviet situation is, in our opinion made all the more difficult and unsatisfactory by endeavouring to weld the communist countries together not in a unity of relative diversity but in a rigid uniformity. The strength of Socialism lies in the expanding minds, self-reliance and energy of the people. The Sov. Gov is weighed down internally with a bureaucracy and a large number of Party chiefs in the middle ranks who are more remarkable for their adherence to their jobs than to the Marxist dialectic, the basis of which, is nothing less than the inevitability of change and the necessity of men and women using the probabilities of change to advantage their own condition.

There is a great deal of fear, I think, in the hearts of our financiers, stockbrokers and economists that capitalism is not going to stand up to the strain of the immense differences noticeable [between] the immensely rich and the horribly poor. For instance we have large blocks of flats and offices unlet while not so far away men and women sleep destitute or in the filthiest slums. Crimes of violence increase, unemployment increases and there is very strong opposition to any increase of money to be devoted to what is blazoned abroad as the welfare state. Mr Wilson has caused an enormous amount of dissension and anger among working people over his intention to reduce wage increases while inflation became more and more apparent and prices went up like rockets. Now he feels the danger that the next election in about 12 months will put the Tories back in power.

Despite Mr W's sad shortcomings that would be a bad day for both you and us, for the ill-concealed enmity in Conservative quarters, both for our people and for the socialist countries, would spring into happy openness. There are many signs that certain sections and reactionary leaders wish to shackle the people, to relieve their own taxation by taxing the poorer sections of [the] population. We can hope therefore that people of every sort will make greater and more insistent demands for peace negotiations that will bring the peoples of our countries together.

The continually increasing economy of the GDR may well cause some headaches in Moscow. For 16.5 million people, apparently tied to Moscow, they have done remarkably well. There the Russian soldier is largely taken for granted; some questions are asked but their departure will not be achieved until we have brought the capitalist governments to realise we do not like war and prob. will not fight. In Britain we cannot recruit 37,000 troops a year for our military forces. Yet some people want us to go and fight for Singapore – where we have £250 million invested.[53] Even 626,000 men unemployed won't join. What about you? Very welcome?

I must go, this is self indulgence.

Leslie P.

---

[53] On a visit to Singapore on 7 January Edward Heath, the Leader of the Opposition, made a commitment that, if elected, a Conservative government would reverse the proposed disengagement of British forces from Singapore and Malaysia and keep troops there indefinitely.

28

Shoreham-by-Sea, Sussex, England
31 January 1970.

Dear Paul,

My feeling, and it is hardly anything more than that,
is that reaction is crowding in on us somewhat. In this
country there is a gentleman, an M.P named Enoch
Powell, who is busy raising all sorts of wicked prejudices,
primarily against the coloured of whom we have about
3.5 million all told. Many of these live crowded together
in the slummiest parts of our industrial cities with
consequent effect upon their education and outlook.
Mr. Powell feels that more austerity is called for, less
cozening by the (alleged) Welfare State, loans to students
instead of grants, a rigid putting down of 'hooligans' and
demonstration – both under the same condemnation.
We have also two v. right wing organisations (one called
the National Front) that wish to go jack booting along
with Mr. E. Powell. There is another hardening of the
Police in Northern Ireland, though they have not yet
been rearmed, but behind them they have a solid body of
pig-headed Protestants who hate some men more than
they love God. There are also some who amazingly wish
to 'make the British Empire what it was' though they
can see what sort of messes the B. E. made in Nigeria,
Rhodesia and India.

   We in this small town rather badly run by a small
council have lately witnessed an all out attack on one
very outspoken Labour Town Councillor – a woman –
by 12 Tory councillors who after a secret conclave by
a vote in Council robbed her of her right to vote on
Council committees where most of the work is done.

My wife went to a public meeting almost spontaneously called in defence of the lady but I think the caucus will hold out. The Tories are indeed rearing up their heads and flexing their muscles for the General Election in about 12 months time when they expect to get back into Parliament [government?]. Then we shall see the money fly – into the wrong pockets and the curtailment of Welfare 'benefits' that already lag well behind those of Holland and Germany. It isn't of course that there are any more actual Tories but there are large numbers of people who vote first this way and [then] that way; and also, of course, many traditionally Labour supporters are so disgusted with Mr. Wilson's curtailment of wages but inability to keep down prices that they are refusing to sally forth and vote. The screw will really begin to turn if the dreaded but 'impossible' economic recession starts. Home markets have declined in some foodstuffs but particularly in cars and other durable goods, particularly those made of steel. The capitalists are always between the devil of imports and inflation and curbing them and unemployment and [the] continually lessened buying power of the masses. We shall see.

There has been a great to do about Nigeria. Ojukwu,[54] who hoped to lead the Ibos into a secession from the Nig. Federation and is I think very much of a go-getter, a sort of adventurer [...] after the oil wells and [...] large deposits, has had to skedaddle and 'the noble McGowon'[55] reigns supreme – with the help of British

---

[54] Chukwuemeka Odumegwu Ojukwu was a military officer and politician. He served as the military governor of the Eastern Region of Nigeria in 1966 and led the breakaway Republic of Biafra from 1967 to 1970.

[55] General Yakubu 'Jack' Dan-Yumma Gowon, head of the Federal Military Government of Nigeria from 1966 to 1975.

arms and Russian planes. 'The imperialists are beaten,' cried Pravda. This means that France and Italy and the Pope were shown the door. I presume Italy will get back her oil concession if the Italian govt denies the Pope. The Pope has been very naughty by practically accusing the Noble McG of wishing to massacre all the Ibos. Anyway the USA happily sitting on the sidelines can now enter into the glory of the greatest of the oil concessions; then Britain now held in high honour by the conqueror will also enter into the joy of the their black overlord. That's two imperialists not yet beaten; perhaps Brezhnev failed to noticed them? Where does the USSR come in? Reflected glory I suppose.[56]

Do not put your trust in Princes nor in any child or man (Psalm of David) but above all do not put your money into USA firms – the Dow Jones Stock Exchange register is down, down, down. Will the stockbrokers drown? Anyway keep your money. I keep mine in an old boot with a hole in the toe. You should follow in my footsteps.

Having engaged our last boy to our potentially last daughter in law, prepared ourselves for the advent of one, two or even 3 grandchildren on September 5th at 6.30 am.,[57] looked at three snowdrops delicately peering at the cold weather and hoped the refuse collector will return to once a week, we have decided to hire a colour television. It will cost the earth or at least my next summer suit, three pairs of shoes and a new umbrella. My wife who

---

[56] As these remarks imply, Britain and the Soviet Union leant support to the Nigerian Government while France led the international defence of the Biafran population. The Catholic Church had a presence in both territories; Pope Paul VI made a number of unsuccessful attempts at mediation and expressed his fear of genocide as the war entered its final stages.

[57] For the significance of 5 September, see letter 29, p.131.

has the delicate madness of an artist for colour says it
is very good. I look at it myopically and say look there's
the sea sparkling away like mad somewhere near Tahiti.
Alas however there are no Hula hula girls in grass skirts
– merely fat old men like me in Panama straw hats.
Anyway it makes the adverts more disgusting – horrible
little boys ungrammatically praising the most nauseating
foods or frantically enthusiastic young housewives
proclaiming with bright insincerity that margarine is
much much better than butter. You would really like our
adverts. Herewith the Guardian. Don't trust old Zorza too
much. He really rejoices when the USSR finds a difficulty.
How he can show such joy over shortage of labour when
we have nearly 700,000 men out of work I don't know.
Or rejoice at the proposed increase in the GNP of 6%
when our increase has been 11/4. I think that the USSR
is about to enter slowly into a state of affairs when
the central and regional planning boards must enlist
the mass of the workers to counteract the increasing
tendencies of managers to please themselves. Up to a
certain state of production directives and bureaucrats
more or less call the tune. When production enters into
a highly complex stage of multifarious production,
particularly for consumption new factors enter in
and problems increase. After that introduction of
innumerable computers and the attempt to solve many
problems with central computers and a populace
demanding [fair] distribution and, as we say, the fat's
in the fire.

The bureaucrats are just about learning that you
cannot [play at] science – any sort of science – or indeed
call a few formulas philosophy forever. They took the
peasants' holdings, or half of them, away and they were
two million cattle down; and sheep and goats. They
told farmers wheat would grow where only roots would

grow and vice versa, and they tried to treat the land as though a boot factory could turn out motorcars. And of course keep rural wages low and restrict rural education. One girl took her chairman of the collective to court because he wouldn't let her go to a university. She won. They at least know that they can't take out an appendix with a directive. However they've still got something like that to learn here, where in an endeavour to make one casualty ward serve at least 100,000 they proposed to denude one town of 20,000 and another of 60,000 of their casualty wards so that anyone involved in a serious accident would have been forced to travel 30 to 40 miles, The official mind never dies alas – not even in tragic circumstances.

My wife says my modest supper is ready. We wish that you were both here or even all here so long as our 'all' too didn't suddenly walk in. Kippers! A highly smoked, very flattened herring. Not bad in front of colour telly! It really makes your mouth water?

I see Alexander has gone to Ankara.[58] He was warmly mobbed by bourgeois newspaper men. Cernik has gone too. But no one seems to be thinking of the economic revival.

Affectionate greetings to you all.

Leslie

---

[58] Alexander Dubcek was made ambassador to Turkey. He was recalled in May the following year before being expelled from the Communist Party.

29

Shoreham-by-Sea, Sussex, England
Undated [*c*. 7th February 1970].

My dear Doctor,

When you are ninety and society considers that it will
no longer entrust its members to your operating table
will you please consider enunciating a Law (note the
capital L) which very properly and in a highly Marxist
way correlates decreasing capacity, reduction in output,
and contrary desires with the energy generated. Since my
'do' in September I lie in bed not listening to Bach and
Beethoven, though they in turn gently hold forth from
the radio, and produce endless disquisitions on Party
strategy and Party Government and refute some choice
items in Garaudy[59] or Gramsci. I also lie in bed and write
very enchanting letters to you, to my children and the
Clerk to the Local Council.

By the time I have struggled with my bath, my clothes
and apologised to my wife for being almost quite useless

---

[59] Roger Garaudy (1913–2012) was one of France's most
distinguished and prolific philosophers, and the author of over
50 books. Jailed under the Vichy regime for resistance activities,
he became a member of the central committee of the French
Communist Party from 1945. He was twice elected to the National
Assembly and then to the Senate. In the late 1960s Garaudy was
best known in British left-wing circles for his promotion of Marxist-
Christian dialogue and a humanist presentation of Marxism.
He was expelled from the French Communist Party in 1970 (see
p.135) because of his critique of 'normalisation' in Czechoslovakia,
accompanied by equally strident criticism of the Party's General
Secretary, George Marchais. In 1982 Garaudy converted to Islam,
and his glittering career was all but forgotten when he was
condemned in 1998 for denying the holocaust and stirring up racial
hatred. He appealed all the way up to the European Court of Human
Rights, which decided against him in June 2003.

I sit down and if I am not careful about 100 miles from
the typewriter.

You will notice however that my meandering mind has
at last won the day and I am not only sitting down to the
machine but I am writing in a proper revolutionary colour.
Or is that because I have made it a red letter day! Except
for my elder son's part of the family we are all normal.
He and his wife however provide our greatest departure
from the normal by a cryptic note 'Baby expected
September 5th'. While we rejoice in the actual commitment
to parenthood we feel that his Marxism has been
supplemented by the use of some soothsayer or of a crystal
ball. September the 6th perhaps: but the 5th! With my
younger son getting married in October and a new baby
squawking away in September we shall have something
not only to look forward to but to save up for. When my
younger boy started to take his place in the hospital wards,
I warned him about kissing nurses in the dead of night.
Whether he took notice of this warning or not or whether
he sampled more than one not unwilling young lady I
do not know but a nurse he certainly has determinedly
attached himself to. So far as I can gather she should have
gone to a College of Music rather than to succour the
halt and the lame. She is a very quiet girl and was only
just beginning to assert herself in our rumbustious and
talkative family when she had to disappear again. She has
however accomplished one record already. She is the only
member or near member of the family that has shouted at
him and not made him glum. Apparently he wished while
he was still on crutches to accompany a climbing party
but he said over the telephone with a certain amount of
glee, 'She shouted at me Dad. She shouted at me'. So I
gather she will bring him up a willing provider and one
properly tamed. His future domestically could hardly be
better – in prospect at any rate.

The current number of The Weekly Guardian covers a lot of ground. Some of the items may be of interest to you. I enclose another issue and I hereby declare with my hand on my heart that I will send it regularly.

We can rejoice that the Nigeria war is over and though McGowan [sic] has been very rude to thousands of people who have and still are sending food etc. we can hope the country will now settle down. The morale of the US army is very 'dodgy' and Nixon may be forced to withdraw US troops in increasing quantities for that reason alone. The sooner countries are left to look after their own affairs the better. Northern Ireland is quietening down; British troops are still there but every effort is being made to make them so comfortable that they will forget they have been shot at. Miss Bernadette Devlin, a taut little revolutionary of 22 who led the anti-establishment demonstrations and defence of a working class area in Londonderry, has still Court charges to answer. As she is the only one out of some 100,000 with charges of treason, violence and so forth hanging over her I cannot but conclude she is being victimised.[60] She has also to suffer some criticism from some Marxists who can't see an outstanding working class leader unless she is officially labelled 'Museum Piece – True Revolutionary Marxist'.

My affectionate regards to you all, from Enid and me.

Leslie P

---

[60] Devlin was elected to the UK Parliament in 1969 for the Mid Ulster constituency; she served a short jail sentence for incitement to riot.

30

Shoreham-by-Sea, Sussex, England
14th February 70.

My dear Doctor

It would inspire me if there were something inspiring
to write to you about. The weather is quite cold and my
body doesn't like it. Yet we are fortunate here in this
highly respectable neighbourhood in having, I imagine,
pre-determined middle class sunshine some part of the
day to look at from a warm house within. So far as the
world is concerned we receive the news very much as
you receive it. The Israelites have bombed a Cairo steel
works and newspaper men are mildly, but only mildly,
concerned that this will cause the Russians to assent
to an intensification of the war in the Near East.[61] But
generally all our Tory newspapers (save the indecisive
Guardian) view the affair as a minor setback for the
left wing countries and this they don't mind. Many of
them would not mind a holocaust if they thought their
own jobs would go on afterwards. Newspaper men are
united in one thing, apart from the insensate competition
between themselves, and that is their profound belief
in the sensation of the moment. Or is it so profound.
While some people in the eastern countries may find the
BBC enlightening I find it much too smooth. Generally
speaking it is not possible without effort or added
expense to find a radio that will pick up the important

---

[61] *The Times* (13 February) reported that 70 Egyptian civilians had
been killed and 98 injured when Israel dropped 5 napalm bombs and
several delayed action bombs on a metal works. The two countries
had been engaged in a war of attrition since the Six Days War of
June 1967.

sections of the foreign broadcasts to compare with the smoothed down importance of foreign affairs.

We have recently started reading a book called The Unperfect Society by one Djilas. Up to where we have got we feel we are constantly being assailed with imprecise sentences and sometimes some statements that are quite erroneous. For instance he says that it doesn't matter what religion a country has, it makes no difference to the development of its economy. I think this is nonsense. Those countries that are almost universally Catholic do not show the same the vigour in the development of capitalist industry – eg Spain, Portugal, Italy – though Italy increases its industrialisation rather in proportion to its rejection of the Holy See. It is however interesting to note that in Spain and Italy the investments of the Church in industry are quite heavy. But Catholic authoritarianism together with, of course, the ruling class is a severe drag on industrial development. We think that Djilas after 15 years of imprisonment has had his judgement impaired not only because he has been deprived of facts but because in prison he has imagined conditions of development that are far from actual.[62]

He is a voluminous writer and we shall read some more of his works but while I am in sympathy with him as regards the development of authoritarianism in certain countries I think there are many strands of his

---

[62] Milovan Djilas (1911–95), wartime *partisan*, leading politician, theorist and novelist, was chosen as President of Yugoslavia in December 1954, having served on the Central Committee of the Yugoslav Communist Party from 1937. Almost immediately he was removed from all office because of his developing critique of what he described as Yugoslavia's new ruling class. Djilas was jailed in 1956 because of his support for the Hungarian uprising, and over the next decade his writings earned him 15 years of jail sentences, of which he served nine. In December 1966 he received an amnesty. *The Unperfect Society* was published in 1969.

arguments that are not helpful in suggesting concrete methods of reconstruction. We are awaiting the last book by Garaudy[63] who has recently been kicked off the French CP Executive Committee and looks like being kicked out of the Party. We shall see. The French Party is now retreating to a hard line position.

This probability and the vagueness of Djilas and the obduracy of Moscow will not help us with our strenuous efforts to build up the Party in this country though the possible harshnesses or a future Tory Govt are now visibly showing.

Our Party has never been much helped by Russian developments except around 1921 when the aftermath of the victory of the workers in Russia brought the Party GB to birth and the successes of the Red Army during the last War brought a great influx of members. The savage onslaughts of GB and US papers on the USSR and the onslaught of the Cold War have effectually kept our numbers down. And, I think, quite as effectually caused the political atmosphere of Moscow to freeze. The enmity of the post war Presidents has successfully manoeuvred our own Prime Ministers into their following an inimical anti-Communist line that has done the world no good whatsoever. We in the CPGB are in a nasty dilemma, the horns of which are constantly wounding. On the one hand we are compelled to believe that the future is with the Communist countries whatever their present handicaps and silly quarrels (Peking and Moscow) and at the same time we are compelled to criticise the development of a rigid authoritarianism which has not only slowed down the growth rate of the economy but has ousted the workers from active initiating

---

[63] See note 59, p.130.

participation. We have dulled workers in this country – plenty of unemployed and lower paid manual workers and slum dwellers – but we have many workers and middle class workers whose wellbeing (though possibly in some jeopardy through [the] ills of capitalism) have standards of living much in excess of their parallels in the Eastern bloc and USSR.

We are in fact once more in a ring of strikes. Teachers, car workers, dockers, soon postmen and policemen clamouring for better pay also. Everyone knows that the 'economy will not stand these onslaughts', but nobody believes what everyone knows. While the Govt wishes to placate those middle people who never never grumble but alas carry the too important 'floating vote' by appearing to keep the workers in order they are also trying to placate the striking teachers and the underpaid nurses and the overweening car workers by appearing to increase their pay without actually giving them more than an extra pittance. The point I should like make is that here there is working class vigour and that is more than can be said elsewhere.

The students are now gathering their forces to show the anti-Apartheid cricketers from South Africa that, though this is not a Socialist country yet, it is no lover of oppression.[64]

Our v. kind regards to you and your family. We hope you are well.

Leslie Parker

---

[64] This oddly worded sentence refers to the mounting opposition to the proposed tour of the South African cricket team scheduled for June. By mid-February the number of matches had been reduced from 29 to 11, abandoning those where pitches could not be easily protected.

31

Usti nad Labem, Czechoslovakia
15th February 1970.

Dear Mr. Parker,

I am very pleased with the G.W. and delighted by your
hilarious letters sandwiched into its pages. Knowing that
you were born in 1898 and that you had your 'do' as you
said in your red typed letter, I have the most profound
admiration for your lively mind. I am keeping all your
letters as they are not without literary merit. They are
to me a source-book of good English. If I were Lord
Thompson I would offer you a well paid job on the staff
of one of the many newspapers he owns, disregarding
your age and medical history. Having read all your letters
thoroughly and discovered that you and I share a deep-
rooted common bias I could easily forgive you that you
prefer to express your thoughts and feelings in the idiom
of a doctrine which on account of first hand experience
with socialism I regard as a little bit antiquated. It is
hardly necessary to tell you that Enoch Powell, M.P.
and the National Front are distasteful to me. If I am
passing over in silence slums, unemployment, racial
discrimination, outbreaks of violence and madness,
it does not mean that I am not aware of these evils of
the highly advanced affluent societies of the Western
world. I don't like redundancies. At your end there are
always plenty of ordinary citizens, their associations and
journalists and writers who without fear for their jobs
refuse to become submissive to authority and are going
ahead with criticizing these shortcomings. To condemn
in strongest terms the crimes committed in capitalist
societies while condoning those carried out in the name

of socialism is not my cup of tea! Your great compatriot, the late Bertrand Russell, pointed to the vast difference it makes when confusing 'all Xs are Y' with 'some Xs are Y'. Well, you are probably right that there are some journalists at your end who live by writing to order what they themselves don't believe, with the sole aim of denigrating the achievements of socialism and rejoicing when it meets with difficulties. This corresponds monotonically with the state of affairs at this end with the exception that all journalists are committed to concealing the truth. The little difference between all and some turns out to have devastating effects. As no one gets any knowledge of crimes committed in secrecy, of blunders and scandals hushed up, save by rumours and insinuations, no one is able to raise a protest. No poky journalist has supplied you with facts and details (Safeguard no 1). In view of the imposed regulations no one will anyhow dare to cry out in protest because everyone has got a job and a family to look after (Safeguard No.2). Since this foolproof system, perfected elsewhere, has been imprinted on this country, most people are looking back at the regime of Novotny[65] with mourning. It was a benign and enlightened dictatorship compared with the present state of affairs. I should very much like to go on chatting with you, particularly about the three snowdrops and the official mind that never dies, but time is running out and I have to start work at 7 a.m. with the beginning of dawn. This winter is hell for us. Our backs are aching from carrying coal from the cellar and the ashes downstairs and from removing the snow from the front of our house. I was just told that there was a 6 hours lasting power failure at Prague! While brewing

[65] See note 50, p.109.

my tea in the morning I am getting cold and nearly mad because of the time it requires to get boiling water. This is just to remind you that you are pretty well off even if the Tories will win the next elections!

Affectionate greetings to you all!
Yours

Paul

32

Shoreham-by-Sea, Sussex
20ᵗʰ February 1970.

My dear Paul

Receiving your letters is one of our major satisfactions. My wife says more than once He is so compressed, shall I read it again and I generally reply that I'll chew it over and then we will afterwards.

Of course I am very much aware that that those who have income of any sort in this country have many things that you in CP countries haven't. But I am particularly aware that we do have the opportunity of communicating one with the other despite the capacity of our mass media of communication to trot easily down the scented rose-petalled roads of irresponsibility as though nothing much mattered and if it did all is well, Mr. Wilson or Mr Heath[66] in alliance with our big cousins in the USA will bring all to a happy conclusion. We have in

[66] Edward Heath, the Conservative Leader of the Opposition.

England an ethos, an attitude towards the relations of one human being to another, something that we should value extremely highly. Though the change to a socialist experiment is bound to come, if I were a praying man I should pray that it came before a complete breakdown of the economy and the disintegration of this aspect of our ethics.

There are those, the Bulgarians for instance, who think only in terms of violence; violence in change and violence thereafter. As Bulgaria through the long centuries has known little but violence this is understandable. But in these islands from the doughty Saxons onwards there have always been signs and eruptions of a staunch duty to criticise the government.

In Wycliffe we produced not only the first translation of much of the Bible, but also the first theory of the common ownership or the land and Wycliffe survived to die in his bed.[67] We happily chop the heads off kings, invite them out never to return, invite new ones, demand the abdication of others – all of course bourgeois activities but which have their effect on the people. We lay claim to a history of almost ceaseless industrial assertion, to bitter fighting for the vote and the secret ballot and of course to the suffragette movement. Though we have been hoodwinked by smooth political talk and patriotic war talk we still lay claim to speak our minds, to work when we feel we need it and to a general feeling that the country is ours. We shall therefore be unable to advance politically to a more conclusive ownership of what is ours without the aid of the normal political organisations like local councils and Parliament that the great majority, despite their fierce criticisms, regard as

[67] John Wycliffe (1331–84) completed his translation of the Bible in 1382.

essentially theirs. We shall of course persuade the more irresponsible organs of communication to try at least to publish the truth but we shall recognise that criticism of government measures local or national is not only a right but a necessity.

No people in a highly industrialised state can be turned into surgeons only, reporters only, lathe workers only, refuse collectors only. It has been found that within months of Hitler substituting instructions about the relations of labour and the owners of the means of production negotiations were going on between them in respect of conditions of work and wages. No highly industrialised state could stay highly industrialised unless the workers can walk the earth with a great degree of freedom.... If they [are] persuaded, cajoled or forced to destroy their organs of unified negotiation as well as suffering a great degree of censorship the gross national product will not achieve anything like the potential the forces of production would otherwise indicate. We have recently witnessed in this country a determined attempt to take away from workers the power of negotiation by making the Trade Unions part of the government itself. This has not only been a failure but the workers have reacted to it by making constant demands for higher pay and in many instances a higher standard of living.

The relationship of the government with the People has in capitalist countries so far as economies are concerned has been worked in terms of disputes and antagonisms with the owners of capital in strikes, lockouts, enforced reduction of wages and general reduction of employment. Capitalism until these latter years has not been forced to take a long-term look at the country's economy but the knowledge that capitalism more than ever drives one whole national economy to compete with another drives the capitalist economist to consider ways and means whereby he can at least dominate the output of wages for three or four years. The capitalists and their politicians are now dead set on gaining control.

At this point I had to declare myself unfit for human consumption and after having three pellets of what I think is called Pitutrin [or] similar I went to bed. It is now Sunday, post bath and noon.

I have recently been writing to a young gentleman on the development of Christian theology in the course of which I had to remark that both the heathen and the Christian thinkers were compelled to use the terminology and current of ideas derived from Plato largely, and in Christology from Aristotle. Greek thought was the only tool they had in which to describe or 'project' the new phenomenon.

In the same way I feel pretty well sure that Marxism, or what goes in a variety of differing circles for Marxism, will provide the basic attitude and basic terminology [for] the political ideas and practices that steadily encroach on the capitalist areas.

At the present time there is a fairly fierce undercurrent that shows itself in eruptions like those of Gramsci, Djilas, Garaudy and weakly in Sartre as to what the social implication of Marxism fundamentally are. The eruptions show themselves in the realm of religion, ethics, culture, philosophy and history but particularly in what sort, kind, quality of government a Communist Gvt should be. At the present time the Chinese Maoists proclaim quite simply that the form of the Russian gvt corresponds to that of a capitalist govt though I myself have not seen any detailed analysis by the Chinese. The Russians placate the Chinese more or less and pretend they have no political philosophy.

Real crit. of the USSR gvt comes from Italy, France and Britain. The British Road to Socialism (a booklet) was sneered at by the Bulgarians rather, because it implied a crit of the USSR. But Gramsci who alas is now dead proclaimed a positive humanist quality in govt as being essential to complete communism. Garaudy's[68] latest book I have not yet read because as Enid has to read everything aloud we get through stuff so slowly.

We found the Djilas book a very dreadful commentary on the effect of sending a man to jail for 15 years.[69] Over 50 pages [at the] beginning of the book were full of misstatements, non sequiturs and references to facts that were not stated. I should not say Djilas was a profound thinker but he has been a creator of many books that must have contained many fruitful lines that could have [been] pursued. In this book he appears to think Marx was a good Marxist and Engels a bad one because Engels [wrote] The Dialectics of Nature without reference to Einstein's theory of relativity. I myself rather like Engels. He is much more a systematic thinker than Marx was and a more systematic worker also, though of course he had neither the time nor the bursting creative energy to write Das Capital. Nor was Engels so black and white, so this is Right that is Wrong. Engels too had something of the calm temper of the lucid scholar despite the sarcasm of anti-Duhring.

Anyway – or where were we – all modern movements of revolution against capitalism or imperialism sooner or later speak in Marxist terms and, sooner or later, will defend their particular governments in Marxist or Marxist-Leninist terms.

Ipso facto any crits will have to be made in Marxist terms though what is Marxist, true Marxist, correct Marxist or bad wicked bourgeois Marxist will only be

---

[68] See note 59, p.130.

[69] See note 62, p.134.

determined long after I [am] dead. I feel quite certain about this.

If Lenin is right in thinking that the development or history can be said to go in 'revolutionary jumps' then we must expect that such jumps in the greater application of humanist principles will come about through pressure which will change attitudes. There is an enormous amount of fear in the world and more of it in the European communist countries than elsewhere. In the capt. countries a policy through the means of communication is pursued of soothing the people to the point of hypnosis. In the comm. countries fear is generated from the top partly because that fear is quite real and has factual foundation and partly in order to create a docile people. The production of a docile people is bound to weaken patriotism, socialist loyalty and retard economic progress, culture and that area of science which the top lot think is not profitable to pursue. On the other hand one of the efforts of the top lot is produce an economy with a standard of living that is not only satisfying to their own people but will evoke at least satisfaction in people abroad, particularly their admirers abroad. Admirers are not increasing spectacularly even in the old colonial countries. While many die-hards or hard liners still nourish their youthful hagiographies the worship of saints in the West is not now considered a profitable occupation. Even the Pope has recently deposed 100 English 'saints' and so far as I can gather the Holy Father is himself in some jeopardy.[70]

Rest assured I shall continue to look on the world with as factual an eye as my sceptical mother entrusted to me. I am, because of facts, irreversibly anti-capitalist

---

[70] In 1969 the Catholic Church removed 93 saints from the universal calendar and revoked their feast days.

but I am or try to be a constructive socialist who gives a socialist government no more licence to afflict people than he gives to any other govt.

[Your] letters are a great joy to us also and we read them much more than once. My wife says we have three more snowdrops at the back and some at the front that must have jumped about ten [feet] – an act of faith or blind purposelessness? We also have seven crocuses both blue and yellow and lots of ... grass with a new apple tree that flies to the sky like a gothic cathedral spire longs for heaven. The seller of this [house] says we shall get three different kinds of apples from it.

Nurses have got a 5 per cent rise, the police are restive because they do not earn enough, a massive strike at Fords the motor people has just been averted with a massive rise of £4 per week, the broadcasting staffs are licking their lips in anticipation, so you will rejoice to know that the English way of life goes happily on.

From us both Love to David, David's Mamma, David's Grandmamma, Affectionate regards (note the more manly note) to David's Father and David's Grandfather.

PS You will be glad to know that our coloured TV newly acquired is always going wrong. But Enid isn't at all glad.

33

Usti nad Labem, Czechoslovakia
2 April 1970.

Dear Mr and Mrs Parker,

I have several relatives and more friends than ever
before now in the USA, Canada and the UK but no one
is writing to me. They have apparently given me up as a
'lost case [cause?]'. But you are not failing me. You are
writing to me notwithstanding my own reticence and
your difficulties with typing. I highly appreciate your
untiring efforts to save me from drooping into apathy
and thus you are relieving me from my loneliness and
isolation. There is hardly any family which has not
been affected by the consequences of the occupation
and for a change I have been assailed in the realm of
my work. An excellent assistant of superior qualities
has left my department and went to Prague to take up
a leading and far better salaried appointment than he
had here. These frequent internal shifts and mobility
are, of course, the result of the vacancies created by
the mass emigration of doctors since August 1968. On
several occasions I suggested to the hospital authorities
to offer my assistant a promotion in order to keep him.
But these stupid bureaucrats are lacking in foresight
and sensibility to the needs of the young, ambitious and
capable workers. Now I myself and another doctor have
to cope with an overwhelming demand for anaesthetics.
Coming home at 5 or 6 p.m. I am worn out and perhaps
a bit doped myself by the escaping vapours. I just could
not concentrate on letter writing. I was going to tell you
that I bought Djilas book 'The unperfect society' while
visiting Germany last year. I read it through voraciously

but felt a little bit disappointed just as you did. This is strange as Djilas retraces my own evolution away from wholesale and Utopian social experiments and projects towards a piecemeal, non-violent social reformism. While I was in Yugoslavia I mentioned Djilas name to a young student who worked as a charwoman at our recreation centre to earn some money for her studies. She spoke English very well and that's why we became friends. Distinct pallor and consternation appeared on her pretty face when I mentioned Djilas, not Lucifer! You may have heard that the Yugoslav authorities robbed Djilas recently of his passport and tonight I learned that they searched the wife of Mihajlo Michajlov,[71] took away a manuscript of her husband's and prevented her from visiting her daughter in the USA. As there are still foreign correspondents at Belgograd we are learning about these and similar happenings. But there are hardly any left at Prague and insults of greater magnitude are not being reported. Talking about books, I should like to mention to you [an] excellent English Pelican paperback: An Introduction to Contemporary History by Geoffrey Barraclough. It would be unfair to attribute the prolonged winter to the Russian presence in this country but as a matter of fact I had to remove several inches of snow on Easter Sunday from the front of our house. Only now it is gradually melting and vanishing from the streets. The drudgery of carrying buckets of coal upstairs has not ended either. In the scarcely lit operating theatre I am putting a needle into the vein, guided more by touch than by sight. Should the patient get a little bit blue or

---

[71] Mihajlo Michajlov (1934–2010), a prominent Yugoslav dissident. He served about six years in jail and went to the United States on his release in 1978, but returned to Serbia in 2001 after the fall of President Slobodan Milosevic.

should he be slightly jaundiced, I never could recognize it promptly in our theatres. When the surgeons are getting hot and sweating they usually ask for the air-conditioning to be turned on. For me and my anaesthetic nurse this is the signal to put on a warm pully because we are exposed to the most cruel draught. Having been a surgeon myself it is a great ordeal to observe the tyros mutilating the patients twice as long than necessary. While working at Bristol in 1939 I went along with the late Mr. Priddie to a monastery in order to put a nail into the fractured hip of the abbess. While I gave the anaesthetic he performed the operation on a kitchen table. On reviewing the later made X-ray films we all could see that the nail was driven in perfectly. Now we received an expensive television set from Phillips to see the fragments of bone, their alignment and the path of the screw and the metal. Now the operations take twice as long than previously and many of them are being actually performed double because the direct vision control with the television does not prevent inept, terribly conceited and complacent surgeons from making the biggest blunders. Most of the surgeons are taking bribes and presents from patients and there is a flourishing private practice going on under the cover of [the] Socialist medical service which ought to provide treatment free of charge. When my fellow anaesthetists from other hospitals complained that they are working ten times harder than any surgeon but never getting any 'presents' from the patients I told them that we anaesthetists are actually members of the order 'Opus Dei' who have to labour and to be overtaxed until worn out but in the noble spirit of Christianity to forgo all reward! This is just one example of a situation which exists everywhere and every day. Arrogant, corrupt and inept cliques are again coercing, insulting and bullying the hard working, intelligent and decent people who keep things going. There are no unions and no means of communications from below up the hierarchy to set things right, prevent inefficiency and correct injustices.

Always pleased to hear from you! Affectionate regards to your David and your family!

Yours sincerely

Paul

34

Tuesday [21st April 1970].[72]

My dear Paul,

One of my friends writes to tell me that 'touch' typing will take away much strain but at the present I am obliged to confess that the strain is doubled. For it attains both him that types and him that reads. I can only suggest to you that the fault lies not so much in the humaneness of my urge as in the inability of the technologists to create a machine that has a more instinctive perception of my needs.

I suppose you are now in the most Leninest [*sic*] time.[73] Our celebrations are somewhat subdued although they might gain a little more vehemence in the course of a week or two. I have suggested to some of my friends that they could fortify themselves with some consideration of whether any existent party matches

---

[72] Dated from internal evidence.

[73] The centenary of Lenin's birth was 22 April 1970.

up to Lenin's conceptions and also whether Lenin's conceptions of the Party still meets the needs of our country.

In this green and pleasant land there goes on a furious wordy battle between Mr Heath the leader of the Tories and Mr Wilson the Labour premier. They spit and scratch rather like Kilkenny cats than grown men with the responsibility of millions keeping them awake at nights. While Mr Heath's stupidities are swallowed and regurgitated in his intestines and finally spat out over the body politic, Mr Wilson's long screeds roll out in ever increasing meaninglessness from the TV screen and in the House of Commons and are remarkable for his venom which Mr H is unable to match.

They quarrel over Rhodesia which is now well in the hands of Ian Smith who is searching the mysteries of the Bible to discover whether God in his love allows 250,000 whites to crush 7 million blacks into economic servitude. Technically Mr Smith is a rebel but alas he is also a potential customer.[74] Mr Heath, not too apparently, hates rebels against our Beloved Queen, of course, but he also loves money (from being a comparatively poor man he is now quite rich). Mr Wilson is chagrined. He has, of course, saved the country and as a reward he has alienated large sections of the workers and enraged the trade unions who are now savagely attacking him and demanding higher wages. Northern Ireland is still bitterly split for there has been no social fruition of the truce – no houses, no more work, the military are still there and an exceedingly reactionary section have succeeded in electing one fiery clergyman to the Northern

---

[74] Under its Prime Minister Ian Smith, Rhodesia had declared itself independent in November 1965 while maintaining its continued loyalty to the Queen. On 2 March 1970 it became a Republic.

Ireland Parliament.[75] Nor does the entry in the European Common Market sweeten his coffee for the French do not like either him or us and the tide in this country swells against 'entry' and in all political parties. To suggest a referendum to this lot of Parliamentary democrats is like suggesting freedom of the press and publication to Brezhnev. The tender patriotic flesh winces. It would be a nice thing if our politicians meditated on the necessity of Truth. Very Helpful!

The almond tree just outside my window that presides beatifically over the low roof eaves has this week blossomed into sheer loveliness. From expectant buds tinged [...] a light green the pink sprang forth with the determination of a good fairy, a thousand good fairies. The sun shone in unusual kindliness, the sky was blue and the almost ceaseless wind died gently down and those who care for Nature worship could have their fill. If I had poetry in my power I should always write to you in verse – or, as someone said, 'worse'.

But then I might out venom Mr Wilson or out bludgeon the Kremlin. Of course we had the American astronauts and I am sending you what the boxing journalists call a blow by blow account of the descent which you probably will not have had in your papers. You will by now also have heard President Nixon's world-cast words that never in the annals of mankind has a country spent its lives and its hard cash to save a mere 18 millions from the dire what's-its-names of communism. While he grandly brings home at an unstated date 155,000 fighting men who never wanted to go there at all he spreads the war in Laos and Cambodia. Compared with the Central Intelligence Agency of the

---

[75] The Reverend Ian Paisley was elected as MP for Bannside in a by-election on 16 April.

USA the NKVD are ministering angels.[76] Of course I grant
there are angels black, very black and deadly black which
the imaginations of not even the Manichees could have
conjured up.[77]

Our affectionate greetings to you all.

Leslie

PS If there is a word like xxio8£ or even Jjao56*(you will
realise this is not a new and esoteric language, but sheer
intransigence on the part of this machine.

35

Shoreham-by-Sea, Sussex, England
25th April 70.

My dear Doctor,

If' wishes were horses then beggars would ride and I
should charter a jet plane or a magic swimsuit that
would swish me up the Elbe to your doorstep. I could
then sit on the coal cellar steps with [you] and discuss
the ineptitudes of politicians, the superiority of women
or the beauties of gas fired interior heating systems
whichever gave you the most comfort. Or you could tell
me about your poets and introduce me to substitutes

---

[76] For the NKVD see notes 259, p.387 and 273, p.407.

[77] Followers of Mani, a third-century religious prophet from Persia.
They had a dualist view of the world which postulated a permanent
conflict between the spiritual world of light and the material world
of darkness.

for Scotch Whisky. But as beggars neither fly the skies
nor skim the Skagarrack without the freedom of money
I shall tell you of two non-events (an expressive use of
slang nowadays) of the past week.

The first is or was the centenary of Lenin kept rather
in the capitalist papers than in the issues of the Left
though we did have a 12 pager in the Morning Star which
we have not yet had time for. The other was facetiously
mentioned: St. George's Day – because some restaurant
owner in Manchester on that day gave red roses to his
women diners. St. George has always been, like a lot
of saints, a bit of a mystery and lovers of our nation
had better leave him alone for though he has always
been supposed to have slain a Lion with more than
usual bravado cum éclat no-one knows where and when
precisely this heroism was demonstrated. Nor is it known
who benefited – a fair damsel or merely a fat German
lady who was an ancestor of our round Queen Victoria.
On the other hand Gibbon, the one really great historian
we can lay claim to, describes St. George as a one time
army contractor to the Imperial what's-its-name of Rome
who quite suddenly became converted to Christianity
and then to everyone's astonishment refused either to go
on contracting or sacrifice to the Emperor. Whereupon
the adjacent Roman Governor, after, of course, a highly
proper interrogation, gave him up, again most properly,
to be tortured. Gibbon described the fortitude of this
erstwhile money maker in appealing tones and said, if I
remember rightly, 'even when they set upon his chest a
very heavy millstone he refused to be moved'.

There are of course a number of critical lives of
Lenin on sale and there may even be some such in
the Communist countries though if there are I am not
aware or them. But it will take a good deal of solid
factual writing to rescue Lenin in the USSR from the

iconography and ikonolatry [*sic*] that envelops his reality in that country. Or indeed elsewhere. It is time, as he would willingly agree, that he was decently interred, the worship brought to an end and the reality of history displaced the myth. While St. George may or may not have set someone free Lenin undoubtedly brought about changes the results of which could as a man enrage him and which as a historian he would have applied his great energy to analysing.

It is VERY COLD. The sun shines. Mr Heath and Mr Wilson are still in deadlock and I mean dead and well locked up in their stupid irrelevances. I am still not allowed to do much. My wife is very active and very thin; some doctors are making £3000 a week doing abortions, our almond tree has shed its lovely blossoms on the green lawn and four magnificent daffodils nod at the blackbird sitting serenely on her nest just outside the window. I will however finish with two sayings of Lenin. The first hardly known and the second used very probably by his mysticisers [*sic*] 'Any fool can have children' and 'Children are the flowers of life'. So we must rejoice that we may in some measure make a garden for them.

We both send you our affectionate greetings. We hope the Socialist countries' endeavour will provide a bucket of coal that will give heat for a year.

Yours always

Leslie P

36

Shoreham-by-Sea, Sussex, England
2nd May 1970.

My dear Paul,

The weather people have relented and the temperature
is now gently going up. Today I can sit trying to hit the
correct keys with a small window open and with the
north wind no longer reminding me that I cannot go out.
The almond blossom is now followed by the plum and
our new apple tree about three feet high pronounces that
sooner or later it also will bloom. While I think that the
promise of eternal Springs is somewhat illusory I content
myself with a little soothing syrup that the young are
always with us and what their forbears have failed to
do they will readily accomplish. One of the blessings of
decrepitude is [the] ability of laying one's sins upon the
children though their teeth will thereby be set on edge.

Our souls have very recently been arraigned by
Nixon's entry into Cambodia. I rather fancy that in this
case Nemesis will have something to say in the USA as
well as in S E Asia. We shall see.

The stupid problem that assails us in England at
the moment is the insistent decision of the All England
Cricket Club to invite the South Africans to play cricket
in our fair and democratic land.[78] Cricket is a game
generally played at great leisure and consists of a mad
desire of the bowler to hurl a very hard ball in a certain
way that intimidates a certain gentleman defending
three erect pieces of circular timber. Six balls are

---

[78] See note 64, p.136.

bowled successively and the batsmen try to hit the ball to kingdom come whereupon he up and girds himself for running like a scalded rabbit between the two sets of stumps. In the latter century this gage was a leisurely pursuit in hot or wet summers for the upper classes but since then it has become commercialised and international teams have disported themselves to the benefit of a paying public. As you know the whole frantic and handsomely profitable economy of South Africa depends on the extraordinary exploitation of black natives of S. Africa who have little pay and no political rights. The democrats, the anti-racialists, the revolutionaries, etc. etc., including my humble self, are distinctly anti this method of making money. So when the S Africans send a team of cricketers to our fair and democratic isle we are definitely against black and coloured people being excluded from participation. The Govt has hedged on this though many coloured once colonial peoples have withdrawn their teams from the Commonwealth Games soon to be held in Edinburgh, Scotland. Since when the Prime Minister – generally a maggot of maggots – has told the demonstrators to demonstrate. Much to the utter indignation of the reactionaries. So we await with expectation the appearance of crowds and crowds of people, all action to stop the cricket and knock off the helmets of the policemen. The magistrates should gather in many fines and give vent to many moralisms [*sic*] from their seats of judgement. In fact one way and the other Morality will be blessed with proponents of about six different points of view about the duties of policemen. I do not however expect a revolution though I do think the superior gentlemen of the Cricket Committee will be reminded that they cannot talk one day of Democracy and then proceed to trample on it the next day as though they were politicians.

To the politician we may reserve the propriety of proclaiming his latest explanation as being historically inevitable and largely the result of his enemies but not, alas, to the gentleman cricketers. Anyway, I expect that the result of this cricket affair to be rather more soul and empire shaking than the invasion of your country. Nor am I being wholly facetious.

In exactly what relationship to the cricket convulsion is the present invasion of Cambodia I could not say. Our politicians except for a few of both Parties are well on the side of the USA. Morality was certainly never invented by politicians. Our own, ever since Churchill started off the Cold War with his Fulton speech, have licked the backsides of various Presidents of ever decreasing calibre and the present desire on the part of this wonderful British nation to out-USA the USA itself is nothing short of amazing if it were not so utterly nauseating. More lives lost, more bombs of course, Bigger and Better and more money wasted. The fatuosity [sic] of [the] human race to watch these stupidities makes my throat dry and my head ache. The manufacture of one single honest leader of the people seems to be beyond the wit of man – or woman.

Your snow will have melted by now and vernal winds will be welcome as a sign that coal getting will soon be a thing of the past.

Please give our affectionate greetings to your wife and to all your family. We are conscious of you very frequently and it is our sincere hope that both your family and your Country will face a year that will bring some measure of joy and a promise of noble things.

Yours sincerely

Leslie

37

Usti nad Labem, Czechoslovakia
9th May 1970.

Dear Mr and Mrs Parker,

Once more only you saved me from extreme solitude and
boredom. I am most grateful to you for the Guardian,
including your letters and the snap of your pretty
house. As the 'glorious days of May', as they are called
here, were coming near I grew more and more restless.
The postwoman, who formerly, especially in 1968,
complained about the heavy load of books, journals
and letters she had to deliver us, has been consistently
passing by. I thought we might have reached the final
stage of 'consolidation' i.e. sovietization and that the last
liberty to communicate with friends and relatives abroad
has gone to the dogs. On April 27th returning in a very
bad temper and gloomy mood from a staff meeting, I
found the 2 small parcels from you. I grunted with great
satisfaction: 'After all, mail is still coming in!' The staff-
meeting was interesting because we were told that the
bonuses we were receiving for the doctors who had left
the hospital and whose work we obviously are doing,
are to be abolished. This would certainly lead to a strike
in every western country but how much the bosses and
bureaucrats are relying on the submissive attitude of
this nation shows the fact that at the same time we were
invited to participate in a celebration of the anniversary
of Lenin's birthday. The celebration took place on April
30th while I gave anaesthetics for plastic surgery to badly
burned and injured children. On May first the sun was
shining and very definite signs of the arrival of spring
were already noticeable but it was still grimly cold. My

wife called me while I was shaving: 'Come quickly and look at our occupants!' Looking through the window I saw a group of Czech officers and at a distance from them a group of Russian officers and soldiers in their best uniforms and behind them, mingled together, went their wives in elegant dresses. That's all I noticed of this year's 1 of May demonstration. After shaving I started to make firewood as we ran out of coal. Sawing and chopping keeps one fit. Although I already passed a sort of tribunal there are rumours that the purges are to go on for ever. The odds in my favour are, however, that the bosses will prefer a Czech speaking specialist and a safe anaesthetic while their prostate is being removed. In the afternoon I was told that there [were] very few marchers this year, that all kept silent and looked pretty sullen and there were no choruses in response to the recitals of the speakers. Amidst all the festivities and red flags Richard ordered his expeditionary force to march into Cambodia and the whole of the States plunged into riotous madness. Alexander the Great[79] countered this move merely by holding a press conference. He correctly said that the Americans have no right to police the peoples of South-East Asia. Being a journalist and present at this conference I would have asked the question – what right has the SU to police the nations of Eastern Europe. Although he condemned the Americans, I am sure he was secretly applauding and blessing them for becoming deeper involved and diverting the attention of Red-China from the Sino-Soviet frontier. Secretly remembering that the Soviets invaded not so long ago not a supposedly neutral but allied country, he said to himself, we are square again and the SALT talks can

---

[79] Probably a satirical reference to the Soviet leader Leonid Brezhnev.

continue.[80] It was getting really nice and hot after the distinguished visitors from the Empire's capital had left this country again.[81] Most people were furiously digging their gardens while others were just enjoying the first sunshine when we were reminded of the achievements of socialism by having the water supply turned off. For at least 20 years the chronic shortage of tap water is bedevilling this town and each year water is being rationed just when it is needed mostly, on Saturdays for having a bath, on Sunday mornings for cooking a dinner! You are pulling the chain on the w.c. in vain and opening the taps you get just a few drops of rusty water! To have a shower or a bath is a bourgeois luxury and all you can do is to board an overcrowded bus and go to the river Labe! Love never linked this country to the S.U. but there may have been genuine friendship before August 1968. Now the Russians have demonstrated to the world that they hold the method how to enforce love and friendship where there is only fear and hatred. For the love of love some keep the decorum but they know as well as I that one hates which one fears. We are sitting back and consuming more beer and rum than ever before and waiting until the deployment of Russian pilots in the country of the overflowing Nilus and sweet, good Isis will lead to the next crisis.

Our affectionate greetings to you all – and much envying you the Sea!

Yours, Paul

---

[80] Strategic Arms Limitation Talks (SALT) began in November 1969 and resulted in the Anti Ballistic Missile Treaty of 1972 between the Soviet Union and the USA.

[81] Brezhnev was in Prague for the signing of the 'Treaty of Friendship, Cooperation and Mutual Assistance' on 6 May.

38

Shoreham-by-Sea, Sussex, England
Monday [11th May] 1970.[82]

My dear Paul,

The almond blossom has gone, the plum blossom has
gone, the apple blossom is daunted and the sun refuses
to shine. And it is Monday. And for the weekend we had
my second son's proposed in-laws and we ate a lot and
my stomach is fatigued and possibly the domestic purse
is consequently empty. And it is still Monday though
perhaps the morning will pass.

The newspaper retailer (known in Eng as the
newsagent: but not to be confused with a news agency
which is for instance Reuter) has resolutely refused to
bestow upon us the Weekly Guardian so we are sending
you the Sunday Times less those parts which deal with
stocks and shares and the benighted condition of the
USA stock market. You will gather that all Britons are
adamantly uninterested in Mr Nixon's latest exposition of
dialectics as he proceeds to demonstrate that by putting
an invading force in still another country is saving lives
and actually withdrawing his armies. In the past we
have had wars to end wars, wars to make Britain fit for
the 2 million left lying quite dead in Flanders; the mind
boggles at what the politicians will think up next.

We have heard lately the triumphal entry of your
allies and we have seen photographs of foreign governors
stern, unbending and apparently far from home and not
quite happy about it. Of course we do indeed rejoice at

---

[82] Dated from internal evidence.

this farther example of fraternal care that ties you closer than ever in brotherly if military bonds to this bastion of social advancement. And we all hope that you will all thrive together.

I once had the happiness of a friendly bout of wrestling with a man twice my size. It was quite comfortable until the squeeze came. The rest was oblivion. But I cannot refrain from remarking that to exchange the Warsaw Pact for a particularly friendly contract is an honour that one hardly expects.[83]

We hear intransigent things of Romania and must say cavorting with the capitalists has its limitations though it may oil the bonds and make relations more tractable. At the moment the choice between Vietnam or Greece and the position of say, Montenegro, is not a happy one.

It is still Monday and I am still deflated.

We have Barraclough's book on Contemp. History and are nearly through one chapter on the Balance of Power which ought to be Balance of Powers but which I do not believe in much as a concept based on fact. Few governments have a continuing logical policy and certainly no country that changes its government from time to time. Nevertheless I shall continue with Barraclough.

But I must stop now because my head is as empty as a balloon.

With very kind regards to you all from us both

LP

---

[83] Presumably a reference to the 'Treaty of Friendship' of 6 May.

39

Shoreham-by-Sea, Sussex, England
17th May 1970.

My dear Paul,

I said to her a propitious beginning to a solemn Sunday
may be assured by any dutiful wife provided she springs
from the marital couch at the proper moment. Though, I
continued, this moment has, as yet, not been determined
by the philosophic nabobs of the Party it is now easily
determinable in this house for it is obviously unfit that
a mere woman should listen to the state first of the
weather and then of the world in general. Besides it
is nine o'clock and you will need an excellent meal in
order to fortify your frail constitution for the effort of
retailing the news in a Sunday newspaper whose contents
could easily be curtailed to a quarter of its rhetorical
superfluity. No, I replied, the time has certainly not come
for any emancipation of the female and stronger sex to
seek for emancipation on the Sabbath. It's up and away
and I'll have champagne, followed by grapefruit, grilled
trout, mushrooms and best Danish bacon with best
Egyptian (or Israelite) coffee and if I am still awake the
news in brief.

In the end it was china tea and scrambled eggs and
I found the kitchen rather cold and isolated. I shall
certainly inform my tender and younger son that women
and/or marriage is or are not to be trusted. We have
at least sufficient water in Shoreham for all necessary
purposes. There is oil for the gathering, floating in and
out on the tide, which it certainly would be unable to do
were it not for the sea water. Then beneath the oil there
is a fructifying mixture of sewage and sea water upon

which the vessels from Germany, Holland and the USSR bring their schnapps, vodka, timber. [There is water] in the River Adur which pursues its way from the interior of Sussex loaded with effluents both human and inhuman, with a white tide of detergents and a subtide of weed killer, bird killer and a subsubtide of other chemical agents deployed for the ostensible use of mankind but fulfilling the excellent moneymaking plan of the ICI. Fortunately a little is left over in which we can either boil our miserable bodies in the bath or some miserable hen's egg in a saucepan. I am therefore very sorry that we are unable to let you have a bucket of our more usable water for you to cook your potatoes in. I suppose you gentlemen and ladies of the Continent do eat potatoes. Or are there any dialectical reasons why this useful tuber though it was found by that bourgeois idol Sir Walter Raleigh,..... (I cannot remember the beginning of that sentence therefore I cannot finish it. Writing letters nowadays is like cycling in the dark with your hands tied behind your back).

Politically we are now in the midst of the greatest confusion that the Tory Party has ever experienced. Neither Heath nor Wilson the great protagonists seem to care what becomes of the country so long as each or both 'get in'. But alas Wilson somehow has turned the tables on the full mouthed Heath and it looks as though the Tories will not win the next election. Mr W also refuses to tell them nor anybody when the election will take place.[84] All the newspapers, mostly Tory inclined, are mad about this for they made the scare by prophesying an election in June and they are left flying their kites without any conceivable string attached to them. Very amusing if

---

[84] Harold Wilson dissolved parliament on 29 May.

---

unedifying! Those that boil potatoes should take care not to let the water run dry.

We have read more of the Barraclough book, actually starting at the beginning for a change. It is quite enlightening though I still think he is mistaken in assuming that the balance of power in Europe was either consciously created or consciously maintained. The English had always been exceedingly conscious of their colonial policies and the money which they brought flowing into London, Bristol and Hull. Every major war in Europe initiated or maintained by Britain was not only for the purpose of trying to make sure that no nation in Europe became dominant but that no nation in Europe was able to acquire English colonies or even very large slices of countries not dominated by the British. In this last they failed to some extent.

Period for engaging in eating, conversation on the pavement and reflections on the Sunday Times and forgetting where I had got to in this epistle. No matter. Nothing is very important. It is Whit Sunday (White Sunday), the Feast of the Holy Spirit. The other day I asked my brother-in-law who is a Christian whether he ever said his prayers to the Holy Spirit. He said not and I said that's the bit of the Trinity that looks very much like a leftover for the theologians to nourish or be nourished by. All our lively Christians are now intellectuals or of the variety that cannot get over Bonhoeffer[85] being killed by Hitler. Many dabble with Marxism in an endeavour to believe that in the day of Revolution they will know the way and be saved for socialism eternal.

My little boy is shocked that for a whole week he has been on duty at night admitting patients into a

---

[85] Dietrich Bonhoeffer, German Lutheran pastor and theologian, executed by the Nazis on 9 April 1945.

big hospital in Birmingham and at other times acting as casualty doctor. He has over a year to do before he goes on to do his last qualifying year in hospital as a Houseman. He told my wife that it wasn't at all like the book. So we learn that praying is not like theology or being a politician in the USA is not at all like upholding the constitution. This demand for model or modelled men seems universal. When I was in the Church I saw priests thinking all the time that a good Christian was the ecclesiastical Christian and now I'm in the Party I see good Marxists always damning those members that do not match up to their Marxist model. Trim the human soul and be damned for damning the souls of others. The Chinese yell because the Russians are not Chinese Marxists and the adolescent rages flow and the words fly. Ever since some ass said God made man in his own image men have been damning men for not staying in God's image. Then when you ask them what that is they [say] Oh the efficient Salesman, the efficient Manager, the ungrudging Workman, the Lovely Slender, Beautiful, Childbearing Soothing Eternal Feminine. They think they can take men down from a shelf at the Gumm Shop or from Woolworth's stores whereas the revolutionary man is very individual; yet he would hardly recognise the future man for whom he died.

God save us from Marx, save us from all conservatives, from bad drains, myopic eyes and from clipping the wings of angels.

Do you want us to send you that Barraclough book?

Affectionate greetings to all your family ...

40

Usti nad Labem,Czechoslovakia
20 May, 1970.

Dear Mr. and Mrs .Parker,

From your note of May 11th I see that you are concerned
about our well-being. I hope, you received my letter of
May [9th] 1970 in the meantime. I have not been able
to write as often as I wished because we are passing
through our cultural revolution. We are alright. In our
garden the apple and plum trees are in full bloom and
the lawn is sprinkled with dandelions. David is getting
frequently into troubles with my wife as he is persisting
with throwing his ball into the flowerbeds and breaking
and tearing the tulips and the budding peonies. I am
sure, he is dreaming of throwing stones as pebbles
and stones are for him the most important and most
beautiful ingredients of this world. His father Ian is not
very different from his son as he thinks that the world
revolves round the reeds for his B-tenor saxaphone,
size No. 3, which are unobtainable here. To get some
rest from the little rascal my wife went to Prague for
3 days. She visited the theatre each night because the
stage is the only outlet of culture now at Elsinore. She
has just returned with 3 cartoons of Kelloggs cornflakes,
one cartoon of Pickwick Tea and last not least with 5
golden boxes of the delicious Benson and Hedges special
filter cigarettes. As I have just glanced at the statistical
yearbook of Health for 1969 and noted that the average
life expectancy of a Czech male is only 67.3 years and I
am 58, I am puffing one of these carcinogenic cigarettes
and thinking, why not have a bit of euphoria. Yes, why
should any citizen of this socialist republic want to

write to his friends in the capitalist countries and receive letters from them, if you can have red radish and Hungarian sausage-salame? Isn't it stupid for a man who has only 10 years to live, according [to] the statistical yearbook, to wait patiently 3 years for an exit-permit while the most sexy girls in their miniskirts are walking through our streets and parks? Which truly socialist citizen is longing to travel westward-bound if there is so much good Pilsner beer? Only a very few citizens can justly claim that their journey to the West is really in the best interest of the State.

After all, can any one citizen be really quite sure that his behaviour abroad will be as impeccable as not to do any harm to the good reputation of this socialist republic? Foreign currency proves to be the greatest inhibition to travel for to live in hospitality with one's friends and relatives would be a disgrace to this ever so rich socialist country. Looking through the window, I can see not only flowering trees, blocks of flats with cranes still sticking from the roof tops, but also a blueish range of mountains. It's this damned range of mountains which makes one think of travelling and thus spoiling any attempt for achieving euphoria.

Well, while we are having our fun with our hawks, you are going to kick Heath into the pants and to give Harold Wilson a big push to the left. I hope I got the headlines of today's Morning Star correctly, did I?

With best wishes
Yours affectionate[ly]

Paul

41

Shoreham-by-Sea, Sussex, England
24th May 1970.

My dear Paul

If you lived in this country and you were in the habit of
administering anaesthetics to the bourgeois you would
hear [them] sometimes murmur in their sleep 'How's
that' or worse 'Owszat' or 'well played sir' or contrarily
'Shocking – only 20 runs in an hour'. These revelations
would tell you where the gentleman's heart was, namely
on the great green cricket field of old England. Here
gents disport themselves hurling a hard ball at three
stumps about 3 feet high and another gent with a bat
attempts to hit this hurled ball into the blue empyrean.
This is our noble game which all the bourgeois have
played since about 1800 and in which they have an
emotionally vested interest. This game, thanks to our
heroic forces that once peopled the Empire, is now
played throughout those dominions, colonies and
whatnots though in this country as a spectacle for the
proletariat it has lessening charm and is sadly declining.
So from time to time our Cricket Council made from
the best willow and, so to speak eclectisised [*sic*] cricket
balls invites teams from Australia, Pakistan, India
and South Africa. But this year the South Africans
knowing that true cricket blood does not really run in
any complexion but that of the whitest white failed
to include in their team one gent somewhat darker in
complexion. So arose a great shout and a stupendous
furore and all racialists were utterly condemned by
bishops, communists, labourites, Swedenborgians,
liberals, trade unions and all those who hate racialism

and Toryism or both. The cricket council hung on grimly for the 'sake of Cricket', hallowed game that has made England what it was, not of course what it is! Miles of barbed wire was brought to keep the sacred turf from the feet of the thugs, vandals and assassins; the police denounced the thugs, hooligans and vandals at their conference; the Tory ministers spoke of the freedom of the Individual, of Cricket, of their grandmothers and their noble Cricket Heritage. All to no Avail. The Home Secretary requested the council in the end to call off all the matches with the South Africans.

Today the Archbishops, the Bishops, the Royal family, the Labourites, the Liberals, the Humanists, the Communists and the Women's Institute in Sludge-cum-Pubsby will join in thanking their respective gods for this benison, while the Calvinists and those who have received the Blessed message of Apartheid straight from their god will gnash their teeth in the outer darkness of gold and diamond mines and the joyous suppression of the Negroes. We shall hear more, I fear.

Tomorrow we shall make enquiries for a reed of beautiful quality which when received will relieve Ian from blowing bubbles through his sax for joy of his son. I've often [wondered] why composers failed to write serious works in abundance for saxophones. Now it is revealed [to] me there are not enough reeds.

I enclose a letter to which I am making a long reply and should be obliged if you could give me some figures about house or dwelling building since say 1952; the fluctuations of the economy; public health service; normal services eg gas, electricity, water, restaurants; goods for domestic use, textiles which come to Mind. Perhaps you could tell me in what condition the Germans took over your economy and in what condition they left it.

I understand that in the last two years of Novotny the rate of increase of production declined to 2 per cent and in his last two years about 50 million crowns were swallowed up in production units with little return.

This week's Guardian is intriguing. I realise that you are very busy and I certainly do not wish to reduce the nine years which you think you have left but if a number of weeks go by we begin to think you have tumbled down the cellar steps with the coal. Thank heavens so far as I know we have done with coal but that is a very sore point with the miners who have been sacked by the 100,000 since the war on behalf of oil our lord and master.

The sun shines, the house swallows are back, the blackbirds sing on three neighbouring aerials and it is time for beer or rum or some such.

Leslie

My wife is 65 today and despite an uncertain amount of whisky makes me feel both very young and very old.

42

Shoreham-by-Sea, Sussex, England
Undated [*c*.2 June 1970].[86]

We are now in the midst of two nerve shattering obsessions in this fair isle which God himself has planted in order that the Chosen of All, the true man-eating or man-loving Britisher may declare to others their true

---

[86] Dated from internal evidence; the previous page (or pages) is missing.

path and show the Light thereon. We have a la commencer THE WORLD CUP OF ASSOCIATION FOOTBALL; several hours of it per diem. Adding to our glories, as yet hardly discovered, we have a terrifically phoney election in which we have to choose either the black pot or the black kettle. Hours and hours of this per diem. So much so that our sometimes equally phoney drama has to be resuscitated at a later hour. Mr Wilson snipes Mr Heath from behind a mindless mind while Mr Heath blows off his major guns with all the startling sound of a damp firecracker. Meanwhile Lima is destroyed and Romania is drowned and drowning.[87] Our minds dully perceive the enormity of both disasters but our hearts are with the gallant kickers of the football and we bite our finger nails (and would indeed bite our toenails if they were more accessible) and listen to the critics and hope that the Brazilians will have smallpox, the Czechs dysentery, the Romanians [a]erophobia and the rest of the opponents measles, apoplexy and hallux valgus acute,[88] chronic and undiminishing.

Meanwhile our best relief Organisations are putting their best foot forward but as yet Mr Heath has [not] accused Mr Wilson of sending or not sending several million pounds to either Peru or Romania.

And again meanwhile, the Irish darlin' Bernadette Devlin[89] stands for Parliament again amidst shot and

---

[87] An inaccurate reference to the Great Peruvian Earthquake which hit the coastal town of Chimbote, Peru on 31 May 1970. 70,000 people were killed and 800,000 made homeless. But Lima – some 400 miles away – was largely spared. In Romania floods which began on 12 May and continued to mid-June killed 209 people and damaged 41,000 houses, leaving at least 265,000 homeless.

[88] Bunion on the big toe.

[89] See note 60, p.132.

anger in Northern Ireland and we hope to Marx and Nemesis that she will come to no harm for 22 is no age to get shot in the back.

And still meanwhile the sun shines upon the Tory and the Social Democrat with undiminished zeal. We have once again too many little plums on our brave tree, too many cats sitting on pergolas or pekagoniums [*sic*] or persimmons or whatever my wife grows in her garden and a blackbird on our TV aerial that sings enough to either break your heart or make you grow two hearts. We also have blue clematis as wide as wide and looking like flaunting or flirting fairies. Even I can see them as I sit here drinking whisky and orange juice and trying to see well enough to type to you.

Summer is with us and how we super cited souls love the change of the seasons. We hope that the coal is piling up in the cellar for next year and that you are not forced to carry it upwards, that David's ball is not smashing down the tulips and peonies that you are all well and love each other so that life becomes bearable and that you will find some time to write about your country for we seem to hear of it less and less in our papers.

L

43

Usti nad Labem, Czechoslovakia
June 5th 1970.

Dear Mr. and Mrs. Parker,

Yesterday I received The Morning Star and found the
quoted passage in the editorial. I turned eagerly to the
article by Sam Russell,[90] well known and locked in the
heart of the few who know about the way he reported
events in this country. Today arrived the 'enormous'
packet with the excellent French reeds, the Guardian
and your interesting 'frivolous' letter. God bless you and
international solidarity! It did me a lot of good to see
once more that it isn't a fraud, after all. Ian hailed the
reeds and international solidarity with more wailing and
bellowing than at any time before. Believe me or not!
For the first time I could endure this sort of vile sounds
without getting barmy. I can stand [it] for a while when
Ian is playing with his band in a concerted harmony but
the daily exercises on the solo instrument is torment
to me. Ian knows of Bach and Beethoven as little as he
knows of Marx, Lenin or Brezhnev but he could probably
play to you many a piece of the Beatles or Big Beat or on
the clarinet of Acker Bilk. It is quite probably a torture
to our neighbours as well when he exercises as their
boys are retaliating with running the motors of the two
mopeds day and night just under my bedroom window.
By the way, we noted how carefully and skilfully you
are always wrapping the packet with the Guardian. For
the first time it happened that the packet was obviously

---

[90] Sam Russell (1905–2010), renowned journalist of the *Daily Worker*
and then the *Morning Star* until retirement in 1984.

opened as it was tied up with a piece of string. I wonder
whether the treaty of friendship and mutual military
aid, recently concluded by the contracting parties, also
contains a provision to ban all foreign political thought
and literature.[91] A German professor of anaesthesiology,
an Indian doctor and some Czech doctors, now in
Germany and Switzerland, were also sending me
occasionally a paper or paperback in collusion with you.
All this has stopped quite suddenly beginning of May!
Through the radio I can still learn in what a mess the
politicians got the world and in particularly, what the
chief editor of Rude Pravo is writing about.[92] Your letter
and Shakespeare prove beyond all reasonable doubt that
English and Scotsmen are the most original and wittiest
writers. You too, Leslie, are too much an Englishman
to bear the impossible constraint of a rigid system of
thought, commonly called ideology! Somebody said
to me the other day: 'Don't think! If you can't give up
thinking, don't talk! If you can't be silent, don't write.
And if you must write, don't sign it!' Very good advice,
isn't it? I felt, however, that I have heard something
similar before. This must be a plagiarism from the
bottomless goldmine of English political thought and
Aeropagitica, Samuel Butler's 'Erewhon' and the name of
Swift flashed through my brain. Now I got it! 'Be a good
girl,' said Mamma to her daughter. 'If you can't be good,
remember the dates.' So here you are, Leslie! However
much you are castigating your money-makers, your
power worshippers, however much you boo and jeer at
your political parties and political system, you can't get

---

[91] Treaty of Friendship, Cooperation and Mutual Assistance between
Czechoslovakia and the Soviet Union, signed at Prague on 6 May.

[92] Newspaper of the Czech Communist Party.

away from the fact, that anything said in Czech or in any other European language, was said better, briefer and more gently in English!

So much for tonight! Looking forward to hear from you soon again,

I am with affectionate greetings
Yours gratefully

Paul
Enclosed 3 snaps

44

Shoreham-by-Sea, Sussex England, the Land of
the Free-for-All
9th June 1970.

My dear Paul,

Our post has been doubly invigorating this morning. Our Medical boy has managed to put pen to paper which he does very, very well. He has just had a month in pathology and succeeded in doing two post mortems himself. He learned a lot from six young and enterprising pathologists. Then he had a week as a locum in a hospital, made only one error, killed no one and now he is 'in' obs and Gynae delivering babies, smoothing the lovely brows of mothers to be and smacking new born infants on their backs. He is 'worn out with work', but managed two late parties last week. He has about another year to go before he sets off as a houseman on his newly allotted salary of £1840 per annum which is about £1600 more than a new

houseman got when you were in England. I have not
mentioned anything to him but I wonder what chance
he has through any organisation of making a cheap trip
to C-S. He is a bit insular and it would do him good to
see anything outside Eng.

Save for one or possibly two weeks near Xmas I have
sent a paper to you regularly. Please let me know should
one not get to you. In future I will put the sticky tape
on the actual newspaper; if you are careful you should
manage not to tear it much.

In the last issue I sent a long reply to Maurice[93]
(I mean copy of) to you. M's actual letter I sent the
week before. One of the reasons why I feel so strongly
about the necessity of good, factual criticism is that
we in England over two centuries have fought for this
and it adds a deep quality to our culture, a sense of
responsibility to our Government and a defence of the
sometimes gullible and often inarticulate millions.
We in England use this freedom so irresponsibly,
preferring rhetoric to logic, and verbiage to theories
and hypotheses established on fact so much that we
are in danger or making the freedom of speech a silly
babbling which people begin to despise then not to
listen to. In many instances the mass media and the
politicians seem to conspire to lead the people away
from central and important national considerations
into labyrinths of nonsense. But please rest assured I
do not attach anything but the gravest significance to
our chance of saying what we like though neither the
papers nor the TV would dream of hazarding their jobs
by giving what we say any publicity. Do I put enough
stamps on your parcels? This week I shall send you the

[93] For 'Maurice' see letter 45, p.180, letter 48, pp.190–1 and letter 81,
p.314.

Guardian – if it is printed[94] – and The Daily Mirror one of our tabloids, nearly 7 million in circulation, designed specially to mislead the workers by sitting on every fence from where, despite a chronically inflamed rectum, it beats the air with a stick of frothy saliva.

The photographs are splendid although I see no bubbles mounting to the ceiling from the sax. The Beatles today are not entirely passé but extraordinary cacophonies proceed from our radio when I turn on the beast. This raucous bellowing about their several sexual disabilities (for I can think no other) has come over from the USA with jumbo jets and dreadful news about the stock market. The heart-rending croaks and the hell fire drumming of a singularly primitive kind can be only the expression of unutterable longing for a quiet spell of bombing in Vietnam.

Our election goes on with Mr. Enoch Powell being so successful in setting black against white in our slummy coloured areas that they say one third of the coloured people are on his side. This is a contradiction that Engels would rejoice in.

Where was I? I said to my wife. Now that's a lovely young woman I'd like to have as my third daughter in law. She said 'I thought you were going to say you're migrating to Usti. In any case you simply can't have all the lovely young women as in laws. I could never have risen to so many occasions.' All the same I cannot understand why a young man needs to go off to blow his trumpet in an army drill hall with charm like that at home. Of course I do agree the nearest I got to blowing a trumpet ever was to harry a kettledrum when I was a Boy Scout.

---

[94] *The Guardian* apparently did not appear from 10–15 June; see letter 46, p.184.

We have 5$^{2/3}$ million little plums on our little plum tree and the blackbird still sings from the TV aerial. Oh Life is rich though Mr Heath is so extraordinarily earnest that he has swallowed his tonsils. This [is] perhaps rather less immoral than Mr Wilson who has swallowed his promises. One question I address to the world is: CAN ANY ONE MAKE ANY IMPRESSION ON ANY BLOODY GOVERNMENT?

My wife says your family is very good looking but where is Paul? And I said Do you think I would send a photograph of myself? Well, she said, that's different.

Affectionately

Leslie

45

Usti nad Labem, Czechoslovakia
Tuesday night, 16th June 1970.

Dear Leslie and Enid,

I am so pleased to have such a conversable [*sic*] partner at the other end of the line that it would be a pity not to reward his untiring efforts with a quick reply. If Hilary is still at the Maternity department at B-ham, please tell him that J. Selwyn Crawford is an eminent anaesthesiologist and the author of a well-known textbook – The principles and Practice of Obstetric Anaesthesia. Should Hilary wish to learn something about anaesthesia in due course, there is no better man than the Professor, John S. Robinson, himself, a keen investigator and the founder of the first unit of intensive therapy in the whole of England at Whiston, near Liverpool. So much for the great ones in anaesthesiology at Birmingham, whose fame has spread across the Channel to our country.

In the issue of the Guardian I found the letter of 'Maurice', addressed to you both but your reply to 'Maurice' with the later issue of the G. has not arrived yet.

I have not met Maurice and I don't know him. As there are some remarks about myself and Czechoslovakia, I am going to say something to you both and to your friend Maurice. But you should know that I am writing to you under several restrictions and constraints. I am at a disadvantage because of the language barrier and it takes me far longer to compose a letter to you than you or Maurice require. I have always to take in account that somebody is peeping into our correspondence. I have to choose my words carefully and I have to avoid certain topics altogether. If l am right in assuming that Maurice is Maurice Cornforth,[95] you may tell him that I am keeping his critical essay of Popper i.e. his book 'The open philosophy and the open society' next to some of Poppers books in my library. I don't think he has succeeded in refuting Popper. Far from it! For the tragedy of the author is that his book made its appearance in 1968. The events of 1968 dealt a mortal blow to a unified concept of Marxism–Leninism. They mark an irreconcilable division between the occidental,

---

[95] Maurice Cornforth (1909–80), Marxist philosopher and prominent theorist of the British Communist Party best known for his books on *Marxism and the Linguistic Philosophy* (1965) and *The Open Philosophy and the Open Society: A Reply to Dr. Karl Popper's Refutations of Marxism* (1968), to which Paul Zalud refers. He mistakenly assumes that this is the identity of Maurice.

more liberal interpretation, which the author exposes
in that book, and the Eastern version. I am, above all, a
professional man which implies that I have great respect
for and some knowledge about the method of science.
Science is to me nothing but the belief that everything is
open to criticism and nothing is exempt from it. The task
of the scientist is to point out that certain facts contradict
this or that theory. This does not mean that the theory
must be abandoned. It can be modified so as to fit new
facts. But if more and more facts are contradicting
essential statements of the theory, the scientist will have
to decide whether the theory is still helping in solving
problems or whether it has outlived its usefulness. It
is at this point that you, Leslie, and I myself disagree
which does not prevent us to carry on the dialogue. I
never claimed to have profound political understanding.
The obstacles to freely expressing my mind, I mentioned
above, can easily lead to the conclusion that I have none
whatever. I neither wish [to], or can, invest my time and
energy in delving into economics and statistics, having
to give anaesthetics for eleven hours daily and keeping
abreast with medical literature. It is quite a different
matter carrying certain principles to their legitimate
conclusions while living at ease, in security and comfort
and in an atmosphere of political liberty than to live and
work in a society so ostensibly contrary to the blueprint
from which it originated. All I wish for is to drive home
my point that certain precious amenities and basic
liberties which everyone ought to possess can easily be
lost for ever! When I awoke from my dogmatic slumber
through the lectures of the late E. F. Carritt of University
College, Oxford on dialectical materialism in 1940, I
decided in 1941 that the political facts are not at all like
the book. Please note that Mr. Carritt's son was killed
in Spain, the other stood as a candidate for the CP of

Gr. Britain at a London district and Mrs. Carritt did as a staunch communist a lot of good for the Basque children in England.[96] Since my age of 15 I have been eagerly reading Marx, Engels, Lenin, Luxemburg, Bucharin, the documents put forward by Trotzki et al. The facts in 1941 were in striking contrast to the expected consequences and the standards of behaviour entailed by the theory. That is why I left the theory and the C.P. Then I was condemned by Dr. Goldstucker,[97] by my two brothers and by my friends at the local group of our Czech party organization at Oxford. My two brothers and all of my former friends adhered strongly to the party until August 1968. Like thousands of high ranking Communists they fled to the West. One of my brothers is at Vienna, the other in your country at Newcastle-u-Lyme, Staffs. Now, Maurice, who displayed more socialist consciousness, myself or those who fled to the West? I did not break away from the wretched people of this country and I am dragging myself daily to the hospital to do my work under the most difficult and stressful conditions. Are those who keep this society

---

[96] Edgar Frederick Carritt (1876–1964) FBA (1945): his lectures on Dialectical Materialism, distilled in his book on *Morals and Politics* (1935), though very popular, formed only a tiny part of his work which was largely concerned with morals and aesthetics; he was not a Marxist, nor a member of the Communist Party, though his wife and children were.

[97] Eduard Goldstucker (1913–2000). A member of the Czech government in exile during the Second World War, he later became Ambassador to Israel. Although jailed for five years under the Novotny regime he remained in the Communist Party.

In 1968 he was both an MP and President of the Union of Writers, which was to the forefront of the Prague Spring. Goldstucker fled to England in 1969 and became Professor of Comparative Literature at Sussex University before returning to Czechoslovakia after the fall of communism.

going and together displaying socialist consciousness
or those who are ad nauseam repeating over and over
again the standing clichés on anti-imperialism cum
vigilance and other esoteric formulas? We have long
ago found out that these formulas are being used as
passwords for the bureaucrats to identify each other.
Their real aim is nothing but to keep their positions
of power and jobs thereby arresting and resisting all
change. Why don't you come to our country and see for
yourself? Everyone with whom you talk will confirm
to you the fact that the atmosphere was never before
so oppressive and stale as now, since the monstrous
rigid uniformity has swamped our society in April and
May last year. You seem to have all prerequisites for a
good apparatchik. You suspect me, an old and lonely,
isolated intellectual, to hand over all Czechoslovakia to
the imperialists because I claim the basic rights such
as freedom of speech, assembly and free movement
which the CP Gr. Br. wants to respect and preserve.
Don't you see, Maurice, that the abuse of power, you are
deploring, is once more flourishing in this country and
why? Let us face one 'superficial comparison'! Since
the beginning of May all newspapers and weeklies,
my friends from abroad were sending me, remained
undelivered, except those letters and packets from my
friend, Leslie Parker. He seems to enjoy a privileged
position with our mail-robbers and I am damned glad
about it. You know the story of Alexander Solzhenitsyn?
He too complained that letters, books, even birthday
telegrams failed to reach him. It emerges that there is a
systematic pilfering of mail going on in order to isolate
certain independently thinking men like myself or the
great Russian writer. There is in my opinion little to
choose between violence as a bedfellow of liberty and
affluence and violence, lawless tyranny as a bedfellow

of poverty, backwardness and stagnation. To show you what the villain looks really like and in what sort of counter-revolutionary activities he is mostly engaging, I am enclosing 3 snaps.

With best wishes and warmest regards

Sincerely Yours,

Paul

46

Shoreham-by-Sea, Sussex England
posting Tuesday 16 June 1970.

Dear Paul

Much to the chagrin of the social democrats and the joy of the Tories the newspaper workers upped the class struggle and stopped the delivery of our newspapers for a day or two. My Tory sister was outraged because she could not read the gossip calumniator in the Telegraph and I offered her the Morning Star. And on her birthday which we all enjoyed.

I am sending you S. Times because there is no Guardian and, today, Monday's Mirror and a paperback agst the Vietnam war by our good friend Fulbright. May these enlighten you in the wicked ways of the wicked imperialists.

Mr. Powell being a good Church of England man has let loose the dogs of war in the Tory Party and the furies of racial strife wherever he can. May he go to a C of E heaven for I can imagine nothing worse.

The Gallop and other Polls are all haywire. The figures of our exports bring transports of joy to them who ought to know better because they are so BAD and Mr Wilson is calmly proclaiming to all and sundry that WHEN he gets back in the Prime Minister's seat there will be much joy for some and heaps of words for the remainder. Quite frankly I would rather lose an ear than my miserable eyesight. Though a nose stopper during this election might save much inconvenience.

During the winter it WAS TOO COLD TO GET OUT: THEN CAME THE SUMMER BECAUSE SPRING HAD GIVEN US THE SLIP SO IT was too hot for me to go out. Now a strong breeze is breezing up from the sea and I cannot go out because I have to go out under lock chain and keyless.

We are now, like our C-S and USSR friends, out of the World Cup. While this will not ensure by any means an economy of words by our journalists it will give great satisfaction to overseas friends as well as our Scottish, Irish and Welsh. We also lost the Wightman Cup again to USA although we had two very lovely girls in our team. O Nemesis why hast thou such a jaundiced eye?

I hear Mr D is on the way to historic immortality...

Our dentists now are getting very uppish. If l am prevented from pulling out all their molars I hope they have eternal toothache with Mr Powell.

Love to David.

L

47

Shoreham-by-Sea, Sussex, England
Friday 19th June 1970.

My dear Paul

We have Gallop Polls and other mysterious ways of
looking into the future and they are now the laughing
stock of the whole world because they told Mr Wilson
and his bonny confrères that they would be returned
to Parliament with the sole opportunity of kidding the
people irrespective of what Abraham Lincoln said about
a government's ability to fool the people all the time.
So the Polls were wrong and all the computers knew it
from the very first figures that were returned. Mr Wilson
is out on his neck and Mrs Wilson who is a charming
woman is packing her bits and pieces and moving into
the poorhouse in which Mr W may write his Opposition
speeches for the next four years.
    Saturday:
    So Mr Wilson kissed Her Majesty goodbye and Mr
Heath put on his cutaway coat and kissed the Queen
'How do', and later went to a royal birthday party at
Windsor. And today the sun is shining and everything is
royal June in a highly Tory England and prices still go
up and the USSR is trying to catch up with the living
standards of the GDR and Mr Heath is determined to
give no post to Mr Powell. I think I shall help Enid to
water the garden so that my strawberries will grow fat
and abundant.
    The British working man has had his belly full of
politics so that he refused to turn out to vote whereas the
USSR people, patriotic to a man, turned out according to
Pravda 99.2% and all the govt was democratically voted

back en bloc. This huge pro-Brezhnev vote failed however to persuade the British working man to put Wilson back so that he could avail himself of an invitation of Mr. Brezhnev to visit Moscow after he, Mr W, was returned to power. Maurice Dobb[98] is our best Marxist economist and is I think an honest man. What I would like to know is something about the distribution of incomes in the socialist countries partic in USSR; the number of dwellings now in building, the quality of goods produced and what pressures have forced managements to grant increases of wages without ensuring increased production. By the way the anti-Lysenko[99] scientist[100] has been released from the lunatic asylum but Grigorenko,[101] an opponent of invasion, is still in such a place. Bernadette Devlin not only failed to get shot in the back, praise Yahweh and his heavenly hosts that she believes in, but in her constituency there was the biggest vote of all, 90%. We are utterly delighted with this result

[98] Maurice Dobb (1900–76), communist economist, Fellow of Trinity College, Cambridge. He was widely known for his historical *Studies in the Development of Capitalism* (1946), but his main interest was in the interpretation of classical economics and the operation of socialist systems.

[99] Trofim Denisovich Lysenko (1898–1976), Soviet biologist and agronomist who rejected Mendelian genetics in favour of pseudo-scientific ideas and claimed dramatic increases in crop yields. Dissent from his theory of environmentally acquired inheritance was outlawed in 1948. In 1966 the pseudo-scientific nature of his work was exposed and he was disgraced. For Mendel see note 274, p.408.

[100] Reference to Zhores Medvedev, 29 May 1970. An internationally respected scientist, he was committed to a psychiatric hospital from May 1970 until 17 June 1970.

[101] Major-General J. P. Girogorenko, founder of an underground dissident group, the 'Union of Struggle for the Revival of Leninism', was twice committed to psychiatric care and stripped of all rank. Released in 1974, he was allowed to visit the US for medical care in 1977, and while abroad was stripped of Soviet citizenship.

though that arch fiend and ultra racialist etc etc etc another believer in Yahweh but probably a different god from Bernadette's [was also elected]. The Lord moves in a mysterious way his wonders to perform. Would you please cut out the Jenkins article when you have enjoyed it and let me have it back. We are unable to obtain two Guardians.

I look forward to the slow rise to major politics of that slumberous Gargantuan the British Working Man and I trust that whatever he does will not impair the virtues of your water systems whether of a heavenly or a less deistic origin. My mother used to tell a droll story about water. A holiday party walking in the hills of Wales, being hungry and tired, stopped at a small cottage and asked whether they could find food and drink there. The woman of the cottage said they could have tea and boiled eggs if they would kindly go to the well about half a mile away and bring back some water with which to make the tea. 'Certainly,' they said, 'but what about the water for the eggs?' 'Oh, that's alright,' said the woman, 'I can always make enough to [boil] them in.'

Salaams to one and all

L

48

Shoreham-by-Sea, Sussex, England
Monday 22nd I think, June I know, 1970 alas.

My dear Paul,

Last week I had a shocking personal week. Analysed
scientifically one cause may be adumbrated as follows:
heretical inconsequentiality, temperamental disability,
philosophic distortion, political enormity, indigestion,
incipient rheumatoid arthritis of the mind, wheezing of
the chest, indigestion, cardiac deficiency, odium omnium,
indigestion, and all my other sins which I refuse to
remember. However soothed by breakfast of raw carrot
and invigorated by reading your letter of the 16th I now
return to the battle of the suburbs determined to put
down noisy motorcycles, stinks from the soap works,
all pro Tory somnambulisms [sic] and ultra dirty lawns.

Your use of the English tongue could not be bettered.
We are always amazed at the vigour with which you
use [it] as well as the exactitude. You have the very
rare gift of combining in your argument, restraint, fact
and opinion.

I am indeed very fortunate to include you among my
correspondents. When I entered the CP in the thirties
I was always regarded as having done so because I was
intellectually attracted. This opinion was held in the
belief that I had taken over lock, stock and barrel the
tenets of the moment. This was never so. I blame myself
for not thrusting deeper into Marx and Engels rather
than taking it for granted that what I held socialistically
was to be found there or what the Party held at any one
time was also to be found there. I entered with certain
unassailable convictions as an amateur historian. First

that though historical evidence is difficult to come by and needs quite a lot of sorting out no view of history could be achieved without. No hypothesis is completely unassailable nor is any practice founded on it. I view specialists with enormous suspicion. In this I think we agree 100%. But, and this 'but' is considerable, I did not join the Party for purely intellectual reasons though what organisation I did join had to live more or less in accordance with my intellectual pretensions. I had been a priest in the Church of England for 10 years and left it because though it was a highly respectable institution as an organisation it cared not one jot for the common people of whom I was surely one. I do not therefore look upon the people as so many production units or zombies characterised by cloddish obedience. I believe that what they know, the amount they know increases the efficiency of every stage of socialism. If we may have access to knowledge then we can form our opinions; though we know that the mass of opinions will never individually coincide they will form a bulwark of the social condition of which they are part.

In practice both the people and the govt must compromise for while discussion may go on for ever decisions have to be taken. Undiscussed decisions are liable to grave error not only in the realisation of the substance of an hypothesis but in forwarding the comfort and happiness of the people. I sent you a copy of my indictment of Maurice about three weeks ago and as a matter fact a copy of a circular I had sent to a number of my friends in early 1968. The latter was quite sucessful in stemming the local tide. As I have often mentioned, those of our persuasion are in a double difficulty of cracking open a society which shows every sign of clamping down on the living and intellectual conditions of the people and in the face of this maintaining that certain rights and freedoms are utterly vital in any new society we may be able to promote.

We are comfortable, as Maurice is, in our present petit bourgeois way of life but we are by no means as comfortable as we were say in 1956 or even 1960, incomes being equal. We are very uncomfortable in the face of continued slums, poor efforts to supply municipal dwellings, 2 million undernourished children, over half a million unemployed, the complete obliteration of non-Tory papers except The Guardian (500,000) and the Star 30,000. Do not underestimate these threats that go along with friendship for the USA, South Africa, the Greek junta, Portugal and Spain. I am also afraid that, perhaps after my lifetime, should the present attempts at constriction develop into suppression, the people, when they rise, will not care two hoots for freedom of information etc., so long as they get rid of their oppressors. Therefore while I am deeply concerned with preserving the best or some of the best in our present society I am consequently concerned with the creation of those 'bests' in other societies. We cannot demand, as some think we can, something for 'A' while agreeing it must not be present in 'B'. My wife says my last indictment was very strong but it is unlikely that Pravda will translate it.

I shall give your information (many thanks) to Hilary who we think will become a (good) GP. Our doctors are on the ramp tor higher salaries. Three-quarters of our consultants spend three quarters of their time dealing with private patients. Others are utterly devoted and hard-worked, some over worked. We have a scarcity of GOOD GPs.

Thank you for the photographs. Do you bind as well as gag your more adoring nurses? While I am highly suspicious of doctors – how the devil do you know what they are doing to you? – I adore nurses.

No, that Maurice told me that I had not the apparatus for a philosopher. This one is a lecturer in economics and is going to do just that in the GDR. Has no idea of what goes on in a human being. Anyway preserve the fragments and love from us both to you all. By the way there are 4000 private enterprises in GDR and it is 8th down in the international table of national production.

Maurice is v anxious to know why?

L

49

Shoreham-by-Sea, Sussex, England
23 June 1970.

Dear Paul,

Now 26th June still the same year. If you were to take my head and shake it would offer no evidence of substantiality, no not even if you were to inclined to drill holes through its external structures – there would just be a hissing noise of noxious gases escaping. On the other hand if you were to examine my bloodstream you would [find] all sorts fizzings and multicellular excitements, inarticulate indignations and a general turmoil of eructations, eruptions, all entirely due to the stupidities of those who by some mischance appoint themselves our guardians. And for which we pay them. Abraham Lincoln in a moment of great unwisdom essayed the opinion that though you can fool some of the people all the time and all of them some of the time you couldn't fool all the people all the time. I doubt this encomium very often though I know in my saner moments it is true but what Mr Lincoln failed to say was what every politician knows you can by means of stratagem, lies and brutal force keep most of the people from altering their condition once the conservative rot has set in. Otherwise we should translate Nixon to Vietnam, Brezhnev to Northern Ireland and Heath and Wilson to some tropical island where they could continue their endless squabbling as to the best ways of deluding the people that the sole object or their being in Parliament is to 'set the balance of payments right'.

Anyway I started with my empty head and there I intend to stay. But until I write to you again I shall let my blood cease its turmoil and flow in silence for the wounds of your country. No matter what the pseudo dialecticians aver or the saviours of humanity proclaim – either in their endless columns or through their endless gun barrels – there is being hounded to political humiliation one Alexander Dubcek who deserved honour from his colleagues and joyful acclamation from all those who stretch mind and sinew to bring into being a noble life to the afflicted everywhere, to all those in bondage.[102] To those enduring unendurable frustration, to all the aspiring he rose as a beacon over dark and stormy seas. Of all contemporary statesmen he said what he meant and he said it and meant it because he cared. 'I shall not be satisfied,' said some Lord of the Dunghill, 'until he is a chauffeur.' This same gentleman is now on his way to the Red Square to enthuse over the bust of that great mastermind. The Communist world may well consider whether the trade of taxi driving or the Red Square is the more ennobled.

---

[102] Dubcek's expulsion from the Czech Communist Party occurred three days later.

One thing is certain: easily the greatest factor that inhibits men and women flocking to the ranks of the Communist Parties in Britain, France, Germany and the USA is not entirely unconnected with these elevations or degradations that events give witness to. I think I should go before my blood twists itself into entirely unconsidered hypothetical knots.

Leslie

50

Usti nab Labem, Czechoslovakia
June 27th 1970.

Dear Mrs and Mr. Parker,

Your letter with the very nice photos reached me yesterday. My wife said you both are looking exactly like she had visualized you. I think you are looking far smarter and even younger, than you yourself described in one of your letters. I only now realize how much there is in a snapshot. To have a person in his physical likeness in front of one's eyes quite definitely underpins the relationship based only on the exchange of views and words. I therefore include yet another picture from the 1 May procession in 1962. The picture is remarkable for two reasons. First, that we were able to smile under the rule of Novotny. Secondly, it depicts the only two fellows from the medical staff of our hospital who were members of the CP-CS before the war. The man, carrying the poster on the left, marked with a cross is the chief of the neurological service. He was like myself a pre-war member of the CP but has left the party in 1969. I am

very sorry that our erratic postal service failed to deliver
me the copy of your own indictment of Maurice's letter.
Having your reply, I would feel no need to assail him as
fiercely as I did. I always feel sorry after getting cross
or being rude to a Nurse or to David if he is naughty. I
always feel like apologizing which I often do, after the
outburst of anger. I too am very happy that I can write to
you and that I am receiving very stimulating letters from
you. You will hardly believe me but I have no one to talk
to here although I have several good and trustworthy
friends in the hospital and among the local people. A
strange disinclination to talk, a sort of paralysis has set in,
perhaps because there is no input from the environment
worthy to talk about. Ian and Zdenka have gone away for
3 days and there is no bellowing of the saxophone. My
wife took some of the white, pink and red roses which
have just come out in the garden to Peter's grave and she
took David with her. So there is no crying and yelling
when something offsets his play. Bright sunshine and
tranquillity invites to meditations. We both have reasons
to be sick and disappointed. You about the outcome of the
elections and I about the expulsion of Mr. Dubcek. I don't
like to meddle into party affairs but Mr. Dubcek belongs
as much to the CP-CS as to the great multitude of right
wing forces as we are denounced in the party gibberish.
Why is it necessary to hurt and humiliate that man still
further after he has been deprived of all power and has
been singled out to suffer more than anyone? What right
have they who elected him against his own expectations
and wishes as their first secretary on January 6th 1968
to use him now as a mean for the purpose of their badly
needed scapegoat? I have just seen a fairly recent copy of
the American magazine 'Playboy' which shows that this
sort of publications manages to pass the filter alright.
In this copy Norman Mailer says: Ultimately polities

denies the rational nature of man. General Charles de
Gaulle said once: Christian perfection will never create an
empire. The man of action is hardly imaginable without a
strong trait of egoism, ambition, obstinacy and cunning.
Of course, A.D. had none of these qualifications. He
naively assumed that a good leader must serve his own
people first. Even though the world wants to be deceived
it is immoral to do so. Following such outlived and old
fashioned tenets of belief in this age of global strategy he
had to be kicked out. I am really enchanted with the way
you are describing your principles in your letter of June
22nd to which I am going to refer at present. Perhaps A.D.
felt in regard to the policy of the CP-CS so far pursued
just the same as you felt towards the Church of England.
A.D. thought that our C.P. cared far more for copying
faithfully an imported model than for the common people
of which he certainly is one, particularly now. I can tell
you that in 1968 we felt for the first time that we are not
just production- and service-units to be amortised if their
rentability ceases. I wholeheartedly agree with what you
are saying about access to knowledge, about individual
differences of opinion and decision making. I am the
last person – or A.D. for that purpose – who would deny
rationality to those whose observations, judgements
and tastes depart from certain principles. I too, hold
that decisions about what to do are ultimately of more
importance than decisions about what to say. However,
decisions in terms of statements are guiding decisions in
terms of actions insofar as they are informing us about
what observations, experiments to make or where to look
for relevant knowledge. Perhaps next time I shall give you
my views about the 'small economic miracle' (small as
compared with that of the Federal Republic of Germany).
As this is a rather long letter, it will suffice to tell you that
unfortunately the existence of 4000 independent peasants,

handicraftsmen and shopkeepers has not prevented the GDR to become one of the most totalitarian states of Europe. I shall also relate to you my impressions about an interesting book, called 'Programm 2000' by Karl Steinbuch, a computer specialist or cybernetician from the University of Karlsruhe. Don't worry about any fragments of love! I shall go on writing to you as long as permitted and possible. With best wishes and warmest regards.

Yours

Paul

51

Shoreham-by-Sea, Sussex, England
5th July 1970.

My dear Doctor,

Whatever remnant of charm capitalist organisation had retained with [for?] me is now forever destroyed by this morning's discovery that we have been sent a copy of the Guardian that we had several aeons ago. We are now in the midst of a gently worded, half unspoken wrangle [over] whether you should be the recipient of the Sunday Times. Like the problems of the Middle East, Northern Ireland and our Tory govt this problem will sooner or later be solved.

There are so many events spilling over in my mind that I feel I shall not cope with any.

We have recently 'had' Wimbledon – ours and the world's (so they say) tennis championships. This year unless the TV was wrong the standard was unusually high but as no one remained flawless someone in the end won. That old veteran, full 35, essayed for the men's singles but failed (name: Rosewall). The Communist men did not get very far though Metrevelli with Olga Morozova showed up in the finals of the mixed doubles but were beaten by Nastase the Roumanian and a little ball of American energy called – I can't remember. Metrevelli's partner Miss Olga Morozova appeared the complete player. A lady of considerable power and physique and as decisive as a party secretary. If she could get international practice she might be the world winner. I'm afraid the Czech players disappeared fairly early. Perhaps they went to Scotland to play golf and drink whisky with Laver, the deposed champion.

Northern Ireland has erupted; the troops of the imperialists have been increased; the Tory Govt shows little more imagination than Gladstone did in the 1860s though the Home Sec. has already been to Ireland whereas it took Gladstone about 40 years of talking about the 'Irish Question' before he paid a two day visit to Dublin. Many Catholic houses have been searched and a number of rifles etc. found; fewer Protestant houses and less guns. There is talk of re-arming the Royal Ulster Constabulary which is exactly where the troops came in because they seemed in danger in of shooting all the Catholics. We find in today's paper that the social reforms are being deliberately slowed down by the N.I. Govt. In fact no act can be passed until October next. Not a house has been put up though the British Govt (Wilson) was ready to finance half a million in five years. Meanwhile at every eruption Prots kick out Catholics from houses and take them over. Bernadette Devlin, ambushed by the police on her way to her last meeting before going to prison is now in prison and every legal effort is being

invented to not only keep her there but also to prevent
her taking her 'loyal oath' as an MP in order to deprive
her of her MP's salary. Pouring oil on by no means extinct
fires I call it.

I gather that Jodas[103] was so anxious to prove Husak
guilty of pragmatism, pro Dubcekism, right wing
centralisticism, [*sic*] etc. etcetera that he wrote to
Moscow who sent his letter to Husak whereupon Jodas
(really Judas?) beset himself with a heart attack and
promptly died. It is, I fear, a very open question, however
dialectically attacked, as to his eventual interment
in the Red Square though they do say that after an
uncertain time has elapsed, should you be interred
therein or thereunder, you will eventually be kept down
by a heavy if not too artistic bronze bust. As the fat lady
said when offered a still larger helping, 'If you bust I
must'. Necessity is after all the mummy of invention. I
should not be at all surprised to learn that Moscow has
found that using the military to preserve or invent 'law
and order' is not conducive to an enlarged economy.
I understand that several years ago Moses informed
his Egyptian betters that trampling on the proletariat,
even the Hebrew proletariat, was not at all conducive
to making bricks without straw.[104] I am quite certain
that unless the people are involved in the promotion of
production and indeed in every facet of building the new
social order, the new social order will remain as tatty as
the one it has displaced. It were better that Mr. D had

---

[103] Founding member of the Czech Communist Party and in the
years 1968–70 a member of the ultra-leftist dogmatic group known
as 'Jodasites'.

[104] Pharaoh refused Moses's demand to free the Israelites and then
punished them by depriving them of the straw required to make
durable bricks. See *Exodus*, chapter 5.

not been sacrificed on an altar, the god of which had long since been socially useless and discredited but I am equally sure that he and the people will rise again. You and I are often irritated by stupidities but a long [time will] elapse before all the positions of government in our countries are filled with Zaluds and Parkers. Meanwhile I gently rejoice that Mr D appears to be defended by Mr H who has at last got the ear of Brehznev. That this is so is deplorable but it is better than a poke in the eye with a burnt stick. You must have more faith in the people. Just because the people do not have a great deal of political perception does not mean they do not know a good man when they see one. For good men they have an affinity because of their own natural goodness.

I do hope you have received my indictment of Maurice. My wife says it was very strong and if you haven't got it it will have done someone some good anyway. It was quite long and wore me out and my wife told two of my children and today they are in an uproar – long after the event of course. But I do hope you will get it. Maurice was quite impressed. M. is one of those charming people who mostly fail to realise that other people have feelings and [thinks] there is a socialism that can be built without people though it may have some sort of units that look like human beings. In a capitalist country of course a man of your parts would not in the first instance be writing to me. Think of the loss! You would be drawing about £7000 per annum and you would be blowing up the govt to give you another third on top of that. You would also spend half your time dealing with private patients, running a nursing home and making another 8 or 9 thousand on top. You would approve of the BMA telling all GPs to resign from the National Health Service though only the youngest of these got less than £5000 a year and many of them tried to get patients to have this or that done privately so that they could have a rake off. And you would urge that the output of doctors should be kept to the present minimum and all the time tell everybody what long hours you worked. You would have at least a month's clear holiday a year and when you came back or you had overfed you would be rude to your working-class patients and get away with it. And all the time you would tell everybody, particularly the Tory newspapers that all doctors are very much overworked and they should have large increases of pay whenever they wanted them 'without reference to the state of the economy'. Your children would go to a good school (note the 'good'), your family would be happy in a detached house with gas central heating, colour TV, a washing machine and a daily help and two million underfed children, 666,000 unemployed, a million houses not built, men and women living in rooms while the rats ate their bedding and sometimes their babies and the top lot got richer and richer and the bottom lot remained a permanent sediment to nag them while they lived burying themselves in their work, in their private arguments, in blasting young people, all strikers, girls in mini skirts or in long skirts and so on. I cannot and I would not leave my countrymen for I have no hope beyond them. We must all fight our battles on the ground that has been bestowed on us by very dubious history whether we are in the USSR or the GDR or Mexico or Fiji. It is not the will of god but our common sense that dictates where and what we do. So although your smile must be somewhat wry you should smile again. You are a nice man and you should take care you are not ruined by any interloper.

There are many benefactors of history. Today I learned that during the Mexican Olympics the army mowed down 500 Mexican people, men, women and children in an endeavour to stop the students demonstrating during the sports;[105] in Greece it has been established that depriving of several thousands of food and torturing many others still goes on; both North and South Vietnam are desolations, but particularly the North where thousands of square miles have been defoliated. Despite Northern Ireland we in England have much to take care of and preserve in culture, freedom and work and we have to make sure we do that though I think capitalism is in for a major financial crisis. I may be wrong.

I think it is time this machine was oiled or I had some tea therefore I wish you and yours a very good health. Linda is coming tomorrow and we feel very cheerful.

Leslie

52

Usti nad Labem, Czechoslovakia
15th July 1970.

Dear Mr. and Mrs. Parker,

Many thanks for your letter of July 5th. I have had a letter from my brother from Vienna and a postcard from Robert, my elder brother, who spent his holiday in Brixham, Devon with his family. Coloured postcards from Italy, France and Spain are coming in from our former colleagues who are free to see all the nice places

---

[105] The 'Tlatelolco massacre' occurred on 2 October 1968, ten days before the opening of the Olympic Games, when 10,000 students gathered to protest against government repression. Estimates of the dead vary from 30 to 300; over 1300 were arrested.

of Europe, wandering from beach to beach, while we are sweating blood and tears in the hothouse of our operating theatres with their mal- or non-functioning air-conditioning. The hospital is the microcosm through which I view the economy of the country as a whole. I cannot forgo to tell you that the cause of the trouble has been tracked down at last. It was discovered that the fresh air inlet pipe has been passed very close to the hot and pressurized steam sterilizer. Instead of a cool breeze we are getting a stream of hot dust, being sucked in from the nearby building site!! I would, however, not complain if I would find a copy of the Guardian or any weekly or monthly in my mail, which consists lately only of medical journals and reprints of medical papers. I am told in a discrete way to become an idiot-savant, to stick to my business and to become as narrow-minded as a coin to fit into the slot of the social machinery. Furthermore I am thus gently reminded that to receive foreign newspapers is a transgression against the treaty of mutual friendship and defence however much Marx hated and fought censorship.[106] This reminds me of the fifties when I went to the University Library at Prague to borrow a book by Bertrand Russell. I was then told that these books are being lent only to members of the faculty of philosophy or students of that faculty. Anyhow, 'The Arrogance of Power' got through alright and I read it eagerly.

I find myself in agreement with much senator Fulbright has to say. Considering that the booklet was published in 1966, one has to concede that the senator foretold the staggering 'fallout' of the war in Vietnam quite correctly. How important and refreshing newspapers are is clearly demonstrated by the

[106] This is nowhere stated in the Treaty.

interesting background story to Jodas's fatal heart attack.
We have been told that he died from a heart attack and
nothing more.

On July 3rd I visited with a party from the hospital
the international medical exhibition, held at Prague.
We saw the most sophisticated medical equipment,
lavishly displayed and explained to potential buyers at
the West-German Siemens A.G. We were even treated
with beer and coffee – but, alas, their demanding
hospitality was to no avail and entirely wasted on us.
With no foreign currency at hand our pressing need for
complex equipment cannot be met. Walking round I
felt more and more frustrated until I came to the stands
of Portex Ltd and Gillette Industries Ltd. As subjects
of the Queen you will be flattered to hear that the two
British firms got ahead of the Germans, at least at
that exhibition. I was treated with Scotch whisky, with
soda and ice! To these two British firms I owe the only
acquisitions in substance, namely a copy of The Sunday
Times and a most generous sample of fine hypodermic
needles and wonderful sterilized, disposable syringes,
made by Gillette.

After the visit to Mediexpo the dull cucumber
season set in much earlier than usually and with great
suddenness. We are speaking of the cucumber season
when most people are going away for holidays, when
public services are at near standstill because of shortage
of staff and cucumber salad is being served with each
meal under numerous fly-traps, hanging from the
ceiling. I am no longer holding out any hope to receive
your indictment of Maurice and I am very sorry it got
lost while being pushed through the sieve. I doubt very
much that I shall receive any newspapers from you
for the meshes of the iron curtain have been tightened
and made foolproof. The transitional stage from the

Dubcek era to a closed society of the Soviet type is now completed. The cynicism of the petty and top nabobs now in power is astonishing indeed. They are declaring an uncompromising ideological war on behalf of the working class just while at the same time conceding that for the first time in history the CP has lost the confidence of the workers – viz Rude Pravo of 16.7.[107]

There is a grain of truth in Liu Piao's[108] doctrine that the world is divided into cities and the rural areas, lying in self-sufficiency and in an eternal sojourn from progress behind the iron curtain. I really envy you the eventfulness and the exciting atmosphere of city-life, the diversity of opportunities and the great variety of choice open to you in the affluent societies of the West. Each moment you are called upon to decide for yourselves what you really want. You and only you are responsible for your decisions. Each minute you have the possibility of communicating with thousands of people and tell them your consent or dissent. Your independent 'Aye' or your 'Nay' will necessarily shape the course of events. Just now, and probably under the influence of the ultraviolet rays of the sun's energy, cultural, artistic, recreational activities are reaching a climax of activities. The strike of 50,000 dockers is on, the £ is dropping at the stock exchange and a state of emergency strictly for the duration of one month has been declared. Please note that that we are living for one year in a state of emergency, normal legal procedures being suspended for the duration, as temporary as the military presence of

---

[107] The newspaper of the Czech Communist Party.

[108] A reference to Lin Biao or Lin Piao (1907–71), Chinese revolutionary and military leader who became Vice Chairman of the Communist Party, Vice Premier and Minister of Defence before dying in controversial circumstances in a plane crash.

our friends. As men are getting warm, they usually get
excited, even perhaps a bit delirious. In our rusticating
region all creatures are lurching and flopping about very
sluggishly. Workers are not permitted to strike but one
can see them dozing and sleeping on their scaffoldings
in the hot afternoon sun. The scene of Prague, the
landscape on the way from Usti to Prague and our city
appear to have paused for millions of years at the stage
they have once reached. The hospital from the bottom
pillar to the equipment are fossils from the Cambrian
or Silurian ages. What is true for the microcosm applies
as well to the macrocosm of our whole industry and
society. Perhaps in 1000 years when all the barriers will
be swept away tourists from the city will be lured to
the Socialist lands by the countless precious species of
antiquated machinery, houses and transport means. The
zoologists will find evidence that centuries of captivity
and isolation not of their own making caused, through
evolutionary changes, distinct differences in the whole
make-up of technological Man and the unresponsive
species of homo sapiens, dwelling in the rural regions
of Socialism. These queer beings never lived their own
lives but they were lived by others for them. They never
were called upon to make any free choices and decisions
and bear the responsibility for them. They were always
being told what to do and what to leave undone. As
the same convulsive messages had passed through
their nervous network over and over again, at an ever
decreasing speed, an atrophy of the brain might have
developed in the course of the centuries of passivity and
submission. I don't think that even very prolonged lack
of communication can actually lead to brainlessness,
but it remains for the brain physiologists of the future to
demonstrate a slowing of mental activity, or perhaps even
an actual disappearance of certain structures endowed

with independent thinking and recognition of another human being.

I have to ask you for leave and being burdened with this Orwellian perspective of the future of the inhumane socialism of our time I have to go to bed now. I hope to hear soon from you, always looking forward to your letters.

Yours sincerely

Paul

53

Shoreham-by-Sea, Sussex, England
15ᵗʰ July 1970.

My dear Paul,

As I yesterday lay determinedly in bed because it was (and still is perhaps) my meditations on the substance and form of sundry brilliantly impressive letters to Edward Heath Esquire, Mrs Barbara Castle and our highly respected, often vituperative Powellite MP,[109] your postcard arrived. There is in this house an unnatural appetite for picture postcards. Owing to my inability to rush out to buy a card showing the undoubted salubrities of Shoreham, the recently erected and now immortal bridge spanning the Adur, the immoveable oil slick and the highly scented soap factory I had to content myself with a very plain card written in my

---

[109] Captain Henry Kerby (d. January 1971).

own not so plain handwriting the which my beautiful wife presented in due course to the Postmaster General with an urgent wish that he would despatch same to you without delay. Roundabout Christmas I must say that my determination to send you a paper every week though not exactly shattered was a little splintered. Since then I think I have succeeded in sending you some newspaper each week. My letters too have been quite regular and my last note included a letter from our son Hilary who is often called Bill. The only letter perhaps which you have not got was the one which Enid called very strong and this was not addressed to you and which my wife says was posted in mistake. Sometimes your letters come within three days which is good but mostly they take 6. All delays of this kind I ascribe to our capitalist friends in London for the slow aeroplanes they use. And that reminds me that we have just read a long novel hot from America in which the lack of excellency of the USA commercial airfields is vividly described along with two love affairs, one irate wife, one very anxious wife, one poverty stricken wife and one wife who refused to let her husband smoke cigars in bed. For good measure there was a discussion over abortion, a gent who blew up himself and a large hole in the plane and a demonstration about noise. This demonstration of 600 appeared in the airport on the night of the biggest snowstorm in USA history along with a lawyer who hoped to collect a fee of about 7000 pounds sterling. If a certain lady could get two years in a labour camp for demonstrating on her own what should not these marauders have received?[110] What is

---

[110] Probably an inaccurate reference to Larissa Daniel, which Leslie repeats below (p.255) and for which no evidence is forthcoming. See letters 62 and 64 and notes 134, p.245 and 140, p.255.

justice anyway? Most properly represented perhaps by
that blind lady standing on the top or the Old Bailey
our criminal court, holding a pair of scales. She never
[even?] demands in a stentorian voice 'Who shall dare
to put on the weights?' They do dare, however, as we
have recently witnessed. Seven undergraduates from
Cambridge recently received 'exemplary' sentences
for smashing up a few plates and glasses at a dinner
called to give publicity to Greece as a touring centre
when daily we hear of countless tortures to both men
and women in that country. VIOLENCE – that's what
they were accused of.[111] Has every and any govt the
right to inflict violence on those with they disagree?
Despite intra and international protests we are selling
arms to South Africa. Nor are our protests helped by a
certain communist country trading with Greece now.
Our Bernadette[112] is still in prison and the Speaker has
ruled that there is no constitutional way of bringing
up her case in Parliament because 'Northern Ireland is
not a colony nor a dependency over which we have any
legal control for the powers of the Commons were given
over to the Stormont govt in 1920'. The Governor of
Armagh jail is according to one MP never to be found.
Bernadette's plight is in my mind because we have
just said goodbye to Linda who has been with us for
a short time, ... pretty well exhausted ... because [her]
neighbour had drowned in the Yorkshire river Ouse
leaving a wife and five children. Quite a shock. Linda
slept a lot and read a lot and went off fairly rejuvenated.

---

[111] Fifteen students invaded and attacked the hotel where the dinner
– part of a Greek week – was taking place on 13 February. They were
accused of causing over £2000 of damage. On 4 July six were given jail
sentences of between 9 and 18 months, and two were to be deported.

[112] Bernadette Devlin, see note 60, p.132.

Bobbing about in my mind are conjectures on
the necessity of art to a society aspiring to advanced
technological production. It is easy to say that the
decadent art (I might explain the term on some future
date) now exhibited in GB and the USA, for instance,
reflects the comparative stagnation of the economy
but it is not easy to say that a wholesome economy can
only be achieved when art is free from dogmatically or
arbitrarily disposed boundaries. Art at its best under
capitalism is dragged down to pounds sterling at its
worst to bed-scene cinema, vulgar double- entendre on
comic TV, sheer pornography in literature etc. etc. which
again is regarded as successful according to the amount
of money it makes. While of course in England there
are millions of highly respectable people (like me) and
there are many thousands who have [a] high standard
of art and behaviour and, in addition, many striving for
betterment and revolutionary change, I consider our
society decadent. Perhaps no worse than ever it was save
for this difference – in the 19th C particularly as well as
in the 18th and vigorously so in the late 16th the whole
of society was forward looking – despite enormities of
social disfigurement and injustice. But today England
has no future that is not wrapped up in a bank balance,
a mortgage and the cost of living. Though the sun shines
and the fresh breezes blow and children are lovely I think
ours is a decadent society. It has no future. The serenity
of age is even no longer with us for every day we over a
productive age are told that we are expensive, live too
long and even stifle the aspirations of the young. They
say beauty is in the eye of the beholder but those who
say it often forgot that the eye needs something to rejoice
in. Long, long ago I had joyfully anticipated that the
communist countries would long since have been gloried
over with an outburst of art that left the ebullient life of

the Renaissance only a splendid memory. We
are still, however, turning our longing eyes backwards
to Praxiteles,[113] Michelangelo and, now, even the Incas.

Our affectionate greetings to you all. I thought
the other night as I lay in the darkness that I heard
coming down the wind the herald of the dawn tuning
in his saxophone.

Leslie and Enid

54

Shoreham-by-Sea, Sussex, England
21 July 1970.

My dear Paul,

The delinquencies of the capitalist post and mail workers
must be experienced to be believed and I shall most
certainly complain to the H.M. Postmaster General that
your letters have not been coming through promptly
and properly. I cannot conceive that the corresponding
workers in a socialist country should be so dilatory as
to delay the delivery of my letters. The complaint must
be made this side and I shall certainly do that. I shall
also write to the Czechoslovakian Embassy who will also
doubtless be suffering the same inconvenience with their
inland mail as we are in this country benighted with a
Tory dominated Parliament, the pomp and circumstance
of the Royal Family and so on and so forth. I have been
in the Communist Party for 35 years now and have no

---

[113] Attic sculptor of the fourth century BC.

small influence in the south-eastern area of England
not only among Party members but also in concomitant
organisations and associations. I am as a matter of fact
writing today to the Circulation Manager of Morning
Star asking if there is any impediment to the Star leaving
these Tory dominated islands. If there is one thing that
I cannot stand it is the steady outpouring of words
defending the status quo however that status has been
arrived [at].

Blackstone, you remember a jurist of the 17th
century[114] whose words have penetrated even the
fastnesses of Peking and Albania once said 'Justice
must not only be done, but must also seem to be done'.
Contrary to the ideas of Plato, that besotted idealist,
in this case the appearance is to the human being as
important as the act. Indeed Marx himself is eloquent
on the subject of the objectivity of the subjective – a
contradiction that is on paper utterly irreconcilable but
which in practice as Marx, that great genius, knows
(forsooth he is eternal) is solved only in practice. This
predisposition to the eternal has, however, been thwarted
by the dogmatists and stupid jealousy of the unutterable
bourgeoisie. The plenitude of their egotism is only
balanced by the historic sublimity of that inestimable
paragon of Marxist purity Rude Pravo. I personally like
no colour more than Rude though in our language that
word spells out another meaning, the which we must
not only ignore but definitely repudiate.[115] However,
to get back to our original contention about the mail

---

[114] Sir William Blackstone (1730–80), Tory politician and jurist of the
eighteenth, not the seventeenth century; there is no evidence that he
uttered this phrase.

[115] The title of the Czech Communist Party Newspaper means 'Red
Justice' or 'Red Truth'.

conspiracy I have no doubt that since the advent of the
Mr Heath as our Lord and Supreme enchanter there
has been a tapping of our telephone, a reduction of the
exercise of our minds and subterranean attempts to
divert our massive thinking from being distributed to our
friends and allies. Nevertheless we are not disheartened
because we know that in the end Truth itself will prevail.
Though our despicable government sells arms to the
even more despicable South Africans a great preliminary
joining of the forces in Greater Africa will quickly
balance this infamy.

[...] What I wanted to say there before the machine
went wrong was that the utterly decadent imperialists
will fall before the wide open discussion and healthy
discussions that go on in every walk of life within the
communist countries. I am glad to hear you say that
in the country of which you are so integral a part the
respect given to the communist is enthusiastic and
warm. I am also glad to be able to tell my friends that,
although the rate or production of the C-S economy has
been disappointing, the workers are setting to with a will
to produce goods for export to Russia and other great
countries who have hardly any need of what so small a
country as C-S produces. Nevertheless we must be guided
by the supreme wisdom of the Soviet Union whose
recent treaty of friendship has shown the world just
what friendship is. And what a wonderful word that is.
Before the clouds of darkness the illimitable ignorance of
the deists and the dogmatists flee before it. Never in the
whole history of your country has it known such a warm
friendly embrace. They speak in our imperialist country
of the Great Russian Bear with great reverence because
they speak only of its massive armies which lie as it were
from one end of the Globe to another. Before this might
both friends and enemies gasp with joy or fear and I am

sure you must be proud to see the officers of this mighty arm of freedom and equality marching down your streets arm in arm with your noblest and most beautiful girls. In our country the army is a threat to our inheritance, sending our brothers to the far countries in which we have no interest or gain and indeed by doing so acquire a reputation for arrogance. There are no heroes of the British Empire as there are heroes of the Soviet Russia. The people here look with almost unearthly expectation to the coming of Socialism though I must say they would be somewhat surprised to see a flotilla of Russian ships ascending the Thames. Doubtless the Elbe supplies a better and more handsome field of glory than our mean and wholly commercialised Thames. However, now I must leave but not before I do say that since March I have written quite regularly and sent either the Guardian or the Morning Star with regularity certainly since then. You are quite right, our national newspapers are totally unreliable as are our politicians, our road sweepers. Yet I am constrained to say though we do not always have ice because my wife is not devoted enough to get it out of the refrigerator we do mostly have whisky. We recently gave our friends: grapefruit from Azerbaijan; caviar from USSR; wine from Yugoslavia and GDR; venison from Siberia, potatoes from Byelorussia, raspberries and strawberries from Romania and cheese from Slovakia. It is a pity that we had to have coffee from Brazil. Life in an imperialist country has not many compensations. The aeroplanes are always unexpectedly coming down where they should not; the rich abound particularly in the political parties.

I am indeed particularly glad to hear that in the Communist countries Party members take the smallest salaries and always, so to speak, put themselves at the end of the queue. This tremendous ... respect for the people they help to govern has always been a mark of the true nobility of Party members. In England our Party members [officials?] have much less in salary than the average working man and certainly much less than the average man or woman in the professions. But in your country the workers and the professional men are regarded almost with reverence. Many professional men like architects and doctors surgeons and lawyers must have a wonderful life in every communist country but those of China and Albania – those heretics and enemies of the truth and the Good of the people.

I was delighted to receive your letter of July 15th and in the course of time I shall reply. Until then you may rest assured that in matters both small and great – from, as you say, the small almost irrelevant matter of the ventilation ducts to the wise government of your country we are in agreement. Here, in imperialist water because we no longer have Communist wine, I drink to you and your noble country. As Lenin himself said, Power is to the People and the People will prevail.

My wife sends you her love and the Portslade and Brighton Branches of the Party send their comradely greeting.

And I remain your sincere friend,

Leslie

55

Shoreham-by-Sea, Sussex, England
23 July 1970.

My dear Paul,

In my last undedicated epistle I sent by mistake two
pieces of newsprint giving the address of an agency
thorough which I may procure extracts of a general
nature from soviet journals. As extracts of this kind are
difficult to come by would you please return them unless
you have thrown them away.

I have been in touch with the Morning Star and find
that up to date there is no Czech embargo on the Star
so we shall send you that journal until you find that you
are more occupied with Pravda, that – to use Milton's
phrase – two handed engine standing at the door ready
and willing to smite with unexampled patriotism those
to the left and those to the right leaving those alas too
unconscious of their happiness at dead centre.

I am exceedingly sorry that a letter from Hilary to
us – he's the Medic at Birmingham – which I sent you
because of your professional interests has not reached
you. It must have been sent by some Corborus[116] to the
far-flung boundaries of dreadful night. Should this letter
turn up may we have it back too?

You must have missed a number of my letters which
until about three weeks ago were generally enclosed in
the Guardian which, as I have already explained, save
for Christmas, 1 have sent almost as they arrived.

---

[116] Possibly intended to refer to Cerberus, the mythological three-
headed dog that guarded the gates to hell.

I have started rather haltingly on the second part of my indictment in which I wish to prove the indivisibility of art i.e. communication not only by music but by word from ... all social (including economic) growth or decadence. It is particularly difficult to say when art is decadent though there are plenty of people both in the East as well as in the West who are quite convinced they can do this without paying any regard to any other factors in society. Here provided you can get a stage or a printer you can publish anything. Ever since Sherlock Holmes crime has been advertised with excitement, murder has come in for wide public support as a basis of fiction. But today we have gone over to sex – [greatly] and clearly disclosed on stage and [in] drawing. We have apparently now running in London to high prices a comedy in which men and women walk the stage naked to the unredeemed laughter of the middle-aged, the positive enjoyment of the young and to [an] increase of interest [by] readers of dramatic criticism. Lennon, one of The Beatles now posing in bed with Yoko on behalf of peace, had his private parts drawn and etched (but not amputated) for display in a public gallery. The police, an easily outraged section of humanity and wanting an easy kill, took the lot home to the Police Station for a closer look perhaps, but had to return them without bringing a case to court. Decadence, I suppose, is to be reckoned, but not easily, when art fails to bring to light anomalies, how people battled to right them, as well as to inspire people with visions of the good life.

Provided people have a vision of a wider, happier, freer life they will work for it until, as we say, they drop. But the promise of greater things must be perceivable in the present. Marx, and it is well to remember this gentleman, said that the transcendental (heavenly) transcendence of Hegel was in reality the conception of a project that mankind desired to put into execution. Men, at least since they lived in societies, have always had this great gift of' projection which the animals have never had. The trouble with planners is that they can only see a definite, highly circumscribed programme, whereas a vision includes many programmes as yet hardly conceived. It is necessary, as Engels says, to have a transcendence that is not heavenly transcendence, a philosophy of subjectivism that is not subjective but subjective enough to be creative and individual enough to be made social.

Of course we get post cards from here and there and we have travel books and films and brochures of where we could go if we had the wherewithal. In my first seven years of work I had a week's holiday each [year], except one year when l was done out of it by a crafty firm. While we have holidays with pay we still have some millions who cannot go abroad. Of our 60 million only two million get abroad. Blackpool and Brighton are our biggest tourist towns and they take about 1,000,000 men women and babies between them. We have about a million that are unemployed or so little employed that it don't matter. I have never asked my children because they are professional people to believe that all the things of the earth are theirs for the taking. I get annoyed that David will receive only about £1300 per annum as a lecturer in Leeds University whereas Hilary as a GP after three years work will get £5000 per annum. But I do not think it is earth shattering nor does David. Professional people need wide information, access to books, some travel for research, some knowledge of the polloi and so forth.

But so do work-people. I have no patience with those from one country flaunting the riches of the other as I have no patience with the upper crust of our own medical profession demanding more and more both from the State and from their patients. The other day I had a barium meal after eight months of waiting! A fortnight before I had it the doctor came round and said I could have it done privately at a cost of £25 if I wished. No, I said, and would have said no had I been Croesus.[117] To do anything else would be socially retrograde. We have consultants making £10,000 from the State and the same from private patients – their underlings are given most of the State slog. We have private abortionists that can easily make £3000 per week and then fiddle their income tax. 'I find out what a girl has in her bag and then take most of it,' said one of these healers. I don't care if your writers of postcards get millions a day and lie with the loveliest women on the most entrancing beaches so long as you don't want to be like them. They still have their fight coming: even the sycophants will not escape the crushing mills of the future. I have no bitterness and bitterness did not make me a Communist but I hate all those capitalists and communists alike who make people bitter. One of the causes why things go wrong is that all rationalists think that reason is the only criterion whereas the final criterion is humaneness – in so much as you did this unto one of my little ones ...!

Affectionately

Leslie P

---

[117] King of Lydia 560–547 BC, renowned for his wealth.

56

Usti nad Labem, Czechoslovakia
29th July 1970.

Dear Leslie and Enid,

Your letter of July 21st arrived yesterday and your letter
of July 23rd today. This is not bad going. I think I have
received all your letters in addition to a letter obviously
not belonging to me and addressed to comrade Jack
Cohen. Most of the newspapers, especially the Guardian
Weekly, also reached me and I feel that your rancour
against your post and mail service is not well founded.
I have positive evidence that at least some of my letters
are being read by a third party. Before launching
your complaint I should like to remind you what the
Postmaster General of the Soviet Union replied to an
angry protest of some writers about sluggish delivery
of inland mail in the SU. He replied in effect, and with
typical cynicism, that writers of his times are not writing
as well as Chekhov did. Enclosed I am returning the
piece of newsprint you wanted back and I enjoyed the
funny kitchen sink story from Yugoslavia. In these days
of tension and worry a bit of humour, gushing from a
jovial heart, is very welcome. Following in the trail of
your humorous writing I must tell you a story I heard
recently. A meek and much harassed Czech undergoing
a loyalty test is making all sorts of evasions and in
particular is excusing himself by pointing to official party
statements made in the first half of 1968.The chairman
is getting impatient: 'Haven't you got any independent
views of your own?' he shouts. 'Oh yes, but I don't believe
what I think!' was the reply. In the Guardian Weekly of
July 4th I found an article 'Loyalty tests on Czech party

members' describing the situation with brilliant insight. However, the report contains a serious flaw by stating that 'unless in prison you are a collaborator' ... and that it would be better if the C-S prisons were full of active resistance fighters. In fact, only a small minority in relation to the whole population is truly collaborating. 14 millions of Czechs and Slovaks can neither all leave the country nor hang or burn themselves to death. They have to work and carry on with their daily activities in order to survive and thus defending the integrity of our society against all sorts of onslaughts. If all dissenters would become resistance fighters the C-S jails would have to detain 7 million people, small children and old age pensioners excepted. This peculiar misconception proves that the special correspondent of the Guardian in Prague is an Englishman who is unable to comprehend the nature of the totalitarian regime in which the State owns everything, even the smallest tobacconist shop, the tiniest hair cutting saloon, every pub and every petrol pump in the country. Wherever a kicked-out person turns he will always be at the mercy of the same employer. You would do much better to point this out in a letter to the Editor of the Guardian than to complain to the Postmaster General or writing to the C-S embassy.

Much acrimonious feelings have been caused by the interviews for the admission to Universities. A stupid and dogmatic admission policy, long ago given up in the Soviet Union and in the GDR, has been reintroduced. The aptitude test is not decisive, but pupils of working-class origin as well as children from the countryside and from divorced families received preferential points in their favour, whereas in pupils being descendants of the intelligentsia points were subtracted from the aptitude test. After the social revolution in 1948 universities were widely opened to all those who could not complete their studies during the Nazi-occupation. The new working-class intelligentsia was created. But these doctors and engineers, mostly dedicated to the CP, have now children about 18 years old and eligible for admission to the universities. Many of them were refused because their fathers, although descendants of poor peasants or workers, are by now doctors, engineers or intellectuals. The logical, or better illogical, conclusion of this policy is that in Socialism subsequent generations have to be recycled between intellectual professions and workers, each 30 years! Let it be! I hope that, until David will grow up, the view will prevail that no country in this world can afford to waste any talent. I wonder whether your David at Leeds could possibly get hold of a booklet by Donald M. MacKay, professor of communications at the University at Keele with the title: Information Mechanism and Meaning. It was published in Cambridge, Mass. in the U.S.A. at the price of c. 3 dollars. If this book is available in the UK I would be very interested and would very much appreciate reading it.

Affectionately

Paul

57

Shoreham-by-Sea, Sussex, England
30 July 1970.

My dear Paul,

If I could write to you about the numerous things that spring into my mind when I am not writing to you, you

would never cease reading. Limitations are the essence
– if you will forgive the metaphysical term – of sanity.
To start with I must express the girlish enthusiasm of
my wife for your postcard. She was truly delighted that
you should in the midst of your important work think
of her and her delight in decorating the mantelshelf of
our lounge or living room with picture post cards. We
imagine that Usti is [a] most important river port and has
about 80,000 inhabitants who largely live on playing the
saxophone, enjoying anaesthetics and singing the Red
Flag. Enid adds to these constant admiration of the sky,
walking by the river and drinking Pilsner and Riesling.

I am sending you a Guardian today and 1 sent you
one last week on hearing that you had received two
together with a belated Sunday Times. You will perceive
the eyewash over sending military forces to Malaysia
which will cost an unnecessary £100 million [and]which
a highly intellectual government intends to find by
spending that amount less on our educational estabs.[118]
There is also an article on the USSR fleet now operating
throughout the oceans which until now have always been
considered the mares nostrae of the Anglo-Americans.
There is an underlying arrogance in this article that
bodes ill for peace. I do not suppose your newspapers
carried Castro's offer to step down from the leadership
of Cuba because he had been persuaded to take wrong
advice about the possibility of harvesting in 1970 ten
millions metric tons or sugar. He only managed just over
8. There has never been such an offer or resignation
from any Party leader ever before.[119] Humility is in the

---

[118] On 28 July Lord Carrington, the Secretary of State for Defence,
held talks with Malaysian leaders about continuing Britain's
participation in the defence of Malaysia and Singapore.

[119] See The Times, 28 July 1970, p.5.

offing and I should warn you that if you cannot remove 5 thousand legs, 65 kidneys, etc. etc. this year you might well find yourself 'door keeper in the House of the Lord'.

Meanwhile on our own struggling patch the Dockers in high rebellion have 'seen reason', 'bowed to the country's needs' and otherwise been persuaded to take up their burdens, save the fresh fruits, the patience of the government and the future of our trade balance and go back to work. It is amazing how quietly the nation has taken this strike; I think everyone waited to see what was going to happen when the Government put the troops into the docks which I must say they never threatened to, save indirectly through some newspapers.[120] The Govt however still labours under the Foreign Secretary's determination to sell arms to South Africa but it is now being said that the Foreign Sec will be hived off to Washington to become our Ambassador and doormat in that highly reactionary capital. On the Continent, though, our country has been forced to change the negotiator as it is making almost frantic efforts to get into the common market. While everyone knows that achieving this aim would put up our cost of living by about 30% everybody is also wondering how long all these friends and fierce competitors can take in each other's washing. Exporting is sometimes achieved by one country supplying what another country has not got but mostly by each country trying to sell in the others the very same kind of goods that those countries themselves produce. For instance, last year Vauxhall Motors in England lost 3.5 million pounds sterling but Volkswagen managed to sell almost half as many cars again in this country as they did the year before. It is of course because of this overlap in

---

[120] The dockers had been on strike from 15 July, leading the government to declare a state of emergency.

similarities of production, as well as the fear of being
swamped with British capital, that France is trying very
hard to find sufficient arguments with which to keep
Britain out of the Common Market. On the other hand
France needs capital to increase her factory production
and to modernise her agriculture. France like Russia has
about 50% [5%][121] of the population in agric but they
cannot transfer large masses of this agric. force to factory
work. In any case, many of the capitalist countries will
have sufficient production power to meet more than the
basic needs of their populations and much more than
enough to supply those who have the purchasing power.
It does seem, however, that the capitalist countries
are once more being faced with [the] dilemma of
having enormous potentialities of production while an
increasing number lack the necessities of life above what
is mere subsistence level. We shall see. We notice that
the Sov. Un. has postponed its meeting of the Praesidium
and conclude that the debate on how to remedy the
slow rate of increase of the Gross Nat. Product is still
going on. With money being poured into a large army,
an ever increasing navy and arms for this country and
that – lunch over – and I am unable to continue with
that line because I cannot read. I imagine any other
line will do. I think it was about 14 days [ago] I wrote
to you after receiving a very disturbing letter [122] from
[you] which I promptly railed over seated on a cloud of
irrelevance filled with whisky in a particularly gaseous
form. I should, I think, hate to reread this effluence of
Haig or was VAT 69 and I should be too fearful of having

---

[121] Presumably 5 per cent, which is the correct figure, was intended.

[122] This appears to refer to Paul's letter of 15 July (letter 52, p.202) and
Leslie's reply of 21 July (letter 54, p.211).

it read back to me but ... if it produced in you some of the turmoil that news of wickedness combined with good whisky, created in me then I am slightly, over so slightly sorry. The most sedate of anaesthetists should, however, be capable of a secondary buffer to life's degeneracies. So I commend to one of your leisure hours Schnapps or cognac or even vodka. Tomorrow my son David and his fair Margaret, great with child, will be with us for the weekend and we shall take the opportunity to drink in Riesling the Good Health of you and your family. You would, I think, like our lot when they are all together; their vigour is notable and their crosschat and backchat highly amusing. One day perhaps. I am sending a Guardian today. Enid insists on reducing the number of my plums. It is a deep plot to rob me of my rights. Today is gloriously sunny with a light breeze; we shall go out and buy a paperback or two. I think we, and you, should be enlightened. I hear that the Sov. Un. is the greatest publisher of books in the world – 78,000 titles last year. The Age of Enlightenment cannot be far away. Ginsberg, now in a labour camp, succeeded in making a recording on a home-made tape recorder and sending it to far off friends.[123] Humanity is fundamentally indivisible, nor shall the gates of Hell, Vietnam, northern Ireland and or of any odium humanum prevail against us.

Leslie

---

[123] Alexander (Alik) Ilyich Ginzburg (1936–2002), Russian journalist and dissident. He was sent to a labour camp three times between 1961 and 1969. *The Times*, 29 July 1970, p.4.

58

Usti nad Labem, Czechoslovakia
2nd August 1970.

Dear Mr. Parker and Mrs Parker,

Thank you for sending 3 copies of 'The Morning Star'
and the paperback 'Revolution Cuban Style'. It is hardly
worth the postage rate to send a daily newspaper from
England to C-S. At the time they arrive here the events
reported are already out of date and I have heard about
them already over the radio. This applies equally to 'The
Morning Star' as to any other daily newspaper. What I am
after are comments and surveys, thoughtful reviews of
books and films such as appear in British weeklies such
as the Guardian Weekly, Statesman and Nation or The
Economist etc.

The book by Gil Green arrived just at the time when
Fidel had to admit publicly the failure of the tremendous
drive for los diez milliones, in spite of enlisting nearly
every human being and all draft animals for cane-cutting
and harvesting. In addition it has been reported that
coffee has to be added to the long list of rationed goods
and to pineapples, bananas, oranges and citrus fruits not
available to those who grow them. While Russians without
vodka or Czechs without beer are simply unthinkable,
Fidel has apparently succeeded to persuade the Cubans
to forego coffee – not a small achievement, indeed! All
Communist countries have developed a calculated routine
for putting visitors in their right place. Notwithstanding of
this precaution a great deal of unsavoury facts are leaking
through the eyewitness account of Gil Green. Cuba's
indebtedness and complete dependency on the S. U., the
German D.R. and other East-European Socialist countries

227

explains why Fidel condoned the Russian-led invasion of
C-S at the meeting of Communist Parties in Moscow in
1969. This, alas, is not to be regarded as 'economism' (see
below!). A doctor who visited Cuba on several occasions
on a Czechoslovak merchant vessel concluded his shocking
account about conditions there with the observation
that the interests of the U.S.A. would be better served by
allowing Cuba to steam in her own juice and act as an
efficient deterrent to any attempt of another revolution
in Cuban style in South America than by occupying it.
A former sister of our hospital, Mrs. Eulalie Machado, the
pretty wife of a Spanish Communist refugee, returned to
this country after a 2 years unbearable stay in Cuba. A
Czech girl who married a Cuban student, taking a degree
in C.S., returned with her child but without her husband,
being unable to withstand the stresses and deprivations
of rumba communism.

From the observations of Gil Green and my own
eyewitness accounts a different image of Cuba emerges.
The regime is more and more relying on the army and
the militias, following in the trails of other military
dictatorships and juntas in South America. The militias
are composed of work-shy people. These men and women
with guns are providing most of the vociferous and
enthusiastic support for the lider maximo at his mass
rallies. They are occasionally taking part in 'voluntary'
work brigades but with the specific task of maintaining
discipline and surveillance of the lax and disgruntled.
We know from our own experience only too well how
'voluntarily' extra work without extra money is being
procured. Here the inconsistency of your Gil Green is most
appalling. He is extolling any strike for any increase of pay
under capitalism. But, after the vanguard is in power, long
hours of work, even during every weekend and Sundays,
ought to be voluntary, the worker and compesino ought to

be ashamed to ask for money, and doctors are 'voluntarily' foregoing the 600 pesos the government had promised to pay them. Yes, someone has to pay the bill for any revolution. Unfortunately most often the bill is presented to the very same people for whom the revolution is said to have been made. After witnessing all the greediness, the lust to cash a tip in the health service or at any other place or office under 25 years of socialism, I am overawed by those well-meaning moral philosophers who are preaching to the poor that the love of money is the root of all evil. With apologies to Samuel Butler I think this dictum to be the fallacy of fallacies, as the want of money is so quite truly too! The rational Carlos Marx who foresaw an economy of plentifulness to the satisfaction of all needs would have nothing but scorn for Fidel preaching against 'economism' and 'selfishness', and he would undoubtedly plead for his immediate excommunication from the Communist party. After receiving intimation that he would be prosecuted, the hero of Erewhon planned his escape with Arowhena by ascending in a balloon in front of his Majesty and the Queen.[124] 'Escape', this is indeed the acid test you should apply in judging the quality of life in any communist country. The doctor of our Merchant Navy told me about the horrible regulations and the law for those who wish to leave Cuba. It is a serious omission in Gil Green that he does not mention this aspect.

With best wishes to you all
Yours fraternally

Paul

---

[124] *Erewhon: or, Over the Range*, a satire on Victorian society by Samuel Butler, was published anonymously in 1872.

59

Shoreham-by-Sea, Sussex, England
Saturday 8th August 1970.

Our dear Paul

May I make one or two communicatory [sic] things clear
and will you please acknowledge them. Since the end of
Jan I have sent the Guardian every week. I only sent the
three Stars in order to find out whether those would be
stopped too for it seemed obvious that the Guardians do
not get through regularly.

Three weeks ago I sent a postcard informing you of
the dates of most of my letters during the last six months.
I have written every week.

I am this weekend sending you a short book on vision
and visual errors; please say what date it arrives.

David, who was here for a few days, said he would get
the 'Communications' book but was a bit puzzled about
its subject ie visual, printed, electronic, neurological
etc. I have just acquired an American book that took
three months to get [here] so please do not think we
have forgotten. From next week we shall try to send you
weekly The New Scientist in the hope that something a
little more neutral than the obviously anti-SU Guardian
[will get through].

I think sometimes that you appear to think that
because I remain in the CPGB that I approve of the
things that many in the C countries are learning to abhor.
I am not in favour of unhappiness or corruption in the
sciences, history, geography, politics, daily life or any
other aspect of human societies. You are not aware of
the sweat, emotional upset and intellectual shocks we
have given ourselves while we have been appraising the

situation by seeking knowledge and talking and writing to those people whom we can influence. We have not hesitated to make our opinion known wherever it has been possible to make them known. The discussion of [the] undiscussible is coming slowly about in certain organs whose editors two years ago were muttering 'that will be printed over my dead body'. We do not influence the course of events by withdrawing from them. There is always some measure of disinclination or not-doing that can be adopted.

But of course I remain in the CP for more than that, for l am convinced that the salvation of this country when the capitalists have brought it to its knees will have to be achieved by the socialist endeavours of the population. Up to the time of writing the CP is the only possible body in these islands that has any idea of what to do in such circumstances. We have hundreds of disrupting ultra lefts who only, so far as I can gather, wish to create destruction and chaos all around them. We have others who think a complex industrial system like ours will either run on its own or can be run factory by factory with no central planning. We have, to be sure, many in the CP who wait for the Millennium – either Socialism by accident or Socialism through the USSR navy sailing up the Thames. And of course among the Labour Party lot we have some who are prepared, as they were in the thirties, to watch the people suffer and 'try to right the economy' and others in the L P who are sound practical, truth-telling, incorruptible socialists. For the truth is that all over the world those of the down trodden rise up against the corruption of the system that quite deliberately keeps them down. If we could choose, of course sections of the world population would first be converted to the highest moral categories that are rather in the books than exemplified in any social economic complex at the present time. In Iraq they shot 42 'spies', mostly Jews, in three weeks.[125] In Iran the Kurds get it in the neck because they are communists. In Brazil, Chile, Guatemala, Bolivia the unlettered poor begin to throw off their 'betters' by force of arms and by force of arms in those in those countries they are bloodily suppressed. In Greece, islands are full of tortured and dying men and women who only want the vote. In Northern Ireland under the flag that flies over me and other liberals, the Govt. refuses to build houses, invest for employment and considers arrest without trial. When many of the people attain their freedom they will not suddenly throw off the desire for revenge or for a better living that they have learned from their capitalist betters. They will be what I would term 'bloody awful', but they will be better than the condition which they suppressed.

The blacks in the USA do not risk their lives and limbs because they are well-to-do or because life offers them endless opportunities for creative activity but because every effort is made to deprive them of their self-hood. There is preparing in the USA the greatest civil war in history and I hope to god it is the last for I would myself much prefer to realise social transformation through startling degrees than through a holocaust. But I feel quite sure that utterly corrupted Kennedys and Johnsons and Nixons and the utterly corrupted tribes they work for will neither relinquish sufficient wealth nor enough power in order to make life wonderfully tolerable for the whole American population who are forced to become revolutionaries and cannot create the sort of revolution which they prefer. The Lenin crowd didn't in 1918 and

---

[125] On 13 April 1969 *The Times* reported that 26 alleged spies had been executed in the previous three months; on 26 August 1969 it gave a total of 51 for the year.

again in 1921. And incidentally the Russians did not create the Cold War.

The revolutionary movement against capitalism is worldwide and if we Socialists in England all turned in our cards, read Woman's World or listened to the silly political persiflage of the Spectator or the New Statesman we should only make the going better, [giving] in the first place great gains to the already wholly corrupted, those in Zurich or the ICI or Lombard Street or British Motors or those in Harley Street or the multiple grocers. Then there would be a still greater explosion and we who believe in happiness, in incorruptibility, in science and the scientific method would have no place.

The truth is we have all got to strive – all of us, workers, mothers, intelligentsia, barbers. Worms in their gardens will simply have to turn. A very great shock has come to the socialists but we have to survive and will do so as long as we are among the people of whom we have a great need and to whom we of the superior education can offer much.

I have said before that Marxism or some form of Marxism will fashion the minds and perceptions of men and women for a long time to come, that is as long as the Great Corruption weighs them down. Therefore, although I personally hate scriptures that dictate what you should think we have to drag from these writings the true underlying hope of the oppressed. A move to this end is made in Garaudy's book 'Marxism in the 20th Century'.[126] This is a thoughtful humane book and should be read. I do not know if I could get a copy through to you.

It is a peculiar thing and one that Enid says hurts her, but when you disapprove of us you always address

---

[126] See note 59, p.130.

us as Mr and Mrs. When one day you address us as Comrades we shall know that we have dropped beyond recall. So we sent you a book on Cuba which we thought would get through to you and you go off like a whirlwind and I shout at my wife and get up an hour too early because the bloody heart is something or other and the typewriter ribbon sticks and god knows what else. A revolution starts where the bloody minded capitalists left it. Cuba was no exception. Unless Cuba wishes to buy no capitalist will consider sending anything at all and the USA utterly refuses to let even its aircraft call there and every citizen who goes there gets no visa, no insurance protection, no diplomatic protection and has to fly to Europe to do so from the USA. Quite frankly you underestimate the enormous pressure of the capitalists and their govts upon any socialist govt. Nixon would sooner see the Cubans rot than offer them a dime and unless my information is absolutely incorrect the Cubans, despite their present low condition, would sooner rot. This desire for freedom is something more than a hatred of striptease joints, of millionaires, of brothels and bordellos galore, of half the population unemployed and so forth. If it were not you would not be so bitter against your present situation. Freedom is something that men like the Greeks or Guatemalans or the Blacks or Manhattan or the fellahin of Algeria or the Sudanese are willing to die for. I do not explain this because I cannot. Your nurse and your lady with baby-less Cuban husband could not feel this in a foreign country – why should they unless they nurtured aims for universal freedom in their breasts? Scores of thousands of Czech intelligentsia fled to the middle-class comforts of the capitalist world but their going only moves them from one social problem to another. They loll back unable to do anything but accept what the capitalists tell them – they cannot demonstrate

234

or become politically active or take part in industrial strife (except on the part of the boss) for otherwise they would be biting the hand that is supposed to feed them. These have no freedom. But their children will have and they, true Canadians or Swiss Yankees, will turn upon their supine parents and their parents will say O Johnnie look we have deep freeze, a refrigerator, coloured telly, two cars and holidays in Miami – Oh Johnnie why do you do it? And Johnnie will tell them. Of course Castro made mistakes and of course he depended upon the wrong people or some of them. He was told he aimed [too high] at 10 million tons and thereby failed to keep an eye on other sides of the economy. But this was not because he was corrupted or because his Party was corrupt it was largely because he had too much faith in the ability of the people themselves to rise from the degradation that providing harlots and prostitutes for America had brought his people to. You rejoice too much in honest failure, in too much aspiration. Revolutions start, and Castro should have remembered this, at the very lowest point that capitalist degradation leaves off.

The filth of the upper classes flowed into Cuba. Yet you appear to think that all that glitters is good. This is not so. I am sorry for your ladies, perhaps now they have got back to their own beloved country they will exert themselves for its betterment. The Cubans will not continue to be dominated by US cash and will never be dominated by the so-called system of democratic centralism in that country which passes for socialist government at its highest. Meanwhile, as your ladies labour, the Cubans will take care of themselves though once they had the appearance of riches [and] are now in rags. The rich Cubans smoking not Havanas but Californian cigars rest in peace as their underlings plot to drench their homeland with blood. 'I would sooner be a doorkeeper in the house of the Lord than dwell in the palaces of the ungodly,' said the psalmist. The poor, the Pope and the capitalists are always willing to have always with them. There can be no end to the striving of humanity and unless the silly sods owning the Bomb destroy the whole world then the people will strive. There is no end to the stupidity of some governments and it is necessary that all of them shall feel the weight of the people.

The dire history of socialism has proved, but not yet too effectually, that it takes the workers a long time to turn out a large number of intelligentsia and it takes govts a long time to learn that the intelligentsia can [not] wholly be bribed by better off jobs, social prestige and the rest. Nor can any country in these days survive without an intelligentsia and that it is simply foolish to choose [them] by social prejudice. The capitalists in this country are preparing to do just that. They surely intend if they can and dare to reduce the number of working-class entrants to the universities. You never come across a working-class origin in [the] higher civil service or Foreign Office and Oxford and Cambridge have only 2% of working-class students even now. We have to fight as best we can and when we can. Democracy, freedom, as Marx says 'a free man in a free state', is not, most certainly not, handed to the populace on a plate. I do not doubt your integrity and for the moment I do not see any cause why you should doubt ours. You may doubt my wisdom but that my Mother did years ago and alas she is no longer with us. We both send you our love.

Leslie

60

Usti nad Labem, Czechoslovakia
17th August 1970.

My dear Leslie and Enid,

I gratefully acknowledge having received (1) the 2 copies
of the Guardian of July 25 and August 1st, (2) the parcel
with modelling clay, bubble blowers and crayon for
David, (3) your kind letter from the 8.8. I deeply regret
that I have through my unwise criticism of the book on
Cuba hurt your feelings. You are probably not aware that
the entire press of the Warsaw Pact countries did not
report the highly self-critical appraisal of the economy
and did not even mention the sugar harvest. Had I known
that Castro is going to allow those who prefer la dolce
vita to leave the country I would have exercised more
moderation in disapproving the book and saved you
from getting palpitations and shouting at Enid. I gave
the book on Cuba to a black medical student from Ghana
who is being trained at our hospital and who was keen to
receive some more information about Cuba. We had him
for tea the other day as he complained of feeling lonely
and of boredom. I don't blame him because this town
is in a drab state. I would not carry on a discourse with
you for two years if I would have the slightest doubts
about your integrity. For 25 years I am excessively poor
and 40 years ago I married the poorest Czech girl there
was, in defiance of my parents but in accordance with
the principles I was then cherishing. I remained beside
her during all the perturbations of the war, emigration
and repatriation with the unavoidable temporary
separations. Never in my life I have been in a brothel,
nor did I ever attend a strip-tease. I have no connections

whatever with the upper classes which flowed into
Havana before Batiste was overthrown. I have myself
been compelled to take part on numerous occasions in
'volunteer brigades' and I sacrificed some Sundays after
ill-spent weeks with drudgery and useless compulsory
meetings. Our women are still spending hours queueing
for all sorts of goods every day as a reminiscence of the
days, not so far off, when we too had food rationing in
this country. I remember with horror that we had to
queue up for 6–10 hours to get a new ration book. Not
so in England during the War. We tossed the old ration
book into a pillar box while the postman delivered the
new one! It makes a lot of difference to have an old
and wizened civil service or a stupid and corrupted
petty bureaucracy. I cannot help to feel sorry for the
poor devils of Cuba who have to queue and do the cane
cutting in shoes without soles. Contrary to our caudillos
Castro has the courage to say: Mea culpa. Ours are
always ready to blame someone else. While he is going
to throw out 'those who have spent themselves', we are
massively taking them in and back, from the highest to
the lowest levels. You very correctly state in your letter:
'Nor can any country in these days survive without an
intelligentsia'. You know as well as I do that the 600,000
managers, professionals and businessmen who fled
after the Cuban revolution cannot be replaced overnight
by ill-trained workers or technicians. But Cuba is not
the sole country where breakdowns and blunders in
most sectors of the economy and in the administration
are due to the lack of professional skill. But what are
our party hawks doing? They have already turned out
50% of all professionals from the CP i.e. from leading
managerial posts. And the other half is being paralysed
by lethargy and disillusionment. I don't see any reason
why there should be a deadlock in our communication

over the Cuban issue. For me Cuba is only an instance, yet another application of a holistic theory of social experiments which are impossible without suppressing public criticism, without destroying knowledge. To your extension of an expression of Marx that a free man in a free state is not, most certainly handed to the populace on a plate, I can only add: 'You are telling me'. By the way, would you regard Shakespeare to have been a Marxist as he wrote in King John, Act V, Scene 2:

> 'I am too high-born to be propertied
> To be a secondary at control,
> Or useful serving-man and instrument
> To any sovereign state throughout the world.'

I have no quarrel with you or Enid over the issue of a distant island but only with closed minds near home.

Many thanks once more! Bohumila and David are sending you our love.

Yours sincerely,

Paul

61

Shoreham-by-Sea, Sussex, England
20th August 1970.

Dear Paul,

The tide of evening descends over this country almost with somnolence. Mr Heath is boating or sleeping, the appeal judges refuse to lighten the rather heavy sentences given to some undergraduates of Cambridge because they disrupted a dinner in aid of the thugs of Greece.[127] The government's greatest concern is to deprive the BOAC (a very profitable airway company but nationalised) of £1 million worth of [routes] in order to give [them] to a concern that is nearly bankrupt[128] but capitalist, fares on rail and underground and bus Up again, prices are Up again, England my England have lost the Cricket Test series, the sun shines, the weather is cold when it doesn't.

Our children come and go. [...] Linda after being in Wales for three weeks, apparently all the time on a horse; Margaret, David's wife, is cheerfully expecting her first baby, Hilary has been fed to bursting and has gone back to Birmingham full of the desire to write to you, kiss his girlfriends, write some letters of thanks for presents received for his October wedding and to overcome the mishaps contingent on being ignorant of the subtler points of childbirth and gynaecology. While he was here he hacked up a concrete path and our small garden looks rather like a bankrupt builder's yard. So we languish here rather alone with a large number of empty bottles, a feeling that we might survive and an utter contempt and dismay in re CPCS. We are chagrined by the latest news from your country. Two years after we see only greater deprivation, a slowing down of the economy, a reduction of the party itself. No one save a few purblind idiots who confuse the proletariat with the top pyramid have anything but the gravest disquiet and contempt for the present slide into political and economic mire in which

---

[127] See note 111, p.209.

[128] In November 1970 the government transferred a number of African routes to British Caledonian Airways representing about 3 per cent of BOAC's turnover. BOAC merged with British European Airways in 1974 to become British Airways.

the best elements of the country could be foully drowned. As a result of this dire condition our own Party and the Party in the USA is easy to ridicule, our newspaper is getting more and more difficult to publish and our numbers diminish rather than increase. And no wonder! In these circumstances we welcome the news of the USA and USSR, those two wonderful 'superpowers', now sometimes talked of with reverence in our papers, getting together over the Middle East[129] and the rapprochement between West G and the USSR.[130] Soon we shall have the invasion of Northern Ireland and Vietnam, and Korea and Czechoslovakia and the GDR all smoothed away by the gracious permission of the big boys. With one half of the world hungry, 40% of the SU population on a very low standard of living, with 20 million in the USA ditto, and half Latin America more than ditto and 2 million children in this country not getting enough to eat, the super boys could well turn their attention to a few anomalies at present beyond their infantile minds. If you have a grim laugh still left to you, rejoice with the Editor of the Local Newspaper in Azerbaijan when he disclosed that not only had the top party boys given very lucrative jobs to all their uncles, dads, cousins and aunts but had also appropriated government ground upon which they had built two very large houses. What happened to these enterprising servants of the poor was not included in the report. This reminds me of Mr. Geoffrey Johnson Smith[131] who managed while he was a newscaster on the BBC to marry a rich wife and thereafter get into parliament.

---

[129] The Soviet Union offered support for an American plan to settle the border conflict between Israel and Egypt.

[130] The USSR and West Germany signed the Treaty of Moscow on 12 August 1970 to normalise relations and recognise post-war borders.

[131] A Conservative MP.

The result was that Mr Smith had a very large income on which he had to pay a large amount of income tax at 19/6d in the £. In order to reduce this he bought on mortgage a house in Kensington worth £45,000 but instead of paying cash for it he borrowed money at 6% from the Kensington (West London) Local Council and thus reduced the amount he had to pay in income tax for there is an allowance on all mortgage interest in this country. Mr G. Johnson Smith is now looking for a nice job in the present Tory government and as he knows the ways of the corrupt I have no doubt he will get it.

Meanwhile Government and Trade Unions face each other with wary eyes. Hatchets all round.

Affectionately

Leslie

62

Shoreham-by-Sea, Sussex, England
22 August 1970.

Dear Paul

Your letter fills me with a [lot of joy]. I now know that all is not lost and that you were not, or never intended to be, a proprietor of a harlotry establishment in Cuba though the whole place was sweetened by an excess of American-owned best Cuban-grown sugar. All that my impetuous machine did was to describe, or purport to describe, the conditioning of Cuba before Castro. I am glad you married the poorest girl in C-S and rescued her from the vicissitudes of pure village life to a consideration of the disembowelling or at least detonsiliting [*sic*] of the apparatchiks. My wife being superbly Oxford married the most unoxford of men who later through his life declared or demonstrated his complete inability to be successful. In a sort of way we are thus quits.

I enclose a letter from David in which he expressed his opinion of your letter about Cuba and if I can I will enclose the 'Comment' for your black friend who wants to know more about Cuba. We own another book on Cuba which I will send as soon as that Maurice the apparatchik returns it. At present he is in the GDR giving lessons on economics to little German boys in English. .... Apart from this and [sparse information] in our daily papers we do not know a great deal about Cuba. Information is [no] more readily available about c. than about any communist country. On the whole we think that there will be more genuine discussion in Cuba than has been the case in the West C. countries. Castro's offer to resign was, we think, something more than a gesture. It was also a challenge to the rest of the Party organisations that have been made well aware that they also share in the decision to harvest 10,000 tons. As for the lack of shoes. Before the revn. half the population had no shoes whatever. I think what Castro was really annoyed about was the wastage of money and endeavour on the production of shoes that simply did not stand up to their job.

It should be possible for your friend to acquire knowledge through the Cuban-CS committee. Did I tell you that Khrushchev said 'of course the Cubans are not real socialists?' Well he did and then brought the whole world to the point of complete catastrophe by trying to get hydrogen rockets and bombs on Cuba. There are still plenty of CP'ers in this country who still think that in this matter the Russians were blameless.

I should like to emphasise two points. There is no doubt in my mind that many socialist revolutions are now in the making. These movements are the results of the conditions under which people live or merely exist. Lots and lots of these revolutionaries, rightly or wrongly, would rather live under your conditions than under those which oppress them now though they know what those conditions are and though many of them disapprove of them. No power of the capitalist gun nor of Zalud/Parker democratic philosophy can turn them aside. Secondly in some form or another they maintain they are Marxists. They are sometimes Moscow Marxists but mostly they are upholders of Mao-ism whatever that means or some new form of Communist organisation that calls [themselves Marxist-Leninist]. Where was I?

These Marxist-Leninists call the Muscovites Revisionists and our own CPGB 'reformist' because it no longer believes in World Revolution. In this the Maoists and Trots agree. The Chinese and Albanians assert that Stalin was right in his methods; that the doctrine of peaceful coexistence is wrong because it is fundamentally anti-revolutionary and also, worse still, because the two superpowers are concerned with dividing the world up between them. Also Russia is going the capitalist way because it offers greater emoluments to the intelligentsia and worse still to Party leaders. AND the Moscow lot do not attempt to involve the people, having given up persuasion for legal enforcement. Thus they have turned the dictatorship of the Prol. into the autocracy of the top Party/govt. that enforces its ukases with the secret police and armed services. The Albanians declare that the revisionists can only be stopped by the revolution of the proletariat, armed insurrection backed by the 'true and faithful section of the Russian army'. Oh yes, these Maoists or Marxist-Leninists also declare that the splitting up of the world between the Russians and the Americans will eventually turn Russian into a capitalist state whose principal aim will be to unhorse Chinese communism. I need hardly tell you in the face of these warring movements why we are so anxious to bring pressure to bear from our own British reading of Marx and Engels. I am constantly considering the problem of Communist government but one small typewriter tapping away in a small suburban villa amidst this welter of ideologies seems utterly ludicrous.

We have recently received two books of some interest.[132] The first one published in English in the USA is a document by the top class physicist Sakharov[133] which he sent as memorandum from himself and thirty other top class savants, theatre people, writers, artists etc. to the Muscovites. This document calls for the complete stoppage of all Labour Camps, now between 15 and 30, in the USSR, the release of Daniel and Sinyavsky[134] now serving seven years tor publishing scurrilous material abroad and the cessation of such arraignments and sentences and calls generally for more freedom. It blasts with considerable vigour the Chinese as being fascist and anti-USSR and anti-socialist. I find this nothing less than a reflection of the violent anti-Chinese propaganda that has gone on for so long from time to time in the USSR. Sakharov accepts the theory that because of certain technical developments

---

[132] In this paragraph Leslie appears to run his reference to Sakharov's collective Manifesto, written in 1966 and made public in 1970, into a discussion of his book *Progress, Coexistence and Iintellectual Freedom*, first published in the USA in 1968.

[133] Andrei Dmitrievich Sakharov (1921–89), Russian nuclear physicist, member of the Soviet Academy of Science, dissident and human rights activist. He was awarded the Nobel Peace Prize in 1975.

[134] Andrei Donatovich Sinyavsky (1925–97) and Yuli Markovich Daniel (1925–88) were Russian writers and dissidents, imprisoned for seven and five years respectively in February 1966.

in both the USA and the SU the economies will become
politically alike or enough alike as to live side by side
presumably forever. Presumably he thinks that problems
like Vietnam and the Middle East can be settled by
happy arrangement between the US and SU. Let the
M-Leninists gnash their dentures! He considers that the
USA contains no revolutionary movements. The Black
Power movement he dismisses as easily as being merely
a racial movement which in time will be resolved by the
increasing living standards of the USA. Quite as easily
he admits that the 40% of the USSR population now
existing on subsistence or less than subsistence level
and the 20% in the USA equally happily situated will in
the course of time have their living standard raised –
how he never· explains. Of course, he says airily, there
are a number of millionaires in the USA who over five
years take only 20% of the national income and this
is to be equated with the higher incomes (apparently
deserved) of the intelligentsia and Party bosses in the
SU. He thinks the difference in the standard of living
between the workers and the Top Lot in a socialist
country quite acceptable – quality furniture, clothes,
housing etc. etc. – and we find this makes our teeth
break into pieces. The document finishes with a highly
idealistic picture of the SU and the USA joining together
in an attack on the poverty of the rest of the world.
Each Lot gives 20% of their national income to save
the little blacks of S. Africa and the little Indians of
Canada and USA and the naughty Indonesians and the
Koreans from their present destitution thus creating
a magnificent standard of living that the world has
never seen before. Selah! Of the wicked Chinese there
is no mention. Presumably they [will] have repented
of their anti-Moscow or anti-USA (is there by now any
difference?) wickedness and eaten humble pie and lie

subserviently on the ground waiting for one or other
Mandarin to kick their rumps or even kiss them better.

I really must go hence and shave.

A young gentleman said over lunch he thought it was
highly probable that as every now undeveloped country
grew stronger it would make a Bomb. So much for the
optimism of the young.

The other book we got promises some lively moments
for it is the first of a quarterly series of a compilation
made from the newspapers and periodicals of the
communist countries. We have seen extracts from your
new laws restricting higher education to the children of
the more reliable workers – in some oases there appears
to be a parallel with some parts of our own school system
which definitely limits the chances of working-class
children. The Tories are now trying to pedal backwards
over the ground made by the liberalisation of our of our
secondary schools. There are, if the Tories have their
way, to be no more comprehensive schools – schools in
which there is not only an almost fantastic combination
of subject choices but in which pupils may go as fast
or as slow as they please and even get into the top
forms without being under obligation to pass public
examinations. The Tories in both our countries will not
be successful. 'Selection' is not good for any economy
and in the end not good for that class which is chosen for
the best honours. I think you need not fear. In any case a
young scholar in your household will have an enormous
start over less knowledgeable families. Have no idea
where I have got to. I cannot send you the Sakharov book
because I'm sure it would not get through but when we
have continued with this new quarterly we might try to
get a copy through. I imagine that we in the West are
managing to accumulate a fair amount about you in the
East and this fact must in the end have some influence

upon the top lot. So must the new negotiations [between] West Germany and Russia, the Middle East and the Salt conferences in Vienna. While the stupid oafs in Tel Aviv, Cairo, Washington and M even begin to talk peace their preparations for war must become a little less ferocious. I sent you a Guardian two days ago.

Four more interruptions – where am I?

Two days ago I sent one Guardian and The New Scientist – the latter because I wondered whether that would get through quicker. Tomorrow another Guardian. Enid says when you don't get one some English-reading postman has taken it home to read himself. I hope he reads my letters too. They should be enlightening about what the large majority of the CPGB thinks [even] if it is not expressed quite so blatantly.

On our radio they keep talking about 'The Anniversary' of the invasion. Enid says this is premature because it happened on August 28th but I think she must be wrong.

If David's new baby is a boy he might well call it Alexander after you know whom. Please send D's letter back.

If we can find some Granmas[135] I will send them for your Ghanaian friend.

Hilary is now doing paediatrics. David, you will see, has had a good provisional offer for a book he should manage. [...]

Enid sends her love to you both and I send mine.

Leslie

PS It is an offence to send liquids through the post in this country. I regret there were no reeds in the pipes.

---

[135] The newspaper of the Cuban Communist Party.

63

Shoreham-by-Sea, Sussex, England
27 August 1970.

My dear Paul,

This week I have been thinking of you more than
I generally do which, I assure you, is as much as I
devote to my uncommunicative children. I imagine you
administering all sorts of new anaesthetics, which of
course I have no idea of, to recalcitrant functionaries or to
little children upon [whom] life has been too hard or upon
anxious matrons whose minds turn towards their homes
much more than they do towards their hurts. I imagine
you highly concentrated, calm but urgent, calculating
the exact dose, sighing with relief when some almost
insuperable job is over, or sighing with sadness because
the job was too insuperable or walking home in gladness
because some almost insuperable job had given new life
for painful old. I do not think of you as the pure savant, or
the idiot savant, but as the personally dedicated [savant?]
to whom every vestige of life is precious, precious beyond
rubies. Every spark can and even may be fanned [so]
that the vigour of love and of intellectual attainment and
continuing integrity can be added to those who have to
know they are compelled to make life worthwhile. On this
sunny day in the calm south east England where the slums
do not intrude nor the working class erupt I salute you as
you drip life-giving mixtures into living blood streams or
pump the gases of salvation into reluctant lungs.

I lay in bed awake for a little after my wife was
persuaded that the nightly reading of the indifferent
novel had driven me to sleep – I lay awake – and said
yes, if there were one communist country in Europe in

which I could resign my limbs in the hour of my demise it would be Czechoslovakia. I felt that I should like to be associated with those have striven for the independence of your country and who are still striving and with those now cast down into gloom, a gloom that has all the marks of eternity. I shouldn't mind looking at the invaders both with pity and resentment. Pity because they think the fight so easily won, freedom in a cup of coffee or in a formula or provided by others, freedom on the cheap. You and I know that what we want and what we need and what we need for those to come is something that has to be thought for and fought for. When conditions demand that we be passive, no conditions can make us intellectually and morally passive. A mental vantage point is easily gained by some and quite as easily held there with the same old intellectual view until they slide into a greater dumbness. But for [others] and I like to think I am among them, every day almost in these maelstromic [sic] days a new fact brings a new horizon, demands a new compass bearing and exerts the mind to find causes not only in order to understand but that we may go forward with others. With others certainly, though they be few.

On the radio last night there was a resumé of the C-S CP's 14th Congress – that fateful Congress held in a factory surrounded by tanks with the enemies of collaboration within and the enemies of invasion just outside on the doorstep.[136] These were brave man and most have gone

---

[136] The 14th Congress of the Czech Communist Party was held in secret in Vysocany, an industrial suburb of Prague, on 22 August, immediately after the Soviet invasion. Attended by several hundred delegates, it appointed a central committee, reaffirmed the reform programme and condemned the invasion. The Czechoslovakian leaders who had been abducted to Moscow were then put under intense pressure to sign a document which declared the proceedings null and void, and to reintroduce censorship. They agreed to do so by majority vote.

into the byways and comparative poverty. There was
one brave comrade with magnificent rhetoric against
the dastardly invaders but [another] who again, quite
as bravely and twice as rhetorical, found the Congress
illegal and the invasion highly necessary. Though the
BBC and the bourgeoisie like to remember the sins of the
SU in order to demonstrate what cads the commies are,
those like ourselves remember your people with entirely
different reasons. Doubtless the BBC would clearly like
to direct the C-S CP and go on about the wicked workers
as they do to us but not to you and help to persuade the
people that their hope lay in taking the crumbs from
master's table and not in carving out their place tor
themselves. The new media are, however, not quite so
free as they were, for our Lord and Masters in the USA
are having nice cosy talks with your Lord and Masters
and what USA likes all the top British like and their
underlings therefore must do likewise. So sometimes the
Communists are even respectable and even from time to
time the proper Communist Party to which I belong is
regarded as rather respectable compared with the rag tag
and bobtail of ultras, Maoists, Trotskyites, International
socialists and anarchists that abound in every coffee bar
and street fight.

Nevertheless, there is good hope. While people like
Sakharov can openly attack the neo-. and old Stalinists
in a memorandum to the Top Party Lot and get the
backing of many scientists throughout the world, and
the necessities of the SU themselves can force the SU to
come to terms with West Germany and the USA (though
they are also themselves forced to come to terms with
the SU) and many writers of all kinds are writing and
publishing Samizdat and waiting in the wings with
books, essays, plays, novels, philosophy of superlative
value, we are far from beaten. Nor must we ever forget

the economy the state of which has put off the SU lot from calling the all Russia Praesidium this year. Not until the scientific hypothesis is in full gallop and the workers can shove out lazy and corrupt managers and functionaries and every man jack is invigorated with the joy of creation shall we be satisfied.

Our own Party here is lamenting its lack of youngsters, its poor showing in the last national elections, its passive branches etc. etc. etc. Though there are intra-national causes of this decline many are [anxious] to smooth over the enormous 'roughing up' that we have received through the lamentable murders of Stalin and the very slow and very reluctant admissions of that wickedness throughout the European and Russian CPs. The manner of communist government, though perceived dimly, is perceived even more dimly by Party members themselves. Facts are not [always] available but they are becoming more available. So available and so indisputable that the cry of Anti-Sovietist [*sic*] will soon scarcely echo in any Branch meeting. I am not anti-Soviet and indeed believe more and more in the councils of the people – on every level from the Army to Refuse Collectors from Nurses to Teachers and factory girls and boys and students. The utter necessity of democracy, if that magic first recognisably inspiring socialist state is to be achieved, is conciliarity – which is a nice new word.

Our love to David, to David's beautiful mother, to his lovely Grandmother, to the Pied Piper and to you.

Leslie

64

Shoreham-by-Sea, Sussex, England
10 September 1970.

My dear Paul,

I generally take my weary bones to the kitchen at 7 in
the morning (BST not GMT) and make the tea which I
then take back in which Enid joins me. When we have
imbibed several cups she says I'll get the post. So she
skips nimbly away. There are bills, bank statements,
circulars; sometimes letters from the children, postcards
from sunny seasides which we cannot afford to visit and
requests for subscriptions. If after seven or eight days
there is no word from you she begins to get fidgety and
says There is no letter from Paul as though you should
produce a letter whenever she thinks I should write to
tell you that things are not so dreadful as they were. Now
this morning she swims into the room saying There's one
from Margaret (she's just had the baby) and one from
Paul[137] – all of course with a girlish lilt in her voice and a
gay swish of her dressing gown.

   We now know that the creation of Laughing Gas by
our cousins across the water in 1872 or thereabouts was
not in vain. The sorrows of Prague have been penetrated
not only with the commercial products designed to
put whole battalions into instant coma but with [the]
laughter of those devoted to these strange devices. I trust
that the science or art of anaesthesia in the Communist
countries has benefited thereby. We rejoice in the
international consumption of Slivovic [...] which we

---

[137] Missing from the collection.

ourselves cannot too urgently wish to embrace topped off course or underpinned with Scotch whisky. This latter drink appears to be one of your favourites. The price of it in England is soaring and utterly monstrous costing £3 a bottle, with Brandy at about £4 when it is good. My own palate quivers and salivates at the thought of you being entertained at my expense if you please at Her Britannic Majesty's Embassy. I suppose some scientific good came from this conference????[138]

Consequently our apprehension is disbursed upon the high winds that come romping down the coast shaking my full red plums from my little plum tree to the delight of the children hereabouts and the refuse collectors who blackmail Enid into generosity. Against this helter skelter that lashed the seas and blew the streets clean of pedestrians I was unable to stand and had to return defeated from an attempt to post my letters. But the sky was red with magnetic blue and the air was pure and inspiring and I wished I were young and standing on a hill looking down upon a great landscape. So your buoyant letter has filled us with renewed zest to do what we can which is little enough. My manuscript adversus Stalinism goes very slowly. I get a good deal of some sort of indigestion owing apparently to a defective sphincter 'at the top of your stomach'. If you have spare parts in C-S perhaps you could prevail upon the Secretary of the Party designated to Expedite the Export of Extra Specially Needed physiologically Necessary Odd Bits. I should be grateful if you will [lobby] her with my precious stomach's renovation as the prime object. I see

---

[138] Leslie wrote to me on 26 September: 'Paul Zalud is fiery now having been stoked up by lots of periodicals left by an international gathering in Prague of anaesthetists. He finished up – or nearly so – overfull of Scotch whisky at the British Embassy.'

from the Morning Star today that an attack on the left in C-S has been made in Tribuna by a chap called Svestka (I hope I have the name right). In this article the writer accuses the hard liners of removing Dubcek solely for the purposes of getting back the jobs from which Dubcek had removed them.[139] We learned yesterday that Daniel who got 5 years in a labour camp is now out of imprisonment and is we all hope now in bliss with Mrs Daniel who also got 2 years for displaying on the Moscow streets a poster declaring that the imprisonment of her husband and his friend Sinyavsky were illegal.[140] We may rejoice. I may have told you that three one-time soviet prisoners also gave television interviews in secret places round Moscow and these appeared on our own television screens about 12 days ago. These were exceedingly brave efforts. If we add to these efforts the very successful appeal by many top scientists and well known people in Moscow for the release of Medvedev,[141] another top scientist, we may take heart. Among other things there is every reason to believe that your party lost some 600,000 members who refused to say that they agreed with the invasion. [...]

My faith for the future of mankind lies not so much in men of the mind as in men of a new mind and humanity. The course of events, the crash of circumstances, the needs of men are breeding these not in singles nor in

---

[139] Oldrich Svestka was the editor of *Tribuna*, founded in January 1969. It has been described as 'the aggressive mouthpiece of the ultras' and 'vehicle of militant pro-Soviet dogmatism'. So the attack referred to here was on the temporising 'realists' around Husak.

[140] Larissa Daniels was exiled to Siberia for four years after participating in a demonstration on 28 August 1968 protesting against the invasion of Czechoslovakia. *The Times*, 20 November 1968, p.4. She was still in Siberia when her husband was released. https://en.wikipedia.org/wiki/Larisa_Bogoraz

[141] See note 100, p.187.

doubles but in thousands. Though they struggle they are there. Sometimes like Dubcek they rise almost meteorically towards the stars and drop because the thousands are not gathered there, are not sufficiently strong in numbers energy and faith to sustain such a one. We had a [defender of] humanity in Betrand Russell but despite his very, very active intellect he failed to solve the economic problem. Dubcek, we can see, was the new man, rising like a star, a strong comet who saw both the social [economic?] problem and [also] felt the needs of humanity. He was exploited unmercifully by the bourgeoisie ... who didn't care two bloody hoots about his love of men but cared very dearly to get at socialist states at any cost; he was also exploited by the hard liners who at their best believed in an order that must pass away and at their worst hated a lover of mankind. The communists have often talked about the new man who makes himself in making the New Society but when he came they failed to recognise him or if they did they hated him for what he was.

The funny thing about Nixon is that he is essentially a dull, uninspired man but as self-seeking as the Kennedys or Johnson. The first Kennedy the great intellectual, the one who could read six books at a time at a terrific rate, the Liberal intellectual of ALL times I say ALL TIME, God his very self, made a mess of America. He failed to provide almost any welfare for the poverty stricken and he created Vietnam the ghastliest and most monstrous degradation of humanity for ages – including the shocking mass murders of Stalin. For Stalin was a dedicated murderer whilst Kennedy was a dedicated liberal humanist. All the Kennedys were full of hubris and the power of' wealth. Now Johnson was a wheeler dealer, a frank liar who persuaded other people to vote for what he wanted by bribing them with State cash. He also appeared frequently on the telly, specially made up in order to appear, when he talked about Vietnam as a soul searching, very, very much injured Jesus Christ. In this he was the supreme actor, the unalloyed hypocrite. He even took his daughter to church and told her, in secret of course, that he might have to make a decision that would reduce all humanity and all that humanity had achieved to ashes. How did this soulful before-almighty-God soul searching, daughter devouring, episode get into the papers?? Through Johnston of course. Yet this unutterable liar did more for anti-segregation in the deep south than either Kennedy [or Nixon] ever thought of doing. And he did more for medicare of old people and for the poor.

Nevertheless neither the Kennedys nor the Johnsons and not even the Nixons, all spawned in a cash nexus, are good enough for the people of the USA or noble enough for the power they should not wield but do. They are all in a glass bowl of money making and cannot get out. No wonder Engels said of Marx that the one supremo discovery that Marx made was the manner of freeing not only the workers from their shocking situation but also the exploiters.

I have more faith in your beautiful black girl and her boyfriends in Black Power than in all the legions of the wealthy. It is, however, not unreasonable of many highly educated men like yourself, Sakharov and the chap who wrote the New Industrial State and of course Brezhnev and co to imagine that true freedom will arise through and from them. True, you are all necessary, not so much for the struggle for a new order which you strive to create but for the scientific methods which you test and, having tested, offer. The upper strata of every social condition always imagine that the cause of freedom which they advocate is the WHOLE cause of freedom.

Sakharov vainly imagines this; so I think did Daniel and Sinyansky.[142] Sakharov[143] for all his detestation of the circumscription of freedom, whether social or scientific, is quite calm in suggesting that the poverty stricken will in the course of tine be rescued. Be rescued by whom? Certainly not by us, though with the help of us, but by themselves. As the primordial thing that lifted itself from the warm water that had hitherto given it its circumscribed life into an environment that could, if it struggled, afford it the means to a greater life, we all, the talkers, the scientists, the intellectuals, the teachers, the strugglers for this or that freedom, we shall afford to those primordials that come forth with the masses the environment which the masses will alter and improve and [in] improving will improve themselves. The really sad thing about the shambles in your country was not the defeat of the intellectuals, though this was appalling and deadly serious, but the stopping of the workers from rising to their feet and defeating the monsters. If we can fill these with vigour, make them flex their muscles, open their eyes to some of life's possibilities we are safe. The top lot may strut for a short moment parading their policemen and their silly soldiers and adorning their feeble minded magistrates with falsities but they cannot in the end withstand the continual needs of a vital part of society which is included in those two neutral words, Culture and Science. But above all the scientists cannot stand nor can the super-culturalists disport themselves socially and narcissistically unless the mass of people are swarming round them taking huge bites of what the intellectuals have to offer and gladly, with comradely

[142] See note 134, p.245.

[143] See note 133, p.245.

but deliberate abandon, spitting out some they neither understand nor approve of. This is not a process of levelling down but a process of concrete aspiration – whatever that is.

I rejoice with you; you give me energy; I salute you, you Friend, Powerful Intaker of Alcohol in Every Form, Lover of Humanity and Devotee of the Truth. I salute you and though your heart may be weary never let it be afraid that those unmitigated Sods will get us down.

Enid and I send all of you our love. We shall come as soon as we are able; when University Grants and Weddings no longer take our margin of wherewithal we shall be on the doorstep. See my dear doctor that you hold in one hand a happy combination of tablets that will rejuvenate an old body, re-inspire a wicked heart and revolutionise a stupid stomach. In the other hand you can hold one bottle of Slivovitz, two of brandy and six glasses.

I would tell you all about the hijackings but I haven't time.[144] But we have ensconced in a cell in Ealing Police Station one perfectly lovely Arab demoiselle that quite a few people would like to hang draw and quarter.

My own belief is that the only safe place for a very lovely girl these days is in bed. Probably not. Well then a statue in Prague Cathedral?

Leslie and Enid

PS: We are sending your letter to David and Hilary. They'll love it.

---

[144] See below, pp.267–8 and notes 150 and 151.

65

Usti nad Labem, Czechoslovakia
20 September 1970.

Dear Leslie and Enid,

Your gracious letter of September 10 helped to extend the
buoyant mood of the congress for the remaining weeks of
my leave. I am only very sorry to hear that you are being
molested by a hiatus hernia or reflux of acid stomach
contents into the gullet. From afar it is scarcely possible
to advise you about your bodily needs, nor can I help
you with spare parts, artificial sphincters or medicines.

The weather has been fine so far. A real Indian
summer, indeed. Being still faced with a heap of
books, journals, reprints and even a few magazines
and newspapers, all gathered at the congress, I feel
well compensated for a year of gloom and hard work.
David has started to attend a Nursery school, situated
just round the corner of our street, for 4 hours in the
morning. At first he cried and protested and his mother
had to drag him there for the first 3 days. Now he seems
to like it. My wife, who had to bear the brunt of his
ceaseless and vigorous activities, and I myself wanted to
prolong the period of carefree bliss for another year and
were against it at first. The result of the conflicting views
about the advantages and disadvantages of collectivistic
early education and discipline was that David got a new
tricycle and several additions to his large collection of
toys from his grandparents. I am enclosing a description
of our Nursery schools by an English lady as a cutting
from the Lancet. At my holiday rhythm of life I am
staying up reading and writing letters till 1–2 o' clock,
but sleeping late into the morning. Between breakfast

and lunch I just manage to post my letters and get me
some cigarettes (Fags!). As soon as Bohuna has fetched
David from school I have to take care of him during
the warmest and most sunny period of the day. I am
pulling him up with a piece of string, up the road I mean,
and letting him go down on his tricycle by himself.
Sometimes we are kicking balls around our backyard or
garden. From 5p.m. till 7p.m. I am getting the news and
at dusk everything dies down here at Usti. A place devoid
of all distraction and social events and duties is ideally
suited for reading and studying. Oldrich Svestka writing
in Tribuna about clinging to jobs as the ultimate motive,
said only what the bulk of the common people found
out already 2 years ago. Every schoolboy in this country
knows that it was not appeal to arguments but crude and
brutal force which drove out D. Right from the beginning
of the tragedy all who proclaimed the beneficence of the
third party to the game were rightly suspect of ulterior
motives, the most obvious are, of course, jobs and
careers. Now a few thousand 'hard liners' are facing a
totally unresponsive silent majority. Overtures are being
tried to induce those who by now have become mere
spectators of public affairs to stir again. A ball is thrown
here and one there towards the unmoved spectators
in the hope they will opt for the least evil. BUT WILL
THEY? My feeling is that everyone has the bellyful of all
manoeuvres by now. Unless something more decisive and
substantial than sweet words are produced no one will
leave his cave.

Best wishes and kind regards to you all
Yours

Paul

66

23 September 1970.

Dear Leslie and Enid,

Having just received New Society prompts me to write
again to you making up for the shortcoming of my last
letter. How lucky you are! On 52 weekends you can choose
among The NEW scientist or NEW Society or NEW
Statesman. All very NEW, unlike Tribune or The Spectator
or Punch. Peeping into the 'Foreign Report' issued by The
Economist you can peer behind the scenes and learn in
advance what will hit the headlines later. I should have
overcome my inborn resistance against the Greek letters!
A man with a passion for truth such as mine ought to read
'Pravda' which ironically stands for truth in Czech too.
You would be mistaken to think that we have in common
with the Russians only this single 6 letter word. There
may be 4 letter words too but I would not know. Instead
of getting the truth, and nothing but the truth in one
sitting I am investing a lot of time and energy by reading
Rude Pravo and Neues Deutschland. I could never detect
any news contradicting the truth which is Pravda in
Czech and Russian in those papers. Recently I have
taken to reading the White Book over and over again.
I understand that the most prodigal contributor to
this publication, Jurist Shukov, is now dealing with
the industrial-military complex of the Federal German
Republic, of which it is said in the said White Book
that it financed counter-revolution in Czechoslovakia.[145]

---

[145] The White Book was distributed in August 1968 by the Soviet
authorities; it should not be confused with the absurdist novel
published by the Czech dissident author Pavel Kohout in 1970.

Mr. Tarasov,[146] head of the Ministry for motor-cars is straining all the resources of the industrial complex of the FRG to finance gigantic plants for the mass-production not of subversion, right wing opportunism, revisionism and other by-products of counter-revolution, but simply of lorries and other consumer-goods.

I am very happy, indeed, that our refuse collectors are not used to blackmailing their customers and that our children are going to school orderly and regularly, instead of demonstrating or taking to the pot or blowing up the classrooms. As an outward sign of the integrity of our society I can hold up also our ambulances which are whistling and rushing through our streets to pick up the victims of accidents or disease. We would be mortified by leaving ten thousands of those plunged into death beyond recall by their own country fellow men just lying in the streets as is happening now in Amman.[147] All the wage earners – and there is no other species of homo sapiens in this country – are going to work and leaving for home, in silence! As you can imagine only the women are squabbling in the ubiquitous queues about such trivialities how to make ends meet with the said wages their husbands are earning by working or just doing nothing! For this reason far reaching measures for tightening discipline are being introduced. Sometimes a suspicious conversation is going on between the railings. Some kind of connection, some hanging together there is. It cannot be said in truth that society is broken up in independent families and that the isolated individuals are indifferent to the neighbour's lot. Watching the smoke rising from our neighbour's chimney, I am expressing

---

[146] Aleksandr Tarasov, Soviet Minister for Automobiles 1970–74.

[147] See letter 67 and note150, p.267.

an infinitesimal grain of truth when I say that socialist
society is indifferent to our needs of warmth with winter
fast approaching. For my wife has done everything
and has not left untried anything to get central heating
installed. But all in vain. The firm entrusted with the
social duty to provide the pipes and the labour to this
purport is falling short of solidarity by being indifferent
to our subjective sensations of cold in the coming winter
and in the winter of the past tense. However, who would
be so ludicrous to charge our well consolidated society
with failures and shortcomings in the tertiary sphere.
The infrastructure is most decisive and the tertiary
sphere is revolving with the largest diameter from the
centralistic plan. To regain some sense of proportion
consider only the thoroughness with which we have
silenced all the idle talkers, writers, intellectuals and
philosophers. There is a two year's cultural gap but
people are now far healthier and concerned chiefly with
feeding, drinking beer and reproduction rather than
with criticizing one another. Men of letters of the past
shaped only an aberrant spirit of libertarianism, a sense
of defiance and resistance to established power. All this,
inimical to the healthy instincts of the common herd and,
of course, imported from the capitalist countries. They,
the talkers, expressed an entirely false and mistaken
national temperament, preferring strongly freedom
of speech and of everything else to the control of all
media by the CP. They uprooted – all according to the
White Book – the idea of the leading role of the CP. Isn't
it shilly-shally to abolish censorship, pointing to the
historical fact that Marx himself did not like it, being
harassed by it all his life? It was most alarming to see
how the counter-revolutionaries succeeded to mould the
minds of the entire population to their eccentric ideas
within a couple of weeks. Thus they were undoing what

we thought we did, not without incurring great expenses,
during the past 20 years. This was, of course, due to
the concerted action of the said counter-revolutionaries
who insidiously infiltrated the highest ranks of the CP
and took possession of the mass media, including the
making of flicks! It must be conceded, however, that
they produced a (false) unity of all antagonistic classes
which were abolished long ago by divesting them of all
property. It is, of course, easier to rid people of property
than of ingrained habits of mind, such as to think for
oneself. Even Oldrich Svestka[148] had to admit that there
was a boundless confidence [in] certain party leaders
and an unprecedented devotion to public affairs which
found expression in the admitted fact that all meetings
were full and people read all newspapers with great
passion. Men, and even women, as the case may be,
contemplated ALOUD the public good which was no
good. A restlessness was created, a sense of impending
change, and we really felt not quite secure. You know
whom I mean! I myself would say that this spectacle,
however short, was not without grandeur! No wonder
more and more foreign tourists were attracted, so many,
indeed, that it was effaced in the end. Amen!

Love to you all
Yours

Paul

---

[148] See note 139, p.255.

67

Shoreham-by-Sea, Sussex, England
28th September 1970.

My dear Paul

On Thursday and Friday we received a letter from you
rejoicing our hearts with a double dose of satisfaction.
We rejoiced particularly in your astringent remarks.
When you are astringent we tell ourselves that you
are not depressed, not too weighed down with the
ills of your beloved country. When you are only hurt
we ourselves can only feel hurt too but when you are
indignant then we realise that our own indignation is
not wasted.

Yesterday we sent you not only the Guardian but
also a copy of The New Statesman. We are able to do
this because we have been able to avail ourselves of a
cheap copy of the Statesman for 20 weeks. So you may
luxuriate in the smartness of the smart set of Hampstead
and Bloomsbury. Our quondam Minister of Health old
garrulous Crossman is now the editor.[149] You, yourself
may feel inclined to lay your life down for the freedom
of this sort of talkativeness but you can rest assured
that Mr C. will not be with you. He will be on a small
pinnacle making up a lot of new theories none of any
significance about what the Government of the Tahitis or
of the Laplanders or that of King Wolobaluga of Africa
should be doing about the distribution [of] anti-herbia
[sic] devices in Antarctica.

---

[149] Richard Howard Stafford Crossman (1907–74). He resigned from
the Labour front bench after the election defeat to become editor of
The New Statesman.

We must warn you however that this periodical will be late as our lovely domestic help One Blonde and willowy Maureen will have to readdress it wherever we are in the frozen and undeveloped North of our Benighted Country. BUT PLEASE EXPECT IT and let us know when it does not come. We are a bit hazy about your postal efficiency. The weather has been unashamedly glorious with golden sunlight that casts doubts upon the rationality of mankind as they kill each other off and their bloody-minded governments jockey for positions from which to take the greatest advantage.

It has been interesting to note that there has been discernible in the CP, the LP and BBC a sense of shock over the Middle East. The Morning Star was ambivalent, not knowing not merely on which side Moscow would come down, but whether there was any partisanship possible. The BBC, now almost arrogantly Tory in its questioning of any non-Tory variant, was obviously appalled at the bloodshed inaugurated by Hussein and his military government yet also much anxious not to appear on the side of the Liberationists or Commandos or Guerillas.[150] They tried to find an orthodox word for a most unorthodox situation. Of course while only hijacking was under discussion all eyes were turned upon Miss Khaled[151] and Mr Heath as though they were entwined in dancing a sort of Death Waltz of the Civilised World.

---

[150] King Hussein of Jordan had declared martial law after attempts to assassinate him and the hijacking of four planes by the Popular Front for the Liberation of Palestine. In the ensuing offensive between three and five thousand Jordanian Palestinians, mostly civilians, were killed; some say many more.

[151] On 6 September Leila Khaled took part in the attempted hijacking of an El Al flight from Amsterdam to New York. The pilot diverted to London. On 1 October Khaled was exchanged for hostages taken in another hijacking. She remains a prominent member of the PFLP.

While the USA and the USSR remained
MUMMUMMUMMUM as mummies, they talked
grandiloquently of THE FOUR GREAT POWERS as
[though] this little England, after having made the mess
it did under Eden,[152] could do anything to balance the
world's diplomacy and wash the blood clean.

Then we had the glory of the homecoming of the
Hostages who utterly worn out with their experiences
were asked a series of questions as though they had been
second-rate actors in a blood and guts second-rate film.
All these Oxford and Cambridge smoothies (begging yours
and Enid's pardon) give feelings of nausea.

Now we know that Nixon is doing his presidential stuff
and the BBC will wallow in Presidential vomit as he goes
his unexciting way from the 6th fleet to Tito and possibly
to Romania so forth and to dine with our Lovely Heath
and our Beloved Queen and over to Ireland, there to rest
his weary head on the tomb of his peasant ancestors.[153]
And meanwhile there will be the immovable Israelites
determined to keep the Palestinians in the Wilderness
as they were determined to keep the Philistines there so
long ago. And the hard-faced of Moscow will look with
impenetrable faces and button eyes at a situation that can
do the people of our various [countries] no good.

You speak of brains doing what is necessary. There are
brains enough. Brains of Brezhnev, Brains of Kissinger,[154]

---

[152] Anthony Eden (1897–1977), British Prime Minister responsible for
the disastrous invasion of Suez in 1956.

[153] Between 27 September and 5 October President Nixon visited
Italy, Yugoslavia, Spain, the United Kingdom and Ireland. He met in
turn the President of Italy, the Pope, President Tito, General Franco,
the Queen and the British Prime Minister and Prime Minister Lynch
of Ireland.

[154] Henry Alfred Kissinger (1923–), National Security Adviser to
President Nixon and Secretary of State.

brains of Meir,[155] but there are ambitions and there are dollars and alas there are racial jealousies and perhaps worse still there are the brains, the impossible brains, of the Commentators. And there is a thick porridge of humanity in messy masses that needs warmth and tenderness and humanity though it has those qualities in plenty. No we shall fight this out; in the new–old way, in the new–old terms with bombs and no bandages, with guns and little butter.

Hilary is being married on the 16th Oct in Leicestershire – right in the centre of England. We go on Sat to York to stay with Linda. After the wedding we go to Manchester for a time and then on to Leeds to see the new baby, Laura, of David and Margaret. Our senses will reel with unalloyed family proximities.

Heaven knows when I shall write to you again.

I have not been well but was very good yesterday when we entertained a woman from apartheid South Africa, and [one from] 'totalitarian' GDR. More about the latter later. You have no idea how preposterous they both are.

Love to David, his lovely Mamma, to your lovely wife, to your saxophonist, to the man on the ladder. And to you.

Albanian newspaper speaking of Russia. 'We must depend upon the more loyal section of the USSR army. There is nothing that they and a firing squad cannot put right.' Verbum sapientis.

Enid and Leslie

---

[155] Golda Meir (1898 –1978), Prime Minister of Israel 1969–74.

68

Shoreham-by-Sea, Sussex, England
3 October 1970.

My dear Paul,

I am trying in a very inadequate way to settle up with
myself and all my stray pieces of paper before we depart
on Monday. As I am expected to fall down more hors
than de combat when I face the packing of my clothes
I had, among other things, better write to you. The
weather though several degrees colder continues sunny
and refreshing though my confounded eyesight can
no longer enjoy clarity of outline or perceive what is
happening or worse still what is beautiful in the distance.
Our garden everyone says has been full of colour much to
the surprise of my wife who has not been able to work in
it as assiduously as is her wont.

David, who has been in London arranging or not
arranging with some publisher about a book on Louis
XIII they propose he shall do in the next year, is
coming to fetch us so that we may take the journey to
the North more easily in a motor car than in a train.
Today, Saturday, he is entrancing the Party Executive
with his ideas on Higher Education about which he is
inclined to think he has better ideas than any other body
thereabouts. He should have a bit of a battle which will
do him good and which he will enjoy, particularly if he
gets his way.

We have just had the Labour Party conference and
it has decided with a narrow majority that it will not
have an incomes policy. After which it proceeded by an
overwhelming vote to elect Mrs Barbara Castle, the
great and staunch protagonist of the Income Policy, to

the E. Committee of the LP. You cannot depend on the English for logic even if you want to.

The air of radical social change is swirling round the grey heads – so wise, so noble, so profound-looking. The young and the just below middle age in the unions are restless because they can see one endless battle for their standard of living. We English can put up with the eternal dullness of eating fairly well, paying the rent 50 weeks a year, having only half a million unemployed but when the Conservatives, after the defalcations of the Labourites wish to shackle Us to the Gnomes of Zurich or the Thanes of Threadneedle Street etc. both now and always their blood slowly rises and, logic or no logic, they begin to dig the heels and toes in.

Furthermore our Beloved Queen, the Acme of Dignity and respectability, has been issued with orders to attend upon the President of the US at the Chequers, the country place of the Prime Minister. All the US horses and all the US sheriffs and Panoply of CIA and bullet-proof cars will never assuage wound[s] to the pride of the British though they may not love their Queen one little jot. There she went to eat as ordered at 1.30 and again she went to her car replete with obedience to her USA Lord and Master. How are the mighty fallen! They should learn to seek their meat from God for the memories of the once magnificent but bloodied empire will soon be lost in the haze of history. Amen.

The mess in the M East has been made messier by the death of Nasser.[156] The papers and particularly the BBC have rejoiced in field day after field day. First they had the hijackers, then columns about the Leila Khaled

---

[156] President Nasser of Egypt died on 28 September, a few hours after holding an Arab League Summit to deal with the civil strife in Jordan. The Palestinians lost their principal protector.

they were not allowed to see, then the danger of the
newspaper men in Jordan, then the battles themselves
which, though they couldn't see, they knew all about.
And now they almost retail the manoeuvres going on,
as it were, behind Nasser's coffin. They plunge for the
USA but then they are fearful of the USSR. No longer
is there talk of Four GREAT powers but once more the
superpowers are there to be blessed or spat upon as
you would wish. Then in the distance China rears her
smooth or lovely or oriental or ugly or inscrutable head
and some gent living no nearer to China than the plushy
environs of Hong Kong tells you what is in the mind of
Mao and how well he swam 6 years ago in the Yangtze
which no longer overflows its banks owing to socialist
enterprise. There is also a lot more information which
you can get from Chinese periodicals, The Times of the
past three years and a small book by Joan Robinson.
Though the newspaper man is ubiquitous it turns out
that he is not omniscient.

Sunday:

David has just arrived and I am therefore compelled
to conclude this effusion somewhat peremptorily for
the which I apologise. I am sorry that your holiday
was confined by circs to Usti but Enid is grateful for
the pictures you sent her. She proudly shows them to
everyone unless they say first Oh you have some nice
cards on the mantelpiece.

I am today sending you an Economist in a different
envelope and a New Statesman and Guardian together
in one lot. Please let me know whether you get them. I
rather doubt it.

I can't help saying the Nixons in Ireland are too funny.
A field has been regenerated wherein there was a grave
that is supposed to house the remains of one of N's
ancestors. A village in the poverty stricken West Mayo

County has been visited by Mrs N in which the villagers are now at daggers drawn as to whether Mrs N has really any ancestral connection with them at all.[157] The English reporters are having a field day and even the BBC joins in [sometimes] with delicate, and sometimes with heavy irony.

Leslie

69

Shoreham-by-Sea, Sussex, England
5 November 1970.

My very dear Paul

This onrush of affection is designed to cover up and indeed apologise for my shocking lack of letters in the last month. This lapse was due entirely to having no conveniences like a quiet spot with a very good light or a quiet spot with a typewriter. We thought of you and spoke of you a good deal. In York a friend of Linda, a maths lecturer in the University expressed a desire to visit you so I gave him your name and address and I dare say when next he wanders round Europe in his little red sports ear he will call on you. He is very talkative, as everybody is in York apparently. He dresses rather in the manner of a dockyard labourer on a very dirty job. He told us that he had recently been to C-S and stayed for a short time with some people whose name he could not spell but sounded like Kallous or Kallou and the gent was probably a surgeon. Anyway I don't suppose he will be on his rounds for months.

---

[157] Mrs Nixon came with three helicopters to lunch with distant cousins in the village of Ballinrobe.

We were certainly on our rounds. First we had a
week on the Northern outskirts – no the south-western
outskirts – of Manchester in a very pleasant house with
a lovely large garden that flowed into a small wood at
the bottom. A week there was our limit after which
David, who had already motored us from Shoreham in
the first instance, came for us. So off we went with Enid
very excited over the immediate prospect of seeing her
grandchild, David's first child, a rather nice girl baby
called Laura. For this journey we went right over the
Pennine Range, up as high as Holme Moss where the TV
mast is for a very wide area and the view is magnificent.
Through Holmfirth a township noted for a disaster in the
last century which arose when a reservoir flooded the
town and the whole valley in which it stands. Then up the
hill and towards where we ourselves lived for ten years
on the next highest spot before Murmansk. Our house
with a specially large window still stands but somewhat
impeded by a shocking rash of bungalows built so closely
together that a man could hardly get between these
'detached and desirable residences'. Three-quarters of
an hour [later] and Enid was holding Laura but for my
sake refraining from making the sort of cooing noises for
which my own Mother was famous throughout the whole
of Derbyshire. After about a week we were spun down the
M1 to Leicestershire to a pleasant hotel and a charming
l3th century church where Hilary was solemnly married
to the sound of Chopin and the general shuffling of about
100 people. The sunshine specially produced by our own
heathen god and having no association whatever with
the Church of England came forth for us in splendour
and joy and everyone took photographs of everyone else.
We ate and drank and afterwards I was herded off to the
hotel bedroom where I held a sort of processional levée
while my wife went off to do justice to a large meal with

the in-laws. These are quite nice people. One the lady, the stepmother of the Bride, is a retired teacher and the gent, a rather quiet, humourless man is the head of the English Department in the local once Grammar now comprehensive school. Next morning the cook rose again and so did the sun and both did us well and off we went to York where we met everybody, drank everything and ate the place out, sent postcards to you and managed to escape from any ultracardia [*sic*] nastiness.

I think Enid became the most expert washer-up in Manchester, York and Leeds and in all places silently wished there were no such things as plates, cups, glasses and cutlery. If you will have children, I said, you wash up for them all your life.

And now we are out of the rather misty North and in the full flood of sunshine that must while we were away have been going on night and day for when we returned our garden in the front and round the side of the house was ablaze with colours. Once again we owe our thanks to our own social heathen and of course Left-wing godlet [*sic*] who has a kind heart and a generous nature.

I am going to send you within a few days a length of the best worsted suiting which some of my good friends in the West Riding of Yorkshire have been able to procure for me. I shall drop you a note when we send it and shall be obliged if you will look out for it and keep your post people up to scratch. We are also sending for your wife some wool for knitting, in the hope that she will be able to make or get someone to make a wool jacket which we ourselves if you remember called a cardigan.

My wife has just poked her lovely head in the room and said 'That's enough' so if you will forgive me I will desist, have a small snort of whisky and then shave.

We very much hope you are all well. As one interested in lopping off limbs and whatnot you will be interested to hear that you can now buy spare parts in England. We have a fine assortment of fingers, toes, feet, foetuses, Mammas with zip down their fronts from which a baby may be extracted, a few hearts and livers to match – all in our glorious toylands and straight from that heart of civilisation Hong Kong and all in the best durable materials guaranteed to keep your child happy for hours.

Affectionate Salutations to Two and All

Leslie

70

Usti nad Labem, Czechoslovakia
Guy Fawkes Day 1970.

My dear Leslie and Enid,

First I should like to acknowledge with many thanks having received The Statesman, The Economist, coloured postcards from Leeds and York cathedral and also your last letter with interesting cuttings. It seems ages ago, although you forewarned me that you will not write for some time. I am worrying about your state of health. You and your eyes deserved a respite from letter writing, not your friend in a frozen world in which nothing stirred and will stir. I hope you feel rejuvenated by watching Laura and David and [his] charming wife across the generation gap, being tendered with loving care by them. I too restricted my correspondence recently being fasting in Lent and preparing myself spiritually for my second loyalty test this year. I thought it might do you good receiving a message from Sirius in the Great Dog[158] after your return from the pleasant valleys of Yorkshire.

A miracle happened on Sirius! Thanks to the toughness and perseverance of my wife we have a central heating installation at last! We were, indeed, very lucky because for the next 5 years no private person will be authorized to obtain the material and labour for such and similar projects. I had to incur a debt of 8000 crowns, to be repaid in monthly instalments, for paying the bill but we are now comfortably warm but far from rejoicing, remembering our Peter. We are mourning for him and thinking how much he used to complain of feeling cold and how happy he would be with this improvement in our household. There is not much time for mourning, however, as there are many holes in floors and ceilings to be patched up and the ugly pipes and radiators need painting.

The inhabitants of Sirius have been haunted by the spectre of Torquemado[159] recently. I received absolution at my loyalty test. My own little future seems assured and the prospects that I might be pensioned off in a couple of years are fair. I cannot lose sight of the numerous victims of the nationwide loyalty testing of non-party members and cannot find peace of the mind, knowing that thousands are in distress because they could not change their mind and choose the right words with equal facility than others. When given the pertinent questions I questioned the wisdom of the questioning. I told my father confessor that I think it ludicrously idle and foolish to ask somebody to expound his innermost

---

[158] Sirius is the brightest star in the night sky, part of the constellation of *Canis Major*, or Great Dog.

[159] Grand Inquisitor of the Spanish Inquisition from 1483–98, once described as 'the hammer of the heretics'.

thoughts and reasonings if the subject is fully aware that a sincere answer might well jeopardize his and his family's well-being. If a psychologically normal person is faced with an abrupt collision of his convictions with the incessant demand, backed by power, to make statements contrary to his beliefs he will make them for safety's sake and for his peace of mind. But what is the worth of such statements in which yes may mean no? Does not such a procedure resemble closely extracting fictitious confessions and denunciations as practised in the trials of the fifties? Was not the first secretary of the CP of Sirius victimized in this way and didn't he and the CP and the people of Sirius condemn these methods? My father confessor is a kind and wise man and in addition a good doctor. He himself was worrying considerably that the testing – too rigorously conducted – could reach very deeply into the personal life of the Sirians and breakdowns of the normal functions of the body–mind relations might result from it. Can you imagine the rapture of the simpletons who were given unlimited power to humiliate at these tribunals all those who by the grace of Nature were endowed with a higher I.Q. and are, perhaps, through striving and learning for years a bit better off than they themselves? At this occasion they could vent their feelings of revenge for having been in a free-floating suspense with nobody to supervise for a couple of months some 2 years ago. To a mere spectator this latest testing of indifferents might appear to be just a continuation of the Big Purge which, however, did not greatly disturb the overwhelming majority of the Sirians. To the participant observer, however, a distinct new quality is discernible. I could advance some logical arguments for justifying the Big Purge of party members but it defies all my rational analysis to justify the testing of non-partisans unless the secular Diamat-Calvinism[160] is henceforth a National Church to which every Sirian can be compelled to pay lip-service. Poor Michael Servetus (1511–1553),[161] you died in vain! It goes without saying that most Sirians feel that this new doctrine is a break with past practice and has been superimposed on our own 22 years long tradition according to which the principle of religious toleration as regards non-party members has never been entirely negated. I recall distinctly that a prominent Sirian party leader declared, when asked about his relations to non-party members: we have to persuade them, of course, but if we fail, make them work and leave them alone! He was thus paraphrasing the saying of your terrestrial Frederick the Great, king of Prussia, who under the influence of your terrestrial Voltaire championed religious tolerance and said: Let everyone pursue salvation in his own fashion! I spoke with a would-be-technocrat, concerned with the chemical transformation of rubber in the process of vulcanization, who was condemned to a menial task in the building trade on answering the pertaining questions. Are you surprised that he was looking back with a feeling of nostalgia to the long past age of entrepreneurs who were so preoccupied with introducing assembly lines and Taylors scientific management[162] that […] were not in the least concerned with the thinking of their workers as long as their output was alright. I am just reading a Pelican Book, 'Monopoly Capital' by Paul A. Baran and Paul M. Sweezy which I received from a Brazilian booklegger. However irrational

---

[160] 'Diamat' ie Dialectical Materialism.

[161] Servetus was burnt at the stake in Calvin's Geneva for heresy and blasphemy.

[162] Taylorism, which took its name from Frederick Winslow Taylor (1856–1915), is a theory of management concerned with workflows, aimed at improving economic efficiency, especially labour productivity.

---

this system on your Earth appears to be the Giant Capitalist Corporations are certainly not wasting a single dollar for questioning their white collar workers about what they think about their most recent merger. Certainly your worst monopoly capitalist would not dismiss their white collar [workers] on discovering non-conformist thoughts under their white collar! I am at a loss whether to call this most recent development on Sirius in the Great Dog the 'Big Split' or 'Anomy'. The latter designation can be reduced to the simple imperative 'Never call a thing, say a spade, with its right name'. The former denotes the advice: 'Never honour a promise – take a somewhat ambivalent attitude or act contrary to it if it suits you!' I am rather concerned about the wider implications and distant repercussions of 'Big Split' or 'Anomy'. The consequences could become quite serious if you come to think of it. 'I love you' may mean 'I'LL KILL YOU' and soldiers rendering their oath to fight to death may think of taking to their heels in their second Ego. Men exhibiting the traits of the split personality will be and are, indeed, most eligible for educating the young. All those most competent in double entry book-keeping will fill the posts at all levels of numerous hierarchies. When the fatal seeds of doubletalk and double-thinking are once sown a babel will soon rage on Sirius. If veritable half-wits are everywhere promoted to high ranking positions the time may not be so far off that one of them will steal himself into a position to put his finger on the push-button. That's why on Guy Fawkes Day I prayed: Oh God Almighty, have mercy with us Sirians and deliver us from the supremacy of the simpletons!

With affectionate greetings

Paul

71

Shoreham-by-Sea, Sussex, England
18 November 1970 [?].

My dear Paul,

It is extraordinary what pleasure the sight of an
envelope from you brings us.

I cannot now write at length because someone is
coming for lunch soon.

We have today sent through our infallible postal
system one round parcel containing a piece of worsted
suiting and a quantity of knitting wool in another parcel.
The suiting should make a complete suit including a
waistcoat. We are sorry that we have not been able to
send you the buttons and linings but hope the USSR
cum GDR economies will readily furnish these in
suitable quality. I understand that Messrs Brezhnev
and Kosygin[163] purchase the cloths for their suits from
the finest mills in Italy. The wool is red not primarily
because of its revolutionary associations but because it
seemed the most practical colour when the knitter is not
here to be asked. I should be pleased to learn whether
wool of this quality is readily available in C-S.

My health is fairly good but there are times when
I am too tired to do anything but lie in bed. My
indigestion dramatically subsided when we were away
and apart from starchy carbohydrates I ate pretty much
what I liked. My eyesight worries me most. It is not only
a great waste of time because I cannot surreptitiously
read when we have visitors but an irritating reduction in

---

[163] The Soviet Prime Minister from 1964 to 1980.

my activities as I am unable to refer to parts of books, reference books and pick up sundry information from newspapers and periodicals when Enid is too busy to read to me which, in any case, I could hardly bully her into looking up for me. She is very valiant indeed, from reading this and that to tying up my shoelaces when exasperation, mortification and what not make me very impatient with both her and myself. But we live.

We have become very interested in Bertrand Russell lately.

Everyone in Usti must know you for a true patriot by now. Not to mention a gentleman of the highest veracity and perspicacity. No tribunal in its senses if it were a Party tribunal could possibly give you anything but an encouragement to continue in your high profession and demand that you continue to abide by those scientific principles which form as Marx himself declared more than once to be the foundation, inescapable foundation of all Marxist thinking. It is a great shame that there are many who have little or no idea that all progress must be built on scientific knowledge of the highest order. To achieve this, discussion among Marxists must not only be Party-wide but also worldwide.

With these beautiful thoughts I commend you to your new heating system, Comrade Husak – to whom be a long life of integrity – and to the humanitarians who govern your sweet country.

Leslie

72

Usti nad Labem, Czechoslovakia
26 November 1970.

Dear Leslie and Enid,

Thank you ever so much for the parcel with knitting wool
and the 2 copies of the New Statesman and your letter
which we received properly on November 23rd and 24th
respectively.

I can hardly describe to you with words the joy and
excitement of Bohumila on seeing and feeling the red
wool. There were plenty of 'Oh' and 'Gosh' and all the
Czech equivalents of admiration from both my women.
We had it confirmed by phone from Prague that wool of
this quality is solely available in exchange for foreign
currency in the special shops for tourists called TUZEX.
The wool available there comes from Holland, we have
been told. The other parcel with the suiting has not yet
arrived. I guess that the custom officials are engaged in
assessing the value of it in order to make out the amount
of duty to be paid on delivery. I am embarrassed by your
magnanimity as I shall be hardly able to return your
kindness, except by reiterating my invitation to be our
guests. The choicest Czech cuisine and some bottles too
will be ready for you! Any of your friends who wishes to
call on us will be heartily welcome, because of you but
also because this house will be for ever hospitable for
anyone from England. It is in a pretty dilapidated state,
I warn you! Even on Czech standards.

I was somewhat surprised by Brezhnev praising the
economic reforms in Hungary at the CP congress at
Budapest and still more by sprinkling holy water on
further democratisation, in Hungary, of course. The

absence of W. Ulbricht or his second men seems to be a sure sign that the GDR is at loggerheads with the SU over her policy towards the GFR. The surprise visit of Gromyko to East Berlin seems to confirm this.[164]

In this country psychoanalysis of the citizens is continuing and there is a welter of jokes and stories going. This is a better way to protest against the abuse of power than bombing out mathematical research institutes and computer centers (Madison, Wisc. USA).[165] When a customer arrived in a shop wanting to buy tea, the shop assistant duly asked: 'Russian or Chinese?' 'For heavens sake, stop loyalty testing with me. I'll have coffee instead,' said the customer. Another one: 'We are building an Underground Metro at Prague. Only one subway with moving stairs is so far completed – to the joy of our youngsters who have never seen anything like moving stairs. President Svoboda is showing Brezhnev how work is progressing. But they are finding only a very few workers busy on the spot and most of them could be located in a pub nearby. Brezhnev, expressing some concern about their findings, gets the reply from Svoboda: 'Comrade, tell me the country in which the ruling class is doing any work'.

---

[164] 'The 10th Congress of the Hungarian Socialist Workers Party was held from 23–28 November. It continued a cautious policy of economic decentralisation while confirming a pro-Soviet foreign policy. The highly unusual absence of Walter Ulbricht, the East German Leader, was generally seen as a sign of unhappiness about the Soviet Union's rapprochement with West Germany. The Soviet Foreign Minister visited East Berlin to see him while the Congress was taking place.

[165] A reference to the bomb attack of 24 August 1970 on the Army Mathematics Research Center (AMRC), located on the Madison campus of the University of Wisconsin. Although the AMRC was barely damaged one researcher was killed, another lost 25 years of research records and property to the tune of 2.1 million dollars was damaged.

I should like to draw your attention to two
interesting articles, of which I read only the first one:

1. 'The Convergence of Environmental Disruption'
(from Lake Erie to Lake Baikal, Los Angeles to Tbilisi,
the debates and dilemmas are the same) by Marshall I.
Goldman, Russian Research Center, Harvard University,
SCIENCE, 2 October 1970, Vol. 170, No. 3953, p. 37.

2. 'Disarmament? The Current state of the Fraud' by
Kevin J. Kinsella, International Research Institute,
Stockholm, Sweden Science Journal, Vol. 6, Nov. 1970,
No.11.

I am very pleased with the heating in our house,
particularly as I feel very cold during my work and in
my office at the hospital. The squalor at the hospital
is most depressing and I am glad to get home and
forget work for a couple of nightly hours. David is on
penicillin because he has been found out to be a carrier
of a streptococcus in his throat. He is playing with an
old-fashioned gramophone in my room and managed
to break one disc by Sibelius and Bolero (don't know
by whom). As you are interested in Bertrand Russell I
wonder whether you have heard this one. A dinner party
on the occasion of his ninetieth birthday was arranged.
A London lady present at the party suggested that he
was [not only] the world's most famous atheist but, by
this time, also the world's oldest atheist. 'What will you
do, Bertie, if it turns out you have been wrong?' she
asked. 'I mean, what if – uh – when the time comes, you
should meet HIM? What will you say?' Lord Russell was
delighted – his bright eyes grew brighter, birdlike, then
he pointed a finger upward and cried: 'Why, I should say
'God, you gave us insufficient evidence!''

I shall at once write to you when we receive the parcel
with the suit to relieve ours and your anxieties. Many
thanks once more!

With affectionate greetings
Yours

Paul + Bohumila

73

Shoreham-by-Sea, Sussex, England
Sunday must be the 28 [29th] November 1970 or
thereabouts.

My dear Paul,

Life goes irrevocably on while I lie in bed or gently
walkabout and quite uselessly think of you, my children,
my friends, the irrational Tories, the stupid social
democrats, the blind communists, people in jail and
sometimes of a few ideas, take a drink of whisky, eat
my meals and go to bed. On the whole books are best,
for when they displease you can put them back into
the shelves there to lie until they disturb some other
enquirer. Some days I think the prospects of humanity
brighten, sometimes I consider very darkly the prospects
are utterly scrofulous. But there we are together on a
planet that shrinks as wool shrinks in water that is too
hot. I see men as microbes mounting barriers upon
barriers to their own progress. Or I see this man hurt
and bewildered in the labyrinth. Or that woman whose
charm never had the opportunity to blossom. That child
so sweetly lying there with a whacking big **?** hanging

like, or worse than, the sword of Damocles over its silken head. They all need care, love, tenderness. Yet people no longer turn to God, for the images that God was [given] have proved besmirched, cracked and even hideous – the image of men revoltingly in search of personal power. I think I shall hie me hence and make what every English woman cries out for in time of need, merriment or exhaustion – a good cup of tea from China they say.

There are lots of countries in which you could be refused a job on account of your political or religious or anti-religious opinions. There is hardly a country in the world which has not a batch of prisoners who are in prison for asserting their political beliefs. The exceptions might be all the Scandinavian countries. Possibly France. In many countries the Government has the power of enacting any laws it likes, of imprisonment without trial, the use of secret police who arrive in the middle of night then beat or torture and so forth. We have in jail in England 6 Cambridge students who were picked out as victims of a demonstration in Cambridge against a lordly dinner held in honour of the Greek government.[166]

The Home Secretary is busy making the life of a research student, known for his revolutionary opinions, miserable with the almost certainty of expelling him back to West Germany where he will almost certainly go to prison. This young man has a wife and a baby, and is suffering from some severe head injury.[167] There is a powerful movement in Northern Ireland to set up a

---

[166] See p.209 and note 111.

[167] Rudi Dutschke (1940–79) was a German student leader and Marxist. He was accepted by Clare Hall, Cambridge to finish his degree in 1969, but in January 1971 he was expelled with his family as an 'undesirable alien' who had engaged in 'subversive activity'. In 1968 he had been shot in the head by an anti-communist and eventually died from the consequences.

concentration camp for those naughty Republicans and Roman Caths who will not keep quiet. In N.I. no Prot gives an RC a job and no RC gives one to a Prot. All the Ulster police are Red, white and blue Protestants of a rabid, imperialistic kind. I need hardly tell you that there are many political prisoners. In the USA one Professor Angela Davis[168] is in danger of being extradited to California where she will almost certainly be tried on a trumped up charge of having weapons in her house and inciting others to violence. She has certainly lost her job which is teaching sociology and philosophy in Berkeley University.[169] We do not seek to look only into the borders to the C countries where on the whole the Govt says You leave us alone and we will leave you alone. This of course I agree is wrong but in the capitalist countries the possibilities of the Govt taking utterly irrational and reactionary steps backwards of being so callous about poverty, slum housing and unemployment impels men and women from all walks of life to make their protests from time to time.

I most certainly anticipate that in England [and] the USA constrictions on the rights of common people will grow. Whether we get into the Common Market or not the capitalists will be more and more pressed by their inadequacy to furnish a good standard of life for all. If the USA erects trade barriers then our case will be more and more difficult.

---

[168] Angela Davis (1944–) was a black communist held in jail in New York and charged with the kidnap and murder of a Californian judge in August 1970. A massive national and international campaign secured her release in February 1972, and the following June she was acquitted by an all-white jury.

[169] Angela Davis actually taught at the Los Angeles campus of the University of California (UCLA) from 1969, not at Berkeley. The University authorities made several attempts to get rid of her and finally succeeded in June 1970, when her contract was not renewed.

In England the papers and particularly the BBC
cannot make up their silly little minds whether to be
entirely inimical to the USSR or to be friendly. The fact
that Britain does another £100 million in trade from
the USSR makes them mad one day and lukewarm and
friendly another.

I know that writers, at least some, do not have a
happy time in the USSR and money-makers in GB and
the USA are very fond of blowing this up as though the
great mass of journalists in this country care deeply
for the truth but are not rushing here and there for one
sensation after another in order to call it news.

Three quarters of this multitude just live on telling
the middle section of the population that all's well so
long as God sends a murder or a story about a stupid
foreign statesman or some politician declaring how
utterly fractious the workers [are] and at least once a
week how wicked every red is wherever and whatever.
If they would become honest it would not only hasten
the reduction of our social ills but would also reduce
the pressure on the men of the Kremlin and give them
time to attack the stupidities of their own bureaucrats
to the relief of us all over the world. The professional
class are so gullible, with most of them smitten with
money and the great commercial magnates, and yet
frightened to death that their opposite number in
France or Germany in the USA will cut their throats;
and so fierce about their dividends that they grudge
every penny given to the welfare doctor or the welfare
dentist or to municipal housing that they are prepared
to rob and pillage the members of their own community,
destroy the successful nationalised industries, give
£350 million pounds per annum to the highest of
personal incomes and so on and so forth. 90,000 old
people die of hypothermia in the UK alone, thousands

from preventable bronchitis. And the whole world is gladdened by one and half million pounds going to Covent Garden Opera House each year and our great cities are [decked] out with inescapable luxuriousness of the most ostentatious vulgarity. And all the time we are called upon to 'save the Economy', that God [that] has no beginning and no ending who is the alpha plus and Omega plus plus plus and who is guarded by all the priests of Lombard Street who take care of the grounds while the poor gather their pennies together to meet still another rise in the price of food.

Against this there is only one hope and that is that the pressures now increasing economically every day, and likely to be increased by legislation, will break their own bonds. This they cannot [do] without the active movement into the offensive by the trade unionists both of the professional classes and the workers. I feel outraged by the betrayal of the workers and devoted professional people the world over. Those people in charge think that God or Mammon or some outrageous mummification of Marx has given them the sole right to manipulate the people of the world for their own silly and futile advantage.

Before I shut up I must warn you that Crankshaw,[170] to make a pun, is more of a crank than a sure man. He is bitterly anti-soviet even if he is well read. One or two of his articles I have read. He has written for the American tired businessman, though in politer language [he] would not for fabrication be second to what China tells the world about Moscow or vice-versa. Whatever he says about certain leaders or past leaders should be taken with a grain of salt. People like him do

---

[170] Edward Crankshaw (1909–84), prolific writer, translator and Soviet specialist.

much damage not only to the cause of truth but also to the possibility of the peoples of the world understanding each other.

We send our affectionate greetings to you all,

Leslie

74

Usti nad Labem, Czechoslovakia
4th December 1970.

My dear Enid and Leslie,

Yesterday I received the biggest Christmas present as far as I can remember, from you! The parcel with the fine English suiting has reached us safely. I am very grateful to you. My best Sunday suit is black, pitch black and served me well during the past 2 years when occasions for mourning were hailing down upon us. Perhaps the time for the discharge of other functions is fast approaching and I assume that you anticipated my need to be clad less sombre than hitherto for them. Apart from needs and wants we deem ourselves blessed for having among the considerable number of relations and friends someone as kind as you. You are caring for us with unending care and very uncommon solidarity, without the slightest regard for the stern law of quid pro quo. Several of our friends abroad, including my two brothers, are feeling morally obliged to help us but being under the pressure to get ahead and to surround themselves with the display of status symbols, such as car and a better house in a 'better neighbourhood' are hardly in a position to back us up.

I also thank you for the 3 great, more sensational than revealing articles from the Times and for 4–5 very interesting cuttings. The cover with the newspaper material looked as though somebody had peeped into the envelope. That does not worry me as long as I am being sustained by information which lend some colour, details and distinction to the news I am receiving on my wireless set from distant stations amidst a welter of atmospherics and some jamming. Poor old Khrushchev. Once he said 'We'll bury you yet' and now he himself was nearly killed off by indignation and a heart attack, provoked by the abominable publication of his memoirs, perhaps not even set down by him or if so not with the intention to be published so soon and certainly not in the west. With Christmas approaching and expecting a visit of Saint Nicholas with three live devils and one angel at our house on Saturday night it really is not my intention to revert to the gloomy side and begin to harp on the same old things. David said he wants a pistol to shoot the boys who are beating him up at the Nursery school and Ian, his father, as well because he is smacking him. At the same time he wishes to be given a horn to accompany his father while he is maltreating his saxophone. Ian and Zdena went to a show in the 'house of culture' last night. We also had to fill in a frightfully complicated form for a census. Among all sort of awkward questions, we answered the question whether a common household for two families agrees with us in the affirmative. The Commissar, collecting the forms in the afternoon, rang the bell again in the evening, asking us whether we really mean it and wanted to make sure by asking Ian and Zdena in person. Most young couples want, of course, their own flats and he simply could believe that two women in one kitchen, notably in-laws, find living together agreeable! I enjoyed running hot water and the bath in our own house exactly for one week when we noted a nasty stain on the ceiling in the room just below our bathroom. By the way, according to the census in 1960, only 60% of all urban residencies in the USSR are provided with running water. Tomorrow a plumber will see to the leakage. Zdena spent nearly all their savings for the central heating and likewise we. She looked rather sad today. When I asked her why, she said that they could not afford any drinks last night at the show while all the young people there did very well with alcoholic beverages. Jesting she said she is looking for a man in his fifties but financially very strong! As a doctor and father I taught her that men in their fifties have either lost their riches or their virility or both. You are not likely to succeed in your extramarital transgressions, I told her and she said Plenty of old bastards about!!! The weather is filthy. It's raining, there is a lot of smog and fog over the town, roads and buses are covered with mud. Dawn and dusk are close neighbours, straining our resources of electricity to the utmost. Our splendid governance has deprived us of leisure during the Christmas and New Year season and are cutting and trimming down our earnings. We hope, however, to find enough time to comply with the customs to send you a small Christmas present, too!

With affectionate greetings
Yours

Paul

75

Shoreham-by-Sea, Sussex, England
6 December, 1970.

My dear Paul,

I was overjoyed to receive your letter as I always am and
pleased that you all liked the wool and I hope by now
you have received the piece of cloth. It is a great pity that
you are compelled to spend more money after l have paid
what I consider to be excess postage. I think and hope
that you will be as pleased with that as with the wool.
I shall send something for David and his mother in the
course of time.

The New Statesman which I have sent you irregularly
since our return from the north appears to be edited
by a man who has no idea that real people exist at
all. Political machines round the Westminster area
and editorial nunks [*sic*] in Holborn. I must say that
we think the N. S. a flaccid and somewhat dishonest
organ purporting to serve rather than serving the Left.
Crossman[171] who is the editor was a principal contributor
before the war and every week came up, with great
display of words and some imagination, with a plan for
making the economy go and everyone feeling fairly safe.
As a minister he failed lamentably. All our politicians are
very conceited now and I think this growth of malignant
emotional obesity is due to getting too much on the telly
as well as getting salaries they hardly earn. I am sending
you some extracts from The Times today following a lot
I sent last week. Please let me know it you don't get them.

---

[171] See note 149, p.266.

I am also sending you two or three Stars in order that you may have at least some idea of the turmoil that is now going on over here in regard to the Tories' new bill which will drastically curtail the freedom of the trade unions.

I think we are getting into real economic and industrial chaos. British Motors are to sack 5000 at least.[172] The Govt refuses to lend Liverpool docks 20 million pounds whereas the last govt lent Rolls Royce £60 M and this govt £40 M and the Bank of England another £18 million. Lord Robens in an effort to keep his job as Boss of the Collieries etc. has called the workers ignorant, downright ignorant, conspiring despicable treacherous etc. etc.[173] Routes have been lopped off the BOAC airlines because the Govt is fathering a broken down private enterprise airline.[174] They threaten to knock the paying parts of the Steel industry and the Post Office in order to make private enterprise competitive.[175] They have put up the price of school meals so that about a million no longer have

---

[172] British Leyland (created in 1968 through the merger of British Motor Holdings and Leyland Motors) had just announced closure of two plants at Coventry in its Austin-Morris group, with the loss of 5,000 jobs over the course of the following year.

[173] Alfred Robens, Baron Robens of Woldingham (1910–99), Chairman of the National Coal Board since 1961. He stepped down at the end of January 1971, at odds with the government over its approach to the industry, including proposals to hive off some activities to the private sector. Since 1961 the number of miners had been reduced by half and Robens' relationship with them was difficult.

[174] See letter 61, note 128, p.240. Leslie is presumably referring to British United Airway's financial difficulties which led to its absorption by British Caledonian in November 1970 – which itself had been consistently profitable since its inception in 1961.

[175] *The Times* reported on 1 December that 'Government Proposals for selling off the profitable peripheral activities of mining, steel and the railways are seen as signs of similar impending moves in the Post Office'. Postal workers feared the selling off the highly profitable telecommunications division.

them. Meanwhile the Labour leaders outside Parliament pretend that all this is not going on and Mr Victor Feather of the TUC is saying shush shush if you make a row boys it will be all the worse for you.

We are going to have an unholy strike on Dec 8 and no Marxist or Tory could say what is going to happen.[176]

Could you find time to write out a statement of the effects of events since 1968? How the Comrades from Russia were welcomed and how they arc received nowadays, how you are helping the SU with exports; the strengthening of your economy; the superlative enthusiasm in both the Party and the workers and of course in the intelligentsia; the increase in production and so on. And of course there is the rejuvenating effect of the Party's restriction in membership as well as in the reduction of the intelligentsia and the general effect on education in both schools and university. My wife would also like to know what the effect is on women generally and how they are affected in their training for certain jobs; teachers, nursing, medical and surgical professions. About 1000 words or so when you could find the time after Christmas, say, because I realise how busy [you] are.

Interruption – anyway I've said enough about that. Have you had news of socialist developments in Chile?[177] Of the attempt to assassinate the Pope in the

---

[176] The strike in December was called by the Liaison Committee for the Defence of Trade Unions in opposition to the Government's Industrial Legislation Bill. An estimated 350,000 took part, preventing the appearance of any national newspapers, bringing the docks to a standstill and disrupting car production. The General Council of the TUC opposed the strike call and claimed that 95 per cent of trade unionists had not taken action.

[177] The Marxist Salvador Allende had become President of Chile on 3 November 1970.

Philippines?[178] Of the bombing of North V. and the attempt to free prisoners of war in N Vietnam?[179]

Please tell your friend from Ghana I am sorry that I have had no more literature on Cuba but I expect that some fairly reliable information will become available soon. Unfortunately we know no one particularly interested in Cuba at the moment. Of course there are books about guerrillas etc but these are too expensive for us to buy and considering my present eyesight much to long for us to read. But we have not forgotten. The movement among the upper scientists in the USSR fluctuates but continues to make itself heard. Solzhenitsyn has been given the Nobel Prize and has openly declared that too much red tape would have to be cut and too much humiliation endured if he determined to go to Stockholm to receive it. So he is going to the Swedish embassy instead.[180] We also understand that Non-Socialist Realist Painters i.e. those who do not paint and draw representationally can make a living though they are not registered practitioners. Apparently they can marry a film star, a ballet dancer or employ themselves in commercial work. Their position appears to be much the same as the same gents in our own country. I'm all for marrying a film star myself, preferably a fair haired, blue eyed, passionate Uzbek who has orange groves, grapefruit, vines and a house in Leningrad for the winter. It is most peculiar how

---

[178] A Bolivian artist dressed as a priest attempted to stab the Pope when he arrived at Manila airport on 27 November 1970.

[179] Over the weekend of 21 and 22 November the bombing of North Vietnam was stepped up and there was an abortive mission to rescue American prisoners from a camp near Hanoi.

[180] In the event the Swedish government objected to this proposal and Solzhenitsyn received his prize at the 1974 ceremony after being deported from the Soviet Union.

actors etc. etc. can become highly paid, the most highly paid, in any country. Downright irritating unless you are a non-representational painter with hardly a penny in his hat on the London Embankment who is whisked off to the nearby Savoy by a dark haired black eyed [lady ?] with lovely legs and an enormous bank balance.

I rejoice that because of my inartistic inability my morals remain pure and undefiled,

Have you heard the funny story about the graves of B and H? No. Neither have I. But it is a good beginning isn't it?

Yours ever

Leslie

76

Shoreham-by-Sea, Sussex, England
9 December 1970.

My dear Paul,

I do not intend to overwhelm you again. My last two letters went close together because I temporarily lost one. Thank you for your last one.

I would plug your leak if I were there, though it valgused [sic] my hallux and entwined my navicular[181] round my scapulae.[182] But alas I am not there but half freezing because the idiot working men, the idiot

---

[181] One of the tarsal bones in the foot.

[182] Shoulder blades.

government, the idiot managers, the idiot idiots of sundry realms where stupidity and stubbornness combine to kill off all old men and old ladies, weak infants, chickens, piglets and those using kidney machines etc. etc. etc. and give hypothermia both to the fat and to the thin. Fortunately I made our early cup of tea at 6.30 this am because the beasts deprived us of electricity at 6.50.

Enclosed is our greeting to the three younger members of your family. We are sending them a small note and hope it will get through. They will thus be able to buy what they wish.

Will write soon

Leslie

77

Dear David, Zdena and Ian,

Enid and I would like you to accept the enclosed piece of sterling in the hope that you will be able to get something or things from the foreign shop which might be more pleasing than anything we chose for you from our own shops, And we hope that you will have a little left over so that you may buy a bottle.

We shall remember you and your country and hope that the wicked will either become virtuous forthwith or have the most nauseating indigestion.

To those like your good selves and our good selves we wish happy laughter, a steel lined stomach and loving warmth.

Yours sincerely,
Enid and Leslie Parker

78

Usti nad Labem, Czechoslovakia
13 December 1970.

My dear Leslie and Enid,

You want me to write a statement about the present situation
in this country. I am afraid I can't for several reasons. The
surest way to end up in jail is to publish an article in a
foreign newspaper for nothing infuriates the KGB more
than an eyewitness account by-passing their censorship.
An essential feature of any totalitarian regime is to restrict
anyone to his own narrow field and to have all activities
shrouded in secrecy. The man in the street is excluded from
all informal communication channels and ought to learn no
more and no less than what the censor decreed to pass on
in the mass media. How can I inform you about the extent
of our exports to Russia or about the state of our economy
while I haven't the slightest idea about what is going on in
the large chemical works only a few hundred yards removed
from our hospital? One must be <u>in</u> to learn crucial secrets.
Besides we are taught that economy and foreign trade are far
too complex for any ordinary citizen to grasp. We are caught
in the notorious credo: The Fuhrer knows best. The excuse –
I am a doctor, not a politician or an economist – resounded
again and again at the recently conducted loyalty tests. It
is explicitly demanded of anyone to be all the time vigilant
for espionage and imperialist subversion and to guard
against giving away any vital secrets about internal matter
of factories or services or the state. At staff meetings we are
constantly told to be very careful in our correspondence with
foreign firms which want to sell medical equipment to us. As
employees of the chemical works are the husbands of some

of our nurses we are learning, however, occasionally that this
or that engineer has been dismissed or demoted. Through
fostering a social climate of fear to commit an offence
against ever present higher secrecy and security interests,
people are immured in isolated areas of life and talk and
mind, moving only in isolated chambers. The other day I
received the statistical yearbook of the health services. Eager
to find out how many doctors have left this country I looked
through all tables and figures. I also compared them with
the corresponding figures of previous years. Everyone knows
that at least 3,000 doctors, if not more, have emigrated to the
West since 1968 but the sole indication of this fact I could
find was that the average annual increase of the total number
of doctors was much smaller than in the past. Our official
statistics are like bikinis. What they reveal is suggestive, what
they conceal is vital. All I know about the economy is that at
the moment there are plenty of oranges, lemons, grapefruits
and Hungarian apples on the market. Contrary to the Dubcek
era when I could buy The Times at the kiosks I can now
spend my money on American cigarettes or on Liptons or
Pickwicks tea bags, on Nestle coffee or on Swiss or Austrian
chocolates. Whereas Bata supplied half of Europe with shoes
in the bourgeois republic of Masaryk and Benesh [sic],[183]
my wife bought me a pair of fine Romanian shoes. Our W.C
is also made in Romania. I hope no one will suspect me of
defaming the Husak regime or giving away vital state secrets
by mentioning these economic marvels. The Husak regime
is out to gain the confidence of the people and was recently
backed up by a visit of Podgorny.[184] It seems necessary to

---

[183] Tomas Garrigue Masaryk, President of Czechoslovakia from 1918
to 1935, was succeeded by Edvard Benes who served from 1935 to
1938 (and from 1939 to 1948, when he was mostly in exile).

[184] Nikolai Viktorovich Podgorny (1903–83), Chairman of the
Presidium of the Supreme Soviet.

attempt to heal the total break and alienation of society from the regime. That's why Husak stuck out against the hard liners after having worked with them in close association to destroy all autonomous institutions of indigenous Czech and Slovak culture. The damage done by this unholy alliance is ghastly. 300,000 i.e 20% of followers of the reform movement were expelled from the party and removed from their positions in the civil service, in industry, in universities and the educational establishment. All those surviving the purge in the party were subsequently removed by the nation-wide loyalty testing. Czech culture has been driven underground. The unions of journalists and film-artists were dissolved. The property of the writers' union was confiscated and the only meeting place for members are the funerals of deceased members. 350 judges and an unknown numbers of deputies of the representative bodies were dismissed and replaced by docile nominees. Just at the time of the meeting of the CC the last remnants of independent associations are being hauled away. The newspaper of the Slovak young writers was stopped and in the Czech lands the Czechoslovak-Japanese society was banned in the name of consolidation. Only someone out of his mind could possibly lose sight of these facts and fall a victim to the oratorical skill of Gustav Husak. Are you surprised that I have become as deaf as a post and as blind as a bat to all domestic communication media since marshal Grechko intervened in April 1969 to impose deadly censorship on all forms of communications?[185] It may well be true that I became ignorant and oblivious of the present state of affairs by default but I cannot help it. I am living the life of a hermit. The first thing striking a visitor's eye are the vows to be united with the Soviet Union in

---

[185] Andrei Antonovitch Grechko (1903–75), Marshall of the Soviet Union and Minister of Defence. Presumably the formal restoration of censorship in August 1968 had not produced the desired results.

eternal friendship blazing brilliantly from all public and
factory buildings. Both fractions, the conservatives and
outright reactionaries in the CP, are outdoing each other
by advertising and idolizing the Soviet Union. There is
no lecture and no public gathering where a set of words
about eternal friendship with the Russians is not stuffed
down your gullet. This ramming down of empty words is
being performed repetitively and monotonously on the
well-known Pavlovian principle of conditioned reflexes.
If you bring up this stuff, it is hoped, that you can be
branded as belonging to the breed of those crawling on
their bellies. One wonders why, after a most intensive
advertising campaign, friendship with Russia needs still
improvement. Ergo, there must be something amiss. Never
in history owed so many so much passionate hatred to so
few inept, dishonest and overzealous propagandists. The
in-vain efforts of doctor Goebbels to overcome a genuine
respect for the Russians in the Czechs and to replace it
with an irrepressibly deeply rooted rejection of everything
Russian has been accomplished – by their deeds and their
overbearing propaganda. Our cinemas are swamped with
Russian films. A few months ago a good lady complained
in the local paper that the cinemas are usually empty
when Russian films are being shown and – worse still – the
comrades whose old membership cards have been replaced
by the new ones are conspicuous by their absence. With TV
head counting is of course difficult but on the whole the
public is fed up with bloody shooting scenes from the war
and the guerillas fighting the Nazis. This is the only safe
topic for an unimaginative author of socialist realism. To
prevent fiasco and a shamefully low return from the box-
offices attendance at Russian musical and art shows and
exhibitions had to be made compulsory for schools, offices
and some plants. The pages of the newspapers are full
with exciting stories about the arrival and departure of an

endless stream of visiting Russian delegations, sponsorships and patronages. The parched mouth of the curious reader is usually dribbling with spittle on seeing these news. For he knows that the dullness of long and languid speeches about better understanding and eternal friendship has to be made good by copious meals and a lavishing flow of spirits and wines. To the best of my knowledge there is very little social trading going on with the Russian soldiers. To make an appearance in public with them would certainly be against the etiquette of this country.

Judging from the heaviness of my eyes and the clumsiness of my fingers I feel I have written at least 1000 words and I shall sum up with answering the question of Enid regarding women. Life has to go on and that's why there was little change in the ordeal of our glorious womanhood. But as a successful woman should leave no gap unfilled, a very few have been seen to disappear in the colourfully painted gates of the Commandatura.

With best wishes for Christmas and the New Year
Yours

Paul

79

Usti nad Labem, Czechoslovakia
19th December 1970.

My dear Leslie and Enid,

It was a courageous undertaking to send us the note and good luck that it got through alright. I hope that you received my note under cover of a second Christmas

card which was not meant to mean anything. Zdena and
Ian wish me to convey to you the heartiest thanks for
this unexpected Christmas gift. At this juncture they will
find it difficult to buy what they wish as there is far more
money among the people than desirable goods reasonably
priced. The queues at the Tuzex-foreign currency shops
are fantastic and before the shoppers reach the shelves
not much is left over. The Christmas market is in a chaotic
disarray. There is a plethora of extremely expensive
goods or junk and marked deficiencies elsewhere. As I
said before food and fruits are plentiful and intellectual
starvation alone will never lash workers and housewives
into a furious uprising. The central idea of the Prague
reform movement is that rigid central planning without
the slightest regard for the consumers and for those
who have to carry out the directives of the faceless
bureaucracy can only be ameliorated in sympathetic
communication with the people and their participation
in the management of the plants. The central decision-
making body needs feedback. In 4 days of bloody riots
this idea was vindicated in a most tragic fashion, but
nevertheless with a clarity which leaves nothing to be
desired.[186] It's no use to fasten the blame on thugs, vandals
and hooligans or on counter-revolutionary intelligentsia,
for the middle classes and intelligentsia of Poland was
wiped out by the Nazis and by Stalin. The simple fact is
that the elite of Polish workers put their foot down when
the foolish governing clique displayed enough arrogance
to decree even the pattern of consumption just before
Christmas and the winter. It is a standing joke in the

---

[186] A reference to events in Poland where food and fuel price increases
of up to 20 per cent led to five days of rioting and strikes, followed
on 20 December by the resignation of Władysław Gomułka as First
Secretary of the Polish United Workers Party.

socialist camp: 'Food prices have gone up, comrade!' 'Yes but railway engines are cheaper!' The oriental despots are not likely to take to heart this new lesson. They will continue to keep hundreds of nations in subjugation with their tanks, lies and falsifications. History will one day contrive a constellation so that the endless series of explosions will spark off a chain reaction. In the meantime they are keeping up the cruel game long after all faith is gone and the whistle has been blown.

Christmas 1970 ushered in with socialist gunfire directed against the workers, with tanks surging against infuriated crowds and God knows how many killed, arrested and jailed. What a shameful and stultifying preface to the feast of good cheer and goodwill!

With all best wishes and affectionate greetings
Yours

Paul

80

Usti nad Labem, Czechoslovakia
Sunday, 27 December 1970, ordinary working day
in CSSR.

My dear Leslie and Enid,

I am not a churchgoer but I like Christmas with all the good things it encompasses. Children of the age of David lack the capacity to think of absent objects and all the feeling of suspense children usually display several days before Christmas was ours. Our anticipation of David's enjoyment was heightened because Zdena managed

through her 'old school tie' connections to secure a
Japanese made 'SpacePacer' with a blinking light, 8
legs, an aerial for radar etc. from the Tuzex shop, thanks
to you! As expected David was screaming with joy and
surprise and soon started to crawl on the floor, sounding
like a motorcycle starting off. There was something
for everyone under the Christmas tree and we were
all very pleased and happy. My wife was overcome by
weariness from all the strenuous exercise and I myself by
postprandial sleepiness. I retired with a bottle of Cognac I
received from a nurse for help with her English lessons.
I listened to carols and the music of Bach and Vivaldi
when I suddenly heard in the midnight news the sentences
of the Leningrad trial.[187] I can imagine how the KGB
placed a rat into the group of Jewish would-be-hijackers
to spy on them and to falter their attempt to escape from
the paradise of workers, ethnic and religious minorities.
It has been done in this way by the Ochrana under the
Tsars,[188] by the NKDV under Beria[189] and why should the
present 'Marxist-Leninist' rulers do away with the police
practices which served so well in the past to keep a rotten
empire together? The rat-spy is the chief witness at the
trial and his voice counts for ten of the accused. They are
obviously out to fix once for all those who are longing to
escape and who are pleading in petitions and letters to
be allowed to leave. So the present rulers of Russia are

---

[187] A group of 'Refuseniks', all but two Jewish and unable to emigrate,
plotted to buy all the seats on a small plane and fly it to Sweden.
Charged with high treason, two were condemned to death (later
reduced to a 15-year jail sentence) and ten others received sentences
ranging from 8 to 15 years.

[188] Secret police force in the late nineteenth century.

[189] Lavrentiy Pavlovich Beria (1899–1953), head of the Soviet security
and secret police apparatus (NKVD) under Stalin during the Second
World War and Deputy Premier 1946–53.

dotting their 'i's to leave no one in doubt that little
has changed since the time of the pogroms, since the
doctors' trial[190] and since the Slansky trial in 1953
in this country in which eleven Jewish communists
were sentenced to death and subsequently executed.[191]
Angela Davis expecting trial, the Basques sentences at
Burgos,[192] Brezhnev felt he must have a hand in this
game too. The civil courage of the 14 Soviet scientists
pleading and protesting with Nixon for Angela Davis
is admirable in its hypocrisy and in the violation of
Lenin's principle to fight first and foremost against
one's own tyranny.[193] Thus Moscow has spoiled and
poisoned my Christmas and that of millions of Jews
and Christians alike. Will they pay any attention at the
Kremlin to what the CP of Gr. Britain and 'Humanité'
had to say to this trial? Justice of the King's Bench and
Chancellor of Exeter Cathedral Henry Bracton started
from the premise that all men by nature are born free
when he wrote the tremendous folios 'De Legibus

[190] In 1952–3 a group of prominent Moscow doctors, mostly Jews,
were accused of conspiring to assassinate Soviet leaders – which led to
the dismissal and arrest of many doctors, officials and others.

[191] Rudolf Slansky (1901–52), the General Secretary of the Czech
Communist Party. On 20 November 1952 he was put on trial with 13
other leading party members, 11 of them Jews, accused of 'Trotskyite–
Titoist–Zionist activities in the service of American imperialism'.
Slansky and ten others were hanged in Prague on 3 December 1952.

[192] On 28 December six Basque separatists were condemned to
death and ten others given substantial prison sentences by a military
tribunal. Two days later General Franco commuted the death
sentences to 30 years' imprisonment.

[193] On 25 December 14 distinguished Russian scientists cabled
President Nixon with an appeal to safeguard the life of Angela Davis.
The US government responded by extending an invitation to them to
attend the trial. See above p.288.

Angliae' in the 13th century.[194] The distinction between
attempted and actual murder is a commonplace in the
West and numerous detective stories are expounding
this principle. The legal system of Russia is based on
preventive terror and it punishes thought or the capacity
[for] or the mere willing of an act of resistance. On the
evidence of the KGB I could be sentenced to death or to
several years hard labour, which amounts to the same at
my age, for having willed to blow up the Kremlin sky-high
at 1a.m.while listening to the news in my room at Usti.
Any judge or jury in the West will never be satisfied with
evidence adduced in this way by an agent of the KGB.
The judge would remain adamant that intentions are at
best conjecturable as the would-be-hijackers could have
been overcome by a wave of fear or a qualm of pity with
the pilot or the passengers at the last moment, preventing
them from the execution of their intention. 'Let them
have the benefit of doubt,' he would say. The multifarious
intervention of free will is, of course unknown to Soviet
judges and they are not concerned with such legal
quibbles and niceties. You can once more see what we
know for certain now, that a vast gulf separates Western
thought from the philosophies of Eastern empires and
that the spirit of Marxism, a typical product of Western
thought will forever escape them!

We send you our heartiest and most cordial greetings –
to you and your whole family

Paul & family

---

[194] Henry de Bracton, (c.1201–c.1268). His unfinished *De Legibus et
Consuetudinibus Angliae* (*On the Laws and Customs of England*), now
available in four volumes, hardly sustains Paul's assertion.

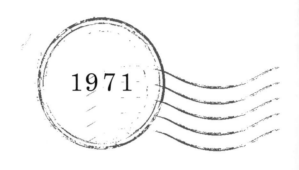

1971

JANUARY TO DECEMBER

The correspondence between the two men was interrupted by the British postal workers' strike which lasted from 20 January to 8 March. Shortly afterwards Leslie and Enid moved to York, where they stayed with their daughter until their new home became available. For the time being Leslie was reduced to writing to Paul by hand, so there are no copies of his letters before 17 June. Reunited with his typewriter, it became obvious that Leslie was having ever greater difficulty in hitting the correct keys. Unable to see clearly what he had written, his train of thought was more frequently broken. The flow of letters continued, however, and with them his graphic accounts of the crises that afflicted the capitalist world and its perfidious leaders. Paul reminded Leslie that it was the much maligned BBC that kept him informed, pointing up the virtues of Western democracies as 'decent societies' where mechanisms existed for the righting of wrongs. His response to Leslie's concern about the deteriorating situation in Ireland was a vivid picture of what a truly Stalinist Ireland might look like, a mirror image of his homeland.

Paul's personal circumstances were deeply distressing: incessant overtime, less pay and a constant battle with failing equipment. If his working conditions were not enough to induce bouts of depression, staff meetings were now used to remind everyone that all personal contacts with foreigners, at home or abroad, should be reported to higher authority. On 21 August, in growing despair over the remorseless measures to limit intellectual freedom and discourse, Paul wrote a sustained critique of Leslie's 'faith that there is a way through history to human fulfilment, a necessity demanding a new way of living without exploitation'. In spite of the good intentions of Lenin 'we are suffering in serfdom and captivity ... That's why I am smoking 30–40 cigarettes. I am often thinking of suicide by taking an overdose. There is so little joy and beauty in our life – I mean the life of an aged intellectual – that death appears as a welcome redemption from eternal want, monotony, drudgery, boredom and sordidness.' Leslie replied with an exposition of the role of necessity in historical change and a passionate appeal: 'I am literally appalled that you should be so at the mercy of your enemies that you have allowed them to condition you to regard self-destruction as your only possible relief. No Stalinist and no bloody minded capitalist would cause me to think that the best thing to do with my life is exactly what they want me to do. Throw your drugs away. Rejoice in your poverty in your freedom of mind and throw your cigarettes away too.'

A bare month later, on 6 October, Leslie, increasingly frustrated by his failing eyesight, went to Shrewsbury in pursuit of specialist treatment. The effort was all too much, and at the end of October he suffered a third heart attack from which he never recovered, dying in hospital on 9 December. Paul's last three letters to Leslie went unanswered. In the final one, arriving too late to be read, he was more positive than for many weeks, celebrating the recognition at long last given to anaesthetics in his country as 'a professional task for a medical specialist'. Leslie would have been delighted for him.

81

Usti nad Labem, Czechoslovakia
8th January 1971.

Dear Leslie and Enid,

Many, many thanks for all the good things you are
unremittingly sending us! I stepped into the new year
with one of my worst depressions. With the windows
thickly clouded with ice I imagined myself to be a
prisoner in a Siberian labour camp, notwithstanding
the pleasant warmth from the central heating and the
numerous cups of tea. Hardly did I start my labour
routine in the operating theatre at the gynaecological
department when a parcel with four most attractive
books was handed over to me by a close friend of Ian
and myself, containing a letter from Maurice. I regret
very much that I could not meet the messenger. If
it is the same Maurice against whom I have slashed
out in anger some time ago, all ought to be forgotten
and forgiven. How small is the world! Maurice was
apparently visiting the family of doctor K. whom I
know since being at Usti. Faced with a mystery, how
persons of very differing outlook can find each other,
I am suspecting a woman behind the scene. I know,
of course, that the daughter of Doctor K. from Usti
is studying English at Cambridge University and
perhaps her heart and that of Maurice are beating
unisono. Having received these precious books I don't
think it would be becoming to pry further into the
circumstances which brought Maurice and the family
of doctor K. together.

I hope you have received by now my letter informing
you that Zdena did very well at the foreign currency

shop just one day before the feast. Our common larder is well supplied with instant coffee and Typhoo tea, not mentioning the space-pacer which is surprisingly still functioning and pacing lustily the surface of our earthly home. Zdena has still a lot of token coupons left, awaiting a more favourable season to spend them. So you need not worry about having made a mistake! I am extremely pleased with the two penguins by George Orwell which I have nearly read through with the greatest enjoyment. As I received from my Black Panther friend from Los Angeles 'The autobiography of Malcolm X' I am also very glad that I am in possession of the continuation of the story in the form of 'Soul on Ice' and Bobby Seales' book.[195] Isn't it a testimony of utter depravity that Soviet authors are busy with issuing books in this country, attempting to show that our dear little counter-revolution – small, indeed, when compared with the Polish events – has been the work of plotting Czechoslovak Zionists instead of translating and making available books such as Eldridge Cleaver's? With all the interesting books on my shelves, I have to sit and sweat 'tears and blood' making out an annual report and a detailed plan for requirements of the anaesthesiology service for the period 1971–1975, being the 5th five year plan. With all the rapid progress in bio-electronic technology the bureaucrats demand a detailed and specific list of all the devices required at all the departments of this region. It seems to me

---

[195] Malcolm X (1925–65), born Malcolm Little, an American Muslim minister and human rights leader, assassinated in 1965 by three members of Nation Islam. The author of *Soul on Ice* (1968) was Eldridge Cleaver, later a leader of the Black Panther Party; Bobby Seale (1936–) was a co-founder of the Black Panther Party in 1966. His book *Seize the Time: The Story of the Black Panther Party and Huey P. Newton* was published in 1970.

ludicrous that the instructions demand that I should make use of the 'modern theory of systems' in working out my plan and report while at the same time we are hourly reminded by the radio to save electric energy! Cardinal Vishinsky and church leaders in Poland are pleading that the workers should not be forced to labour beyond their endurance. We too had actually only one free holiday, and had to make up the rest by doing Sunday shifts. You may also note that the postage rates to Western countries have been raised by more than 200 percent. Rates to socialist countries remained the same. The deadline for my report is January 15th and I shall be very glad to have done with this bloody poetry. Just before Christmas I had two copies of the New Statesman, Galbraith's article was fine! That's it for tonight!

With affectionate greetings and best wishes
Yours

Paul

82

Usti nad Labem, Czechoslovakia
24 March 1971.

My dear Enid and Leslie,

I received your air-letter with great relief. It was, as expected, the first mail from Britain since the strike. During the past 3 months I hardly received any mail, and I shall remember the strike and Mr. Jackson and his union of postal workers as one of the dullest and

darkest periods I can remember.[196] Trying to retrace
what happened locally and to me is a dire business as
each day and each week resembled exactly the preceding
and following one. In essence we are witnessing the
disentombment of the fifties. The new year began with a
campaign of intimidation to communicate with friends
and relatives abroad. Every foreigner is to be regarded
as an enemy and as a potential spy. At staff meetings we
were reminded that the old ukases passed under the reign
of Dzugashvilli[197] are still in force. About each personal
contact with a foreigner, say a tourist or a businessman
from the West, a written report ought to be submitted to
the authorities regarding the subjects of conversations
held with the stranger. Although probably not a single
doctor will be permitted to visit a Western country
this summer, the ukase to report to the authorities all
contacts made and the theme of talks on returning
from a visit to a capitalistic state was well rubbed in by
stressing that even conversations with close relatives
ought to be reported: 'You must be always on guard not
to give away UNWITTINGLY any vital state or industrial
secrets. Insofar as no one of you present at this meeting
can possibly understand the nature of state secrets and
where they are hidden – you have to give a full account
of what was said between you and the arch enemies of
socialism': in this vein the spokesman continued! This
is the APARTHEID of our histrionic internationalists!
I have not touched any local newspapers and I did not
receive any from abroad. Neither do I keep homing
pigeons! And yet I know that the crocuses and daffodils
are out in England and out of work are the workers of

---

[196] The British postal workers' strike lasted from 20 January to
5 March.

[197] Stalin's birth name.

Ford at Dagenham[198] and altogether three quarters of a million unemployed. I also know that Henry Ford II is tired of investing his money into a country with such an unruly working class as the British one. We also learned about the collapse of Rolls Royce and its resurrection by the government of Mr. Heath.[199] You should be just to the BBC as we had these news mostly through them, and the reporters of the BBC spoke truly of a rout, a debacle and a defeat while the other radio stations merely and reverentially quoted Mr. Nixon vows: 'Neither defeat nor a success' in Laos. I could go on and on giving you news about Britain and the world at large, only to point out that the written word, particularly the printed words, are no longer the sole vehicle for global communication. However, there are men on this side of the curtain who still believe they can successfully isolate us from the other half of the globe by suppressing, confiscating and censoring the printed word. In February I received a parcel from New York. In it I found an official notice informing me that 8 copies of Time magazine were confiscated because, according to the press laws of the Czechoslovak Socialist Republic, Time is excluded from postal conveyance. Only the medical journals were left in the parcel. Oddly enough the same men are paying lip service to progress, to the advancement of science and technology, to international cooperation and so on. While satellites are orbiting the Earth and men are prancing about on the moon these men cling to the obsolete notion that they can through oppressive measures prevent an intelligent nation from partaking in the common cultural milieu of mankind. A lot of money is being spent in this

[198] Ford workers had been on strike since 1 February.

[199] Following its financial collapse, Rolls Royce was nationalised on 13 February 1971.

part of the world to close frontiers and to seal off the minds of the citizens from ideas not in accord with centralized power. You will therefore be not surprised to hear that from the beginning of the new year I am not receiving the bonus for extra work which amounts to a third of my salary. The lists of anaesthetics are getting longer and longer and we all are working over-time every day – for less pay. We had to cut down our 'Luxury consumption' and have to go slowly with coffee and tea and chocolates and sweets for David. To the gratification of my Mrs. I also had to reduce wasting money on cigarettes. The picture of the fifties is thus completed. Doctors and sisters and nurses and orderlies will get less pay than any industrial worker. While all our hospitals are lying in shambles the word comes down to the masses that 'the health of the people is our greatest good'. We have certainly made good progress during the past 3 months towards the unchanging fixity of a society resembling those of ancient Egypt, Persia or generally of the East. A small privileged elite sits on the top of the social pyramid and regulates the personal culture and lifestyle of each individual. Dissent is being dealt with economically, albeit otherwise too! We have previously agreed upon who are the powerful vested interests in perpetuating the status quo. Take for example our chief-manager of the hospital. For years I have never seen him inspecting the operating theatres, although his quarters are just across the street. The other day some press photographers came along to take some pictures. To my great surprise the chief-manager appeared in a white coat and putting himself into the picture next to the anaesthetic machine! He has not the faintest idea about what doctors are doing at the various departments and he surely does not know that the anaesthetists are doing daily overtime – unlike the surgeons – because there are so few of them. He can never be reached at his office as he is always attending very important committee meetings (Guess with whom!), but is very demanding in having the greatest possible input of paper-information. He would not feel secure in his office unless surrounded with barricades of annual reports, analyses of the situation, proposals for complex socialist rationalization and five-year-plans. If he would have made an appearance at today's neurosurgical session he could have witnessed the strange spectacle of a nurse holding all the time the operating table. Whenever the surgeon put his burr on the skull of the patient the operating table turned and moved. It could not be arrested and there were only females about and no technicians who could perhaps (hopefully!) mend the defect. Every application of an anaesthetic turns into a fight with technical snags, and still we are doing far more health delivery a day than they are doing in the USA.

I have read 'Soul on Ice' and have lent it to my Ghanese friend. The book of Bobby Seale is interesting for studying the language of cursing (actually 'cussing'). I am discharging my emotions whenever I have to deal with our big bugs by mumbling quietly all the four letter words, and m...erf... and bullshit and dudes and thugs and pigs etc. quietly to myself without being understood. I am most grateful to Mr. Dodson for Thompson's book 'The Making of the English working class', which I am delighted to read just now. It is very interesting indeed, and well written.

I hope you will soon get over your attack of jaundice and that Enid will put on some weight. I am looking forward to hear from you soon again. Remember me to your sons and in-laws, please!

With most affectionate greetings
Yours

Paul

83

Usti nad Labem, Czechoslovakia
12th April 1971.

My dear Leslie and Enid,

Thank you for Enid's letter from York which is the
second letter I received after the strike from you. I
wonder whether my page long letter being the reply to
your first letter addressed to Shoreham was forwarded
to your new address at York. I am very glad, indeed, to
hear that Leslie is feeling better. I am certain that the
cheerful surroundings will speed his recovery. It is very
reassuring to be in touch again with you and that letters
are being delivered again. Maurice will be very, very
welcome. I could introduce him to Nana and Bert, my
cousins at Prague. Nana is English born and working as
a statistician at quality control and Bert is a designer at
Prague's biggest machine-building plant. I hope Maurice
is aware that no entry visas to visitors of this country are
being issued until the end of May, after the congress of
the CP of C-S is over. The sealing off of the frontier may
be a bad omen. The holding of the party congress does
not appear to be a sound reason for closing the frontier
unless the authorities have become a victim of their
own propaganda. The spy-scare is on again. Maurice
may be a safer conveyance for any printed material you
wish to send me than the post. I told you in my last
letter that all foreign magazines and perhaps even books
are being excluded from postal conveyance for fear of
'ideological diversion'. A more likely explanation for
closing the frontier and for intensifying the persecution
of the printed word is that they are up to round up
some dissenters and shut them up in internment camps.

Eyewitnesses have to be excluded from this sort of ceremony. You may have heard how the scandalous way of wiping out Czech culture has affected the international theatre festival at London. An avant-garde and distinguished ensemble, The Theatre Behind the Gate, under the leadership of O Krejca, was booked to perform Chekhov's 'The Three Sisters' for 5 consequent nights at a London theatre. All tickets were sold when the Czech ministry of 'culture' broke the contract and cancelled the tour at the last minute. Krejca lost his party membership during the purge, and consequently also his post as manager of the Theatre Behind the Gate. For obvious reasons he could not be permitted to go abroad. London theatre goers and the whole artistic world can once more see how Socialist governments are interpreting the liberty of artistic creation, the freedom of travel, the protection of individual liberty and all that a free-born Englishman and the French Revolution upheld as inalienable rights of all men. We have made a tremendous leap 20 years back and a number of 'resurrection men' are busily digging the earth for graves and removing corpses and all the paraphernalia buried with them. All this activity is triumphantly declared as a great victory for the working class. I am a damned fool for not grasping this kind of dialectics. At the hospital we have been hard pressed to display more socialist initiative, and at the same time the boss has stopped the payment of all premiums for overtime work which are due to us. As a result we are spending this year's Easter holiday – 3 days off work – in stringent austerity. All the customary amenities are missing. However, David found a few coloured eggs and some cheap sweets lying about in the green grass, being told that the Easter rabbit had laid them there for him. Most doctors have been affected by the curtailment of our dues and we all are discontented and miserable. To be at the mercy of a cold-blooded bureaucrat without being able to take our case to a union or to something like the BMA gets one down. In E.P. Thompson's book I found the remark that combining political oppression with economic exploitation makes an intolerable form of relationship. If the delivery of health care to the people of this country is rewarded by making doctors live at subsistence level, this is exploitation. If I would really stop working next year, I would receive a pension of 1400 to 1600 Czech crowns, which is far below the subsistence level for two persons! In a socialist country a doctor has to work and work until an infarct or a cerebral haemorrhage or a bullet into the head or an overdose of sleeping pills will finish his absurd life. While contemplating these wonderful prospects I am digging in the garden and I am thinking of Hilary and the thousands of doctors who chose to escape from this irrational system. They can at least earn and save enough money to make provisions for their old age. In my self-congratulatory old age I must admit that I should have been much happier on the whole had I stayed on in Gr. Britain in 1945.

I am sending my love to Linda, David and Hilary and to their respective fiancés or wives.

With affectionate greetings to you all
Yours

Paul

84

Usti nad Labem, Czechoslovakia
6 May 1971.

Dear Leslie and Enid,

We received your letter from Leeds of April 19th and the
enclosed note. One person's gain is another's loss, and
we feel it is now our turn to give and divest ourselves
from the role of taking and only taking. But at the
moment we cannot think of anything we could transmit
to you in return for your great kindness. Once more you
enabled us to fit some material comfort to the lovely
and fresh looking natural environment. The Elbe valley
is rather pretty in spring, but looks sad to anyone who
has a lot of bills coming in and nothing but debts and
less and less money to settle them. Your parole: Hold
on and have faith in ourselves! has at least the ring of
originality, and I gladly subscribe to it. The centre of the
town looks like Shanghai or Canton during the cultural
revolution. Posters, placards, slogans everywhere!
People, however, are looking as apathetic as ever. They
make cynical remarks about so much money being
wasted on red cloth, paper and manpower, for useless
propaganda. As expected participation in the 1 May
procession was far greater than last year. Lots of people
were under cross-pressure and reduced the strains by
adopting a position of conformity. Having worked for
two weekends preceding the 1 May I preferred to have
a long stay in bed. Then Zdena, David and I walked
down into town to survey the scene. I do my best to
enrich the sensory experience of David for developing
his intelligence. As the majority of the paraders were
cheerfully shouting schoolchildren in white shirts with

red neck ties, David enjoyed the parade very much. And
the rest of the grown up paraders were anything but
genuinely enthusiastic. Some carried quite ostensibly
the stigma of fear and apathy on their faces. As far as
the hospital is concerned the whole establishment was
present, but the hard working underdogs, representing
only themselves, were conspicuous through their
absence. I know of several doctors in responsible
positions who left the town under some pretext in order
to evade a dilemma. There was also more sick-leave
then usually before a holiday. If I would be questioned
regarding my non-participation, I have my reply ready.
I could point to my regular attendance in the 1 May
demonstrations in the years 1930–1939 at Prague,
when participation required civil courage not fear.
On the whole, I think, Husak can justly claim to have
achieved some measure of consolidation. As everywhere
else, our silent majority regards restriction of liberty
a small price for security of employment and a certain
degree of prosperity. On the other hand, the core of
the intelligentsia is sticking to the belief that without
a free flow of information, without freedom of travel,
without participation in decision-making and without
cultural freedom, we all are doomed to be sterile for
ever. Sustaining this orientation towards cultural and
political liberty is playing a game that we cannot hope
to win under present conditions. Individuals who hold
these views cannot hope to move up on the social ladder
and are in grave danger to be thrown out of their jobs.
There are, of course, many who follow rather self-
interest and seek the approval of the agencies in power.
East Pakistan–Bangladesh has been very much on my
mind. I am pleased to hear that The Morning Star
was the only newspaper of the CP in the West to call
attention to the fact that there is a CP in East Pakistan

which identifies herself with the struggle for liberation. All the great powers, China, USSR, the Western powers keep silent and do nothing against the mass-killings of the East Bengalis by the Pakistan Army.[200] I am fed up with all power politics, ping-pong or otherwise.

Sending weeklies at present would be a sheer waste of money. They don't let pass anything but personal letters which are the only means connecting us (apart from the radio) with the outside world. Please do write soon again and keep the fires burning!

With affection
Yours cordially

Paul

85

Usti nad Labem, Czechoslovakia
20 May 1971.

My dear Leslie and Enid,

Thank you for your letter of May 2nd and for giving me your correct provisional address before moving into your own bungalow. Today I received a letter with cuttings from the Sunday Times. The letter was opened. Considering all your ailments, I think, you have done remarkably well with your typewriter. Typographical

---

[200] The Bangladesh Liberation War for independence from Pakistan lasted from 25 March until 16 December 1971, during which time the Pakistani army systematically slaughtered hundreds of thousands of civilians.

errors don't matter as long as the message with its personal flavour is getting through alright.

As a distant onlooker I see the events in Northern Ireland for which you expressed concern in a different light. The Ulster Catholics are certainly a socially and economically depressed minority, fighting against the privileged positions of old power groups. The use of extreme tactics was probably necessary to make the British government aware of this pocket of poverty, underemployment and iniquity. I wholeheartedly agree with you that the claim of any group or denominational party to dominance is intolerable in a modern society. So far we both agree. But I have no reason to believe that the government, its executive and legislative bodies will remain unresponsive to the shock they have received from the bitter clashes in Northern Ireland. Strikes, demonstrations, the banding together of individuals to make protests and influence voting, that's the way how reforms have always been brought about in Gr. Britain. Only through a perennial struggle has the English working class achieved and maintained its high living standard and the welfare state. My witness is no one less than E.P. Thomson. But there is more to it. The conflicts and demands inspire and provoke tensions from which new scientific discoveries, technological breakthroughs and innovations in social practice inevitably result. Democracy has learned to live and to recognize as legitimate conflicts of diverse groups and interests. It can easily be proved that 50–90% of all really revolutionary discoveries in science and particularly in the social sciences during the last 20 years originated in the democratic societies of Europe, the English-speaking overseas countries and in the USA. I am mostly worrying about the possibility that the unnamed peoples which have sacrificed their liberties to the juggernaut of the totalitarian state will get stuck. Their leaders will say: 'Look at the peace and calm in our lands and compare the stability of our social and political conditions with the turmoil and upheavals over there. Look how everyone is enthusiastically working, fulfilling the plan and cooperating with us in building socialism. Our GNP is steadily increasing 4–8% annually.[201] In the fifties our scientists have broken the monopoly of nuclear arms the capitalists were holding. They have also mastered rocketry and made remarkable contributions to the exploration of outer space. We have created an alliance of peace and order, the military potential of which is second only to that of the USA. In view of all these stupendous achievements the question of the sacrifices necessary, of the quality of life of our people does not warrant the slightest consideration. They are gammas anyhow, according to the classification put forward in Huxley's 'Brave New World'.' You must not attribute this point of view to me and I would take strong exceptions to the last two sentences. Only a very naive social scientist will be deceived by this image. The conflicts and the hoarded grievances are carefully hidden and not allowed to come into the open arena. Being an unfortunate intellectual all depends for me on the quality of social and cultural life. I have more than once indicated to you that I am living in seclusion and working in the narrow space allotted to me. I am a displaced person in my own country and society which is the typical lot of any disposable intellectual who is not a contender for becoming a member of the ruling elite. I have in mind a statement made recently by Doctor Husak

---

[201] Figures born out by later studies, for example Antonin Rusek, 'Industrial Growth in Czechoslovakia 1971–85', *Journal of Comparative Economics*, vol.13, no.2 (June 1989).

at the party congress in Slovakia. He simply said that an intellectual elite orientated towards the West will not be tolerated. This is not just hot air, believe me. The remark of the first secretary presupposes a dividing line, a kind of impenetrable curtain between the culture of East and West. For any truly educated and informed person there is only one common culture, a global or world culture or at least a common European culture. Neither Bohemia, nor Moravia, nor Slovakia has ever been a Duchy of the Czar of Russia. Furthermore it is inconceivable to me how you can reorientate by administrative means, with a stroke of the pen, a cultural tradition, made by history and many centuries. But Czechoslovakia is for you a faraway country and the Irish seem to be close to your heart. I shall attempt to bring home to you the implications of the indicated cultural policy [f]or the cultural front line in Irish terms. Let us assume, for the sake of argument, that Eire has become a totalitarian state with one party rule several years ago. Following the coup, the sacking of politicians and officials, the abolition of habeas corpus and independent judiciary, the declaration of a stage of emergency and imposition of strict censorship were widely publicized in British newspapers then. But interest in Irish affairs waned after the coast guards, customs and other measures, such as the expulsion of the last correspondent of British papers, effectively isolated Ireland from the outside world. Just when the regime widened its originally very slim power base, Eire became a forgotten country. All British news media were also far too busy with the negations for entry into the EEC to devote any attention to Ireland. At that year the government of Eire decrees that the national addiction of the Irish to rebellion and to drink has to cease, once for ever. Idioms such as 'sneaking a drink' and 'watering the whiskey' are to be banned from the

Irish tongue. Some ambiguity, however, remained. Far from denying the medicinal use of whiskey, the new government made it known that it has nothing against the use of a drop of alcohol now and then when you are in low spirits or have a bad cold. But in any of these cases whiskey must not be used as a tonic. Everyone has got to use vodka instead, children included. Then a further decree concerning literature was issued. The works of George Bernard Shaw, James Joyce, Samuel Beckett and the plays of William Shakespeare and the American playwright Eugene O'Neill are to be withdrawn from all public, circulating and lending libraries and the afore mentioned plays must not be performed. Reason given by the Irish Ministry of Culture ran as follows: Shaw was a teetotaller and a Fabian, therefore anti-Irish. Joyce and Beckett betrayed Ireland for living a sinful life at Paris and slandering Eire and the Faith. The latter was not ashamed to receive the Nobel Prize from the Protestant and capitalist Royal Academy of Sweden. William Shakespeare is through his connections to the throne to be regarded as a British imperialist. He also was shamefully seduced by a woman in a cornfield near Stratford on Avon which is against the moral code of the Fenian hero Cuchulain.[202] As regards the plays of O'Neill, he is to be condemned as an American citizen and then for the fact that his daughter married the Jew Charlie Chaplin. The ukaz concerning the exchange of scientific information also deserves mentioning. All propensities of Irish scientists to exchange scientific information with their British and American confrères are to be discouraged, mutual correspondence and the exchange of preprints and reprints are frowned at, publications

---

[202] Cu Chulainn, an Irish mythological hero.

of Irish papers in foreign journals are prohibited and
no papers of Irishmen living abroad will henceforth be
published in Irish scientific journals. The receiving of
free gift parcels of books, drugs, instruments etc. are
to be enmeshed in a great deal of bureaucratic
entanglements. The government ordered a new alignment
for the scientific and cultural community by insisting and
ravishingly supporting the fraternal exchange of scientific
information with Greenland. Irish scientists and the
artists and their creations were badly missed at all
international scientific meetings, exhibitions, festivals
etc. For only a handful of intellectuals received exit visas
in return for cooperating with the cultural media and the
establishment. Modern typewriters, copying machines
and tape recorders, which in the rest of the world greatly
increased freedom of expression and swift and wide
dissemination of news, information, etc. were practically
unknown in Eire. Their use is strictly supervised and
illegal possession of these items is a capital offence in
Eire. Businessmen and the lucky tourists let into Ireland
are saying that the gay, fierce and gregarious Irish have
become lately taciturn, reserved, docile and compliant.
Many people are falling victims to prolonged depressions,
ending sometimes with suicides. However, the national
rite of a lonely and rapid gulp of whiskey is being carried
out secretly.

With affection to you all.
Yours

Paul

86

Woodthorpe, York, England
17 June 1971.

My Dear Paul,

My room in this house is much lighter than my last room.
The window stretches right across it and in the centre of the
window is a glass door which leads into a [fairly] neglected
garden. Getting into the house was nothing short of horrific.
The chaps willing and strong but not skilful arrived with all
the books in massive cardboard cases which they appeared
to relinquish with great gusto, rather to the detriment of the
books and my happily unspoken horror. Many of these are
still imprisoned in the boxes because we never really had
enough bookcases and because we left a good one behind
for the delectation of our usurpers.

   Although the house is built on the same lines as the last
one we have squashed our furniture not too reluctantly
in the available space. We have torn up lots of material,
press cuttings, pamphlets with wild abandon. Some of
these were intended for you and some for the basis of my
reflections on Communist government. Purblindness in
both cases prevents their being used. In consequence of
reflections on Reflections I had a wicked temperamental
morning – interruption – I had a wicked temperamental
morning made no better by [the] heaped up mess of papers
on my desk which I could [not] read. I am now recovering.
The sun shines through my [?] mists. The washing blows
gently on the line next door. And my wife is forgiving.

   Since the receipt of your re-posted letter we have had
nothing from you.[203] Possibly the sanctity of your post

---

[203] The previous letters from Paul eventually caught up with the Parkers.

is rather worse than ours can be if the authorities have one in their little spyglass. The threat of the industrial relations bill had the heat first taken out of it by the resolute attitude of our two big unions and then by the slow workings of the TUC, presided over by a loudly but slow speaking Victor Grayson [junior ?][204] and then by a prolonged, rather useless discussion in the House of Lords – interruption – I have no idea where I was.

The Lords attended when they felt in need of an untaxed five pounds sterling a day to discuss word by word amendments on 162 clauses, some of which are already beyond the wit of the smoothest politicians. The BILL, harbinger of a verbal revolution, will rear up its weary fire-breathing head later in the year, when the Tories will push it through despite opposition from all the organised workers. The Parliamentary Labour Party can blame itself for this, for their efforts, which failed only by a hair's breadth, smoothed the way for this more massive and more vicious piece of legislation.

Not content with this furore the Tories then went in for a confidence trick over the Common Market.[205] The hand was dealt first of all by Rippon who utterly bled red sweat from his last appearance in the subterranean vaults of Europe[206] and we were invited by the Govt, certain Labour Leaders and the BBC to [thank] Rippon who

---

[204] The President of the TUC was actually Victor Feather. Victor Grayson (1881–?) was a socialist politician and MP from 1907 to 1910. He disappeared in 1920.

[205] Formal negotiations about British entry into the Common Market had begun on 21 July 1970.

[206] Geoffrey Frederick Rippon (1924–97), Chancellor of the Duchy of Lancaster with responsibility for negotiating Britain's entry in to the Common Marker. This is probably a reference to the negotiations earlier in the year, which were deadlocked for weeks over the level of Britain's budgetary contribution to the Common Market.

had fought the good fight on behalf of the ill managed
super educated by the kindnesses of the RATEPAYER
– a beneficent god always called in when there is a line
to spare – and wicked, no very wicked workers who
certainly should not get better paid. Well then, after it
transpired that the country was by no means elated by
this vision, in the arena next door to the Quai d'Orsay the
greatest gladiator of them all moved without hesitation,
without thought even and oh so silently into the arena
– for this bull no French Matador had terrors. Anyway
courage was not needed, only stage management.
After two [days] of aperitifs the two heroes came from
their troglytic [sic] conference and produced [some]
of the most resounding verbalisms of all times.[207] No
declaimer in the Greek amphitheatres, no battler in the
Mediaeval schools, not even President Johnson defending
the [surfeit] of blood letting in Vietnam, not even the
most abject demoralised maker of balloons would have
brought forth such wind.

During this mess or message the resounding point of
discussion arose like Aphrodite from a tremulous sea –
whether English or FRENCH could be the true official
primary language of the EEC.[208] Oh Milton, would we
had thy trumpet at this hour – remembering of course
that Milton wrote his more stinging pamphlets in Latin.
Now the troubadour Rippon is sure to clarion forth
his well contrived part of the senselessness conspiracy
while the BBC and some newspapers, deadly afraid

---

[207] A reference to the two-day meeting between the British Prime
Minister Edward Heath and President Georges Pompidou, held at
Paris on 20 and 21 May 1970.

[208] President Pompidou gave voice to French anxieties that English
might become the official language of the Common Market, but it
was hardly the major issue.

of a referendum, are explaining to those who listen to
Woman's Hour and/or pop music or Twenty Questions
that we have no right to a referendum because we do
not know all the facts. Or better, or worse still, we must
remember that we gave this Govt. a mandate to go into
the Common Market OR we must remember that we
being poor ignorant dolly a or poor ignorant housewives
or poor ignorant somebody else having given possibly
with God's help these beautiful, wise all knowledgeable
men and a few not so wise but more beautiful women our
faith, our hope, our eternal forbearance signified by their
arrival in the House of Commons because these gents
and ladies KNOW ALL THE FACTS and will judge to the
greater glory of the Queen, Her Realm and such misfits
as she has the misfortune to rule over.

In all this parliamentary blarney, argy-bargy
and whatnot sounds of sedition ascend from empty
stomachs from more and more unemployed; from
the osculated wisdom over Rolls Royce[209] to whether
Mr Harold Wilson is busier making money over his
memoirs – was it one or two hundred thousand pounds
sterling???, from the browbeating of Lord Melchett[210]
and the probable dislocation of the steel industry and
doom and despondency from the official liquidator of
the Clyde shipping who are found to be 32 million in
debt[211] whilst it is almost certain that the Govt knew at

---

[209] See p.318 and note 199.

[210] Julian Edward Alfred Mond, 3rd Baron Melchett (1925–73),
Chairman of the British Steel Corporation. *The Times* reported on
3 April 1971 that some Labour MPs believed that the government
was deliberately creating difficulties, particularly over steel prices,
in order to force Melchett to resign. Its desire to hive off some parts
of the steel industry could not be doubted.

[211] The provisional liquidator was appointed on 15 June after the
government declined to provide a £6 million loan.

least two months ago; another conspiracy. Meanwhile in order to make sure that we shall have nothing to grumble about should we go into the Common Market prices, particularly of food, is [are] rising like the fires of Dresden and [...] engulfing us all. Nearly 10 per cent in the last month or so.[212] We are now told that there is a world shortage of butter – primarily due to the magnificent planning of world capitalism, though butter in this country is still per long ton £340 while in France £730. But then we are told radishes and onions are cheaper in Europe. We shall finish up eating soya beans, radiograms, pamphlets on the Good European Life and cook with highly vitaminised transistors. We shall sing to each other in our gutters as we did in the 30s, and when we demonstrate we shall be charged down by mounted police, unless London is then full of tourists casting leering eyes on our daughters in Piccadilly. Did I dot two 'i's in that?

Glorious things are promised for the Tories as they lose by-election after by-election, but when in their last year they try to reduce unemployment, ask the food sellers to abate their greed, when Mr Heath is seen dining out or in with Mr Wilson, when the lynx is seen lying down with the jaguar, when mothers bring their babies to be blessed by Messrs David Ryland,[213] the anaemic chancellor,[214] old death's head the foreign

---

[212] At the end of July the government reported that the cost of imported butter, which provided the overwhelming bulk of the country's needs, had gone up by 30–40 per cent over the previous five months.

[213] This is an obscure reference, possibly to a regional official of the General and Municipal Workers Union, and presumably not to a young Liverpool footballer who played only once for them.

[214] Anthony Barber (1920–2005), appointed Chancellor of the Exchequer in July 1970.

secretary,[215] then will the light of humanity shine from the embracing warmth of the greatest pack of liars, cheats and [parasites] that we have ever seen in our mother of Parliaments. Nor do I exclude the liars of old time – Lloyd George, Ramsay MacDonald, Baldwin, Chamberlain and that great shining light of fattened dishonesty Harold Wilson himself.

Anyway other reapers tell us there are too many people in the world so why worry about a few spoiled brats, a few old dears who can't get dentures or specs or many hundreds of thousands who can't get houses.

I am at least well fed. But daily I find this not only surprising but a [...] But rejoice that my irresponsible fingers have not defeated me totally.

We love all beauteous things like Czechs, Latvians, You, Your wife, Your children and grander children, your pussycat and your howling frog. We remember with pride that you keep all sorts alive.

Leslie

87

Woodthorpe, York, England
24 June 1971.

My dear Paul,

There's something in the state of this typewriter which is not wholly due to the typist. Things are sticky, or at least they stick and do not respond to kindly if blundering treatment.

[215] Sir Alex Douglas-Home (1903–95), Prime Minister in 1963–4, appointed Foreign Secretary in June 1970.

I am now in my room with the carpet rather improperly laid and with one change of picture and a bright sunlighty [*sic*] colour on the walls which we found when we came. On my left are two windows about 3 feet square and in between a door which opens on to the garden, which to me is a confused green. Initially the similarity of this house to our last one made this one seem square because it is somewhat smaller and the built-in cupboard space is decidedly less here than in Shoreham. But we shall manage if we do not succumb to the extravagance that we have indulged in. We welcome the absence of traffic which in Shoreham was beginning to get tiresome.

Yesterday we had the pleasure of David's expertise which he rapidly developed after he married. Pictures went up like one o'clock and bathroom appurtenances sprang to the walls and remained as though they had been there all the time.

Did I tell you that my younger son Hilary has now finished his course successfully at Birmingham University? He was much more relieved than we were, for we felt that he had applied himself so well, without being brilliant, that the possibility of his failing was quite remote – although he did have to take another viva voce in obstetrics because after a long night on the wards he was rude to the examiner who called him to the exam before breakfast and who himself had had a very long night on the wards. However, on the second time Hilary said 'the bloke did everything to make it easy. So easy I began to wonder where the catch was'.

Hilary and his wife are in Gozo enjoying Mr Mintoff's[216] hospitality, where the beaches are crowded to the point

---

[216] Dominic 'Dom' Mintoff (1916–2012) became Prime Minister of Malta for the second time on 16 June 1971.

of intolerance and the sea is dead with debris. But they
are young.

Mr Rippon has now returned from a bout of
champagne in the pallid morning and the flush of near
victory and is at this moment being briefed by Mr Heath
as to how and how not he should answer questions in
Parliament. This country is now in the peculiar position
of watching the House of Commons make – oh where am
I ? – make up its silly mind on about as much information
as the general public has. Except of course the general
public has long since made up its mind that Common
Market is [a] common aversion. I myself find the situation
exceedingly [farcical] and much to my wife's alarm look at
the whole affair with its sheer dishonesty, its abrogation
of political power and its improbable benefit to any
nation in Europe as though I were sitting in the shade
on a cool chair somewhere in the rings of Saturn. Apart
from or rather part of this attitude is accompanied by
an intense curiosity as what will? would? happen when
we enter this cauldron of competition. Will the social
democrats continue to sell the people out as they have
done ever since the devil invented them? Will the VIPs
of Italy, France, England continue to stay apart divided
by the greater loyalty or criticism of the USSR? Will the
major capitalists like ICI, Krupps motor people, Unilever
take to swallowing up their counterparts or will they
concert an attack upon the workers? I haven't the slightest
doubt that unemployment will develop on the continent
sooner or later as [it] has done in the UK. Thousands of
white collar workers of medium grade will go the way the
computer etc dictates. Nor should I be surprised to see
a rota system of workers developing in the major works,
with say a man or woman working one week out of three
and being on the dole for two weeks. This will teach the
workers whether they can use their organised strength or

not. It is alas impossible to compare the development of the two UKs – one inside the EEC and the other always teetering on the brink of 'going in'.

Your pundits know what is right for you and also what is safe for them, while our tricksters what is good for money making and immediately beneficial for themselves. There is, thank Marx or God or ???, nothing safe for anyone in particular in capitalism – the only apparent safety is that of the large corporations which fed by human beings care not one jot for any of them – a curious phenomenon. The impersonless [*sic*] of this sort of dehumanised organisation is rather more dehumanised than perhaps – I say this with diffidence – a slave state and certainly more dehumanised than feudalism generally. Blood-letting too in these latter days is more murderous, more ferocious and more intensive than the blood-letting of times past. The Vietnam War or the desperate harm dome to Russia was for instance more deliberately organised from top to bottom than anything Genghis Khan or the Holy Roman Emperors did or could do. War now seems today as something bestially incestuous, for as the world becomes closer knit the concept of the family of man shows itself through the murk as something more than a possibility.

I wonder what human and humane possibilities there are in the European Common Market?

25 June 1971

I find myself isolated from humanity so I shall continue to talk to you, with apologies.

I am sitting by the open door; the birds are a twittering; the grass I can see is green and there is a darker smudge some way off against a fairly blue sky, and I know that [it] is the dubious tree.

As we lay in bed enjoying Chairman Mao's second best tea, albeit capitalised, I said apropos of the Common Market, I find myself in a dilemma so far as our leading politicians go. There is first the smug Wilson sitting on the fence, evaluating which way to jump solely in relation to his political future. There is Mr Heath waiting like a blancmange first for the profits to fall down from treacherous skies, the fascist and racist Enoch Powell against going in coupled with the nauseating smooth Callaghan[217] striving to attain eminence by not going in. But going in there is first the utterly loathsome overfed cunning Thompson [*sic*][218] in alliance with Roy Jenkyns [*sic*],[219] who seems the only one with logical and articulated reasons for going [in] and a man of some integrity, I think, and both of the Labour Party. So far as leaders are concerned, we have a sorry mess of small fry. The world generally speaking is run by a sorry mess of small fry, most of them rather poor in intellect, clever in gathering round themselves men more capable of maintaining their own positions than in enthusing others to build and rebuild. In this country to ignore the populace is to be wise and to rob the lower paid men and women is to be courageous or at least thrifty. Mr Heath, they say, or some say, will be renowned as the greatest premier of this century.

---

[217] Leonard James Callaghan (1912–2005), formerly Chancellor of the Exchequer and Home Secretary, subsequently Foreign Secretary and then Prime Minister.

[218] Almost certainly intended to refer to George Morgan Thomson MP (1921–2008), previously Chancellor of the Duchy of Lancaster and Secretary of State for Commonwealth affairs; subsequently a British Commissioner of the European Community.

[219] Roy Harris Jenkins (1920–2003), deputy leader of the Labour Party, previously Chancellor of the Exchequer, subsequently President of the European Commission.

We have none worth boasting, for Churchill was no statesman and certainly had no [words missing]

Despite the tragedies of assassinations the US has not covered itself in Presidential glory. Now that the New York Times has loudly published revelations of Johnson's miserable lying treachery,[220] in which all the presidents roundabout were implicated, Mr Nixon, that termite, might still prove worthy of commendation by some troglodyte of Latin America. As stars in a murky firmament we are left with Mao now fading[221] and Allende,[222] though Castro could possibly shine significantly. All the women Premiers, Indira,[223] Bandaranaike[224] and the warrior of Israel[225] who is ready to pierce any Hazael temple with a tent peg, fill rather more with stupefaction than with admiration. So much for Women's Liberation for which my wife, having had a life of the sort that has brought her success in work and home that could only be called almost perfect freedom, hankers after as though she

[220] Lyndon Baines Johnson, United States President 1963–9. On 13 June 1971 the *New York Times* began publishing top secret, sensitive details and documents from 47 volumes that comprised the history of the US decision-making process on Vietnam policy, better known as the Pentagon Papers.

[221] Then nearly 78 years old and in very poor health, Mao nonetheless continued in office until his death in September 1976.

[222] The government of Chile's President Salvador Allende (1908–73) was struggling to deal with the effects of terrorist attacks and its lack of a majority in the Chamber of Deputies; see *The Times*, 16 June 1971, p.6.

[223] Indira Priyadarshini Gandhi (1917–84), the first female Prime Minister of India. She was elected in 1966 and assassinated in 1984.

[224] Sirimavo Bandaranaike (1916–2000), the first female head of government in the modern world, was Prime Minister of Sri Lanka (formerly Ceylon) three times: 1960–65, 1970–7 and 1994–2000.

[225] Golda Meir (1898 –1978), Prime Minister of Israel 1969–74.

had been bereft of anything but the kitchen sink for
65 years.

I think I ought to go.

We send you all our love we hope you are all in good
health including the saxophone.

88

Usti Nad Labem, Czechoslovakia
30 June 1971.

My dear Leslie and Enid,

Either a spell of very cool and rainy weather or the
sticky political climate set off a depression with me.
For some time l felt I ought to write to you, but a
uniformly leaden sky does not make a big story. The
numbing routine with no end in sight, the inability
to escape from it and change anything makes one
reticent. Any complaint, even in terms of bitter irony,
appears to be an excess of language when matched
with the ghastly reality. We have again reached
the stage when people are turning their heads and
darting fearful glances about before engaging in
a conversation in a low voice. I am shivering at
the dreading [sic] thought that some stupid nosy-
poker might mistake your typing errors for a secret
encoded message. The first of the 3 letters I received
successively consisted of one blank sheet and one and
a half pages with strings of letters which defeated all
my combinatorial and permuting decoding strategy.
The cumulation of typing errors was clearly due to
your unsettled condition before moving into your new

bungalow. From the words standing out in clarity I guessed that you were writing about our domestic affairs, and even without making any mistakes you always are hitting illegal keys. I find myself frequently pacing up and down cursing myself for having become too vulnerable by possession of a memory and of some ingrained habits of thought. Why can't I stop to be very conscious all the time of the selfsame situation which has not changed for 23 years and can't be altered within the span of my life? 'I told you so,' says Eric Blair to me. 'War is Peace, freedom is slavery, ignorance is strength and you got to love BB.' Why didn't George receive the Nobel Prize posthumously for the best forecast ever made becoming true 13 years before the set term? Secrecy, hate and the fostering of paranoid fears of espionage in order to prevent people from communicating with the outside world, these are the unwritten constitutional principles which are determining policy new development in this country and is the deliberate creation of a highly privileged cast, supporting the local power structure. In the past the 'Faithful' have always received fringe benefits while the principle 'of equal pay for equal work' was officially upheld. In accordance with the big model, members of all professions are openly and without blushing bought off for serving our establishment. The last two letters were nearly perfect. I am over-joyous that Hilary has qualified and congratulate you for having bred two doctors. I congratulate them for being free to pursue their calling and beliefs without restrictions by the state or the police, for being able to protest and enjoy a high living standard without compromising their integrity. The news about the terrible tragedy of the three cosmonauts has come in this morning. The Russians in their space ventures are

winning all battles but the last, counterpointing the
British who always lose all battles but the last.
With affectionate greetings from my wife, David and
the young ones to you all

Yours

Paul

89

Usti nad Labem, Czechoslovakia
4 July 1971.

My dear Leslie and Enid,

Returning from a short visit to Prague I find another
letter from you. It was rather mean to reply with just
a short note 4 days ago, but I simply could not make it
[more] with one of my doctors on vacation and feeling
very tired. Attending the 4th European congress of
neurosurgery lifted up my spirits and gave me some
stuff to report to you. I went there chiefly to meet
Mr. Sweet, now chief of the neurosurgical service at
the Massachusets General Hospital at Boston, under
whom I worked at Barnsley Hall Emergency Hospital
at Bromsgrove while he served as neurosurgeon to
the Queen Elizabeth at Birmingham during the war. I
recognized him at once when he entered the lounge of
the hotel where I was waiting, after 25 years. He [had]
hardly changed at all. Although grey, he is slim and as
full of vibrant energy, while I am white and rather broad
round at the girth. The first night we attended a beer
party at an old brewery. Our American friends enjoyed

the food, but not the cabaret. The band was a half-way house between hot jazz and our traditional brass band. The glamour girls appeared in all sorts of gaudy dresses instead of divesting themselves of them. Although they came at times perilously near to the stage of nudity, they managed to save their dignity. None of my friends is of the type and years to visit strip bars, but they are surely used to more sophisticated shows and musicals. That's why we left early. Next day I myself was shown the historical highlights of the castle by my guest when Mr. Sweet decided to ascend to the castle after having a nap in the lecture room. The ladies were on a congress excursion. At dinner on the steamboat I was introduced to the leaders of neurosurgery of all European countries and met Mr. Faulconer from Guys Hospital, who later gave one of the best lectures on the surgical treatment of temporal lobe epilepsy. Having given up slicing up the brain in the early sixties I was nevertheless very much impressed. But what made me regret forsaking neurosurgery for the first time was a film taken through the operating microscope by the Swiss neurosurgeon Yasargil. This was at least to me the climax of the congress. The farewell party on Friday was too expensive for me to attend and I did not want Dr. Sweet to pay the ticket for me. Then Doctor Sweet read his second paper on treating violent behaviour in conjunction with temporal lobe epilepsy using radio frequency lesions and in-lying electrodes. The advanced technique and the meticulous precision of the procedure, used by Mr. Sweet, was awe-inspiring, and the neurologist from Usti sitting next to me said – we shall do that in 16 years hence. I experienced only one paper read by a stout Russian lady. Although she spoke a little English she failed to understand and answer the questions shot at her paper, even with the aid of an interpreter. Loaded

with bottles of Scotch whisky, American cigarettes and
a beautiful model car with remote control for David
I said 'Good-bye' to my American friends after a rich
dinner at the Yalta hotel where they were staying and
which I had never entered before. I left Professor Sweet
at our state medical library, reading up some papers in
preparation of further lectures to be given at Bratislava
and Budapest. I was very pleased and a bit proud that
the library service furnished him with nearly all the
journals he requested. At Prague I saw for the first time
girls wearing hot pants, but because of the construction
works for our underground Metro, being in the third
year, walking through Prague is hell. I still had enough
money left to buy a good supply of Pickwiks Tea bags
and an automatic rifle, made by the Yugoslavian plastic
industry, for David. This beastly weapon is rattling away
all the time since returning home and during writing
of this letter. Contrary to a set principle of mine and
feeling slightly euphoric from the numerous cups of
Pickwick tea I shall comment on some questions of the
HOMINTERN to which you and I belong. I really cannot
understand why the British public is kicking up such a
fuss about joining the EEC. I feel that a united Europe
is long overdue. President Truman[226] and his secretary
of State Dean Acheson wanted it in return for aid given
under the Marshall plan.[227] At that time Britain and
France were still dreaming their empire dreams. The
continuous squabbling and quibbling among Britain
and France over Germany was agonizing to any good
European living behind the iron curtain. After the

---

[226] Harry S. Truman (1884–1972), President of the USA 1945–53.

[227] The Marshall Plan, or the European Recovery Program, was an
American plan to help rebuild Western European economies after the
end of the Second World War.

rough awakening from their imperial dreaming states following the defeats of Dienbienphu,[228] Algiers,[229] Suez[230] and after Germany became under the treaty of Rome[231] the most prosperous country in Europe yet another dream remained to be shattered. That of De Gaulle.[232] The invasion of this country smashed his illusion that Eastern Europe could regain a measure of independence and France her traditional hegemony over Europe. If you follow the advice of Churchill and look at a large scale map of the globe, you will see that old Europe is but a tiny peninsula of the European–Asian continent. Whatever unites Europe pleases the Lord, and whoever aids in uniting these decent and civilized nations is doing the Lord's work. In his infinite mercy he is commissioning sometimes bloody fools, sometimes wise and honest men and we being ourselves men with but a limited understanding shall probably not always know the difference. I am not against His design of creating countervailing powers to destroy His and our enemies. Those who share the same values should stick together, but in the southernmost corner

---

[228] A reference to the battle of Dien Bien Phu (13 March to 7 May 1954) at which the Viet Minh defeated the French and forced their withdrawal from French Indochina.

[229] The Algerian War of Independence lasted from 1 November 1954 to 19 March 1962, and concluded with Algeria winning its independence from France.

[230] In late 1956 Israel, followed by Britain and France, invaded Egypt to remove Egyptian President Nasser and regain control of the Suez Canal, but were forced to withdraw (see p.373).

[231] The Treaty of Rome was an international agreement that led to the founding of the European Economic Community on 1 January 1958.

[232] Charles de Gaulle (1890–1970), leader of Free France (1940–4), head of the post-war provisional government and President of France 1958–69.

of our Empire [...] manoeuvres [are] going on to which the Yugoslavs are responding by holding their own manoeuvres.

The New York Times and The Washington Post stirred up a hornets nest, but the decisive aspect is that the Supreme Court put freedom of the press first and secretiveness after that.[233] There is no getting away from it: democratic societies are decent societies. The slashing out of the Nixon administration against the freedom of expression is incommensurable with the state of affairs in this part of the world. The recent congress of the Writers Union of the USSR denied creative artists to describe reality in images and visions which pleases them. If they want their work to be published they must conform to hero worship and extolling an idol which is mockery of the external reality. Compare this to the flourishing of pop art, underground literature and newspapers and films, made by dissidents in your part of the world. Artists who are forced to tell lies are driven to suicide – right from the beginning of that system which is always winter and never Christmas.

I am enclosing a snap of David and his friend Michal.

With affection and best wishes
Yours

Paul

---

[233] On 30 June 1971 the Supreme Court upheld the right of *The New York Times* to publish the Pentagon Papers without risk of government censorship or restraint. See note 220, p.342.

90

Woodthorpe, York, England
5 July 1971.

My dear Paul,

The days pass, including two gloriously sunny days
which might well constitute our summer. Though
their very appearance gives us cause for hope.

Meanwhile the world ticks over. Individuals
get along with their little personal affairs and the
great political guns thunder or even whine in the
stratosphere. We have Doctor Hilary Parker full of
beans and his wife Nurse Parker fairly happy to be
with us and very happy to be married to our often
ebullient male child. While Mr Wilson thunders in
treacherous tones that he will not split the Labour
Party – which rather means that he will be prepared to
rat on his long cherished hopes that we shall go into
the Common Market. Alongside him Mr Heath, our
most abhorred of premiers for many years, tells us that
HOPE and Economic Forgiveness (from on high?) is
also just around the corner.

In 1957 Mr Macmillan, better known as Mac
the Knife,[234] also told us that HOPE and Economic
Salvation was just around the corner. And so did Mr
Chamberlain[235] in the 30s and so did any other Premier

---

[234] Maurice Harold Macmillan, 1st Earl of Stockton (1894–1986),
Conservative Prime Minister 1957–63. On 3 July 1962 he dismissed
seven members of his Cabinet, a third of the total, an event described
by some as the Night of the Long Knives.

[235] Arthur Neville Chamberlain (1869–1940), Conservative Prime
Minister 1937–40.

for centuries back, until Henry VII[236] who did not
care a damn and in fact damned those who did care.
Meanwhile our unemployed do not diminish in number
though [they] do in wellbeing and our food prices go
on going up.

Amidst all our smallnesses we learn the tragedy of
the New Mariners, and Russian though they be they
also belong to humanity and humanity is sorry.[237]
And the Capitalists are re-discovering China and the
journalists are wagging on through their columns
about Mao not being so inane as he was or so old or
so decrepit or so this or so that. And the Cultural Revn
did not do the harm that 'was once supposed'.[238] And
how shall we get rid of Taiwan? they ask, and with
the hope of money and consequent [travesty] in their
hearts they will declare, but of course Taiwan belongs
to the Mainland.

And great revelations about Kennedy and Johnson
appear in the New York Times and all the Press Lords
rejoice that the Freedom of the Press is once more
assured though they have long since forgotten any
quest tor truth that such freedom demands.

And that great heavyweight boxer and talker
of all time has been declared immune from rapid
transference to the GI fighting forces and death in
Vietnam because the Supreme Court has declared

---

[236] Leslie almost certainly intended to refer to Henry VIII, not
Henry VII.

[237] This is a reference to the three Russian cosmonauts who lost their
lives on 30 June 1971 when their spacecraft de-pressurised during
re-entry into the Earth's atmosphere.

[238] The Cultural Revolution, or the Great Proletarian Cultural
Revolution, instigated by Mao Tse-Tung in 1966 to preserve communist
ideology by purging remnants of capitalist and traditional elements
from Chinese society, and to re-impose Maoist thought.

that he is against the war by reason of his sublime conscience and most peculiar religion.[239]

Somewhere also in the news are the many deaths and continuing murders of the East Pakistans and denials here and there while political dragons belch forth oracular flames that burn from India and West Pakistan.[240]

No wonder that the Prophets of Israel and Judah cried out 'How Long O Lord, How Long?'

The Day of Salvation is nigh perhaps but remains bafflingly unseen and undeclared.

Possibly Hope comes from the West Lord where the immortal Weevil and Termites bring down their flimsy structures on the heads of millions.

Tuesday 6 July

Your letter came this morning complaining that one of my letters was indecipherable. I am very sorry, and were you not so apprehensive and also that one of my best letters has been despatched via the waste paper basket I should laugh. While it is true that I can no longer see to read even the large letters on my typewriter keys my typing, though far from laudable, is not quite as bad as the messes you received. I think you must have been sent not some secret code but various papers on which I had been practising, or maybe I had over-typed some page by mistake. My sight is circumscribed, I cannot for instance see the

---

[239] On 28 June 1971 the Supreme Court upheld Muhammed Ali's appeal against his conviction in 1967 for refusing to report for induction into the US army during the Vietnam War. The Court found that the government had failed to explain why Ali's application to be a conscientious objector had been denied.

[240] See note 200, p.326.

bottom of the garden which I understand is about thirty yards away. On Friday of this week I am going to see an osteopath who has recently been successful with a case similar to mine. I shall see whether he has more to say than the orthodox man in Brighton. I hope you will not be too ashamed at my venture into heresy. There is a great deal too much of orthodoxy about these days.

Miss Bernadette Devlin[241] is going to have an illegitimate baby in November and we hope this adds to the Republicans and revolutionaries in Northern Ireland. My daughter Linda is also going to have a baby in November and she has left her husband for a young gentleman who is a little keener on her. It has been sad but we are getting over it. We think she will be alright and her husband though lonely is somewhat relieved. He comes to see us from time to time.

I can only say that we are deeply aware of your country's difficulties. Information is to be had from a number of co-sources. We think of you day by day and we shall continue to write too, though our letters from time to time look rather like crossword puzzles in a pre-Mycenaean dialect.

Both of us send you our love.

---

[241] See pp.198–9 and 209, and note 60, p.132.

91

Woodthorpe, York, England
21ˢᵗ July 1971.

My dear Paul,

I really must get Enid to reread your last letters to me.
When a fairly long time elapses between your letters
I become edgy and wonder whether you have been
smoking too much or working too hard or that you are
on a mind-consuming holiday on Lake Ladoga or the
Caspian or complaining to the government about the
shortage of nitroglycerine or whatever you prescribe
for your heretical patients. But when they do come we
can find little time to reread them, though we do in the
end. We respect your quotation from J. Donne Esquire
of blessed memory. Some time ago we acquired for no
particular reason a new book on J. D. and the extract
you presented me with was the first that Enid read. I
do not think that the Common Market can bring either
unity or peace and still less to the people any easement
of the grinding poverty of some. We have a division of
sorts in the family. Enid is against 'going in' and I am
just curious and therefore against the Party line, which
David disapproves of but not too much. I must say
that Mr Heath has done nobody much good and is now
economically or fiscally back-pedalling on his first efforts.
Mr Wilson, on the other hand, is waiting to see how the
cat jumps, but which cat and whose we cannot tell. He is
a slimy reptile. But they are all s.–rs. The whole bunch of
them from Helsinki to Washington via anywhere.
    'The death of any man diminishes me' hit us
appropriately hard. For we just lost a friend of forty
years. When I was a priest of the C of E I persuaded

354

him to become a lay worker in that institution. He was massively apostolic and utterly devoted, not caring for financial enhancement or worldly success. Though he was sad when 1 resigned my Orders he and his wife remained my closest friends and those of Enid when the time came. He had an excellent brain and wonderful memory and had he been born in present circumstances, when education is easy to acquire for those who are able, he would have become a scholar of considerable renown or a missionary of greater renown. His loss has certainly diminished us and it will be a diminution that will never be enlarged. We had seen him a week ago and though he was feeling and looking very weak we sat in his garden, made all the more verdant by an unavoidable neglect, and we chattered and back chattered and indeed had a wonderful time. We had not met for a long time and the renewal of a friendship that needed no renewal was sweet. Then last Monday we buried him. He lies half shaded, half in the sunshine looking over one of the loveliest valleys in the whole of Derbyshire. I wonder whether his imperturbable faith in a future life is to be fulfilled?

I went to see an osteopath of great renown about my eyes. He thought 1 had not got a stretched retina as the gent in Brighton said but a detached retina with a small fracture. He advised me to go back to the orthodox man and ask whether the right end of a laser bean would afford me any improvement. This I am going to do on August 6th when 1 trust a miracle will be achieved that will enable me to write without confusing you further with spellings that are certainly not in the dictionary.

All in all and very expensively we have been spending hours in trains, some of which were rackety and noisy and very jarring to any membranes that might be inclined to shake themselves free from their moorings.

I send you my undistinguished affection – provided I can spell the damn word – and will later drink your health in your favourite foreign concoction. Enid will try the wine of Hermes.

Leslie

PS (handwritten) I can now at least give my address without misspelling it.[242]

92

Woodthorpe, York, England
30 July 1971, 8 pm.

Mr dear Paul

By now you will have received our postcard of the minster which is the cathedral church of the Archbishop of York. While my sister and her husband were here (they went back today) we actually girded our loins and went there to sing psalms and spiritual songs and to meditate on a sermon on St James, whose day it was. The singing was fluty by the boys and growly by the bass and not too determined by the tenors. The altos were conspicuous by their absence. At the end I felt glad we were proceeding to home and a drop of Scotch and indeed a rather more uplifting experience.

In England we are still suffering the pangs of an unrejoicing Tory party who continue their emasculation

---

[242] A reference to the acquisition of an address stamp.

of various enterprises that were already badly managed and costing the country much money. There was hell to play in the Commons over the threat to the workers in the Upper Clyde Shipbuilding area.[243] There was some little hell over the Steel Corporation. There was the initial hell of Rolls Royce, the Great Joy of engineering creativeness. And there was hell over the Industrial Relations Act.[244] And hell still going on over the Common Market.

A tin of coloured salmon is now ten shillings and a half, a leg of lamb over one pound sterling. That word is = pound sterling. Oh, that my fingers are not bananas.

Mr Heath is brutal and Mr Wilson is slimy and things that he should have done instead of harrying the workers are coming home to roost and his hide is as that of an ancient pachyderm.

Despite this we enjoy the golden weather and sometimes sit out on the lawn where we are bitten all over our tender bottoms by minute mosquitoes and other things of prey.

My sister had a good time though she ruined it by having a penchant for not eating at the most extraordinary times. She is however a well preserved woman of 74 plus and was determined to make me a martyr to my own multitudinous ailments, which left me without any enjoyment as I see myself not as a martyr but as a hero valiantly winning over shameful foes.

---

[243] On 29 July the government made it clear in Parliament that the decision to liquidate Upper Clyde Shipyards and restructure them was irreversible. The next day – the day this letter was written – the workers of the Clyde began their famous work in.

[244] The Industrial Relations Act was approved by Parliament on 21 March 1971 despite the opposition of the TUC and affiliated unions. It was awaiting Royal Assent.

Did I tell you that I have now a book-talking machine as dished out to the blind and the half blind? I am at moment reading 'The Golden Ass of Apuleius',[245] the second vol. of a nicely scholarly and thoughtful book on St Augustine of Hippo[246] and a series of documents on King Lear. This trio is somewhat exhausting some days and I look forward to Enid reading a novel 'to send you off to sleep with'. I cannot, however, get a taped recording of the text of Lear. It is splendid to read how splendid Shakespeare is, but much more satisfying to read the actual text.

Saturday morning:

The talking apparatus has broken down. So much for ancient learning on modern technology. And just when I was to be enlightened at the development of St Augustine's considered thoughts on predestination.

I shall go out this afternoon and consider the traders and shopkeepers. And I hope I come back with a few thoughts which I might entertain, which possibly might entertain you or the men on the moon or those who ply their advertisements in little ships.

Sunday:

Waking at 6, I prevail upon myself to stay in bed until 10.30, bath listening blithely to bits of the Holy Scriptures read by Lord Eccles,[247] shave and descend to find this still in the typewriter. Friends never leave you,

---

[245] Apuleius, or Lucius Apuleius Madaurensis (*c*.124–*c*.170) was a writer. His most famous work is the *Metamorphoses*, otherwise known as *The Golden Ass*. The only Latin novel that has survived in its entirety, it relates the ludicrous adventures of one Lucius, who experiments with magic and is accidentally turned into a donkey.

[246] Saint Augustine (354–430), early Christian theologian and philosopher best known for his *City of God*.

[247] David McAdam Eccles, 1st Viscount Eccles (1904–99), Paymaster General and Minister for the Arts.

do they? The lady next door's bed sheets hang limply on the line.

Much later:

To face the truth Paul I shall never get any further. I wanted to discuss the position of our own beloved Northern Ireland wherein the Irish Republican Army are still blowing up all and sundry but with little loss of life in order to ruin the Stormont Government and 'come face to face with Imperialist Government itself'. I do not know whether the blowing up tactics will achieve this. But I am now quite sure that under the Stormont Govt N.I. is getting nowhere fast. No houses are being built, nor factories, and no jobs are being created. It is I think wrong to think that this fracas is merely a row between an oppressive section of N.I. and the depressed and oppressed section which really are still part of the dispossessed and dating back to old Will [Oliver] Cromwell. While the partition of Ireland continues to exist there can scarcely be any general comfort and prosperity for those living in the Irish Republic. I fancy that Mr Lynch the Irish premier is rather bowing and scraping to the British Govt and is only prevented in making more treacherous moves by the strong anti-British feeling in the Irish Republic. The British secretary is probably on the point of ordering Internment Camps and internment therein without trial for all those suspected of IRA sympathies, let alone activities.[248] When will governments learn that internment may kill some people but can never kill their cause – though of course they can delay the resuscitation [of] that cause. The internment camps of Hitler helped to kill both Hitler and Fascism and the

---

[248] Internment without trial was introduced in Northern Ireland on 9 August and over 300 republicans were arrested and interned in Long Kesh prison. Some royalists were later interned.

internment camps of N.I. will help to kill the colonial
policy of Britannia, for they only serve to enrich the
experiences and bolster the faith of the persecuted. The
only possible way of getting rid of the opposition is
Genghis Khan's – murder the lot of them. It is however,
and we may be thankful, almost impossible to murder a
whole nation. While for instance the East Pakistans and
Southern Ireland exist, opposition to the tyrant will exist
also and in these days will eventually be successful. The
path of Democracy that is mockocracy [*sic*] is hard, but
leads to success when a whole people is involved.

I leave you with affection and to your great relief. We
send our love to the Two Ladies, the Larger other Gent
and the Younger Gent and trust that harmony reigns.

Leslie

93

Usti nad Labem, Czechoslovakia
1st August 1971.

My dear Leslie and Enid,

Many thanks for your gracious letter in red. I
congratulate you on your clairvoyance. I am, indeed,
sick from smoking too much. The papyromania
[*sic*] of our health administratology [*sic*], their
incessant pressure to make us do paperwork when
the thermometer was at 30 degrees C in the shade,
their perverse tendency to replace performance and
decisions by paper-images made me crack up about
a fortnight ago when I intended to reply to your nice
letter. After a night of excessive smoking, drinking a

lot of coffee and strong tea, attempting to deliver a
document on the 'modernisation of hospital care and
assuring the fulfilment of the 5 year plan' to an ad-
hoe committee, appointed by the board of directors,
I broke down physically with epigastric pains,
diarrhoea, a skin rash and insomnia from itching
and cramps in the bowels. During the hottest July
weather, while everyone was bathing in the water or
sun, I had to stay in bed for a few days. I was hardly
on the mend when I had to start working again as
one of my doctors went away for his vacations. The
operating theatres are like electric ovens. It fills me
with anger to see how so many people have to work in
the bloody heat because of the incurable incompetence
and inefficiency of our industry and management.
I showed your letter to Doctor Libicky, who is one
of our best ophthalmic surgeons. He is dealing with
about 40–50 retinal detachments annually, chiefly by
diathermy coagulations. He said that a laser beam is
the treatment of choice if there is a small crack in the
retina but not if there is a bulging detachment. Doctor
Libicky is beyond 70 now and received a reward for
uninterrupted distinguished work since 1945. He was
nevertheless refused permission to spend his holiday
in Yugoslavia because his grown-up children have left
this country in 1968 and are now residing abroad. I
have not the slightest desire to go to the Black or the
Caspian or to the Baltic Sea. I can breathe the same
air of scarcity, of queues and inefficient services, of
surveillance of everyone by thousands of policemen in
uniform and hordes of their non-uniformed informers
just as well at home without undergoing the travail and
expenses of travel. We are fenced in, but events radiate
instantaneously all over the world. I was interested to
hear that Mr. Fedosiejev, the electronic engineer who

defected from the USSR, was interviewed last week in
the Sunday Telegraph. He noted the low productivity of
Soviet industry and that the military aspects dominate
all scientific research. I would agree with him that
young scientists and the young generation as a whole
no longer believes in the ideals of communism. You in
England have now the opportunity to read the papers
of the Soviet doctor Medvedjiev.[249] He tells the story of
how irreparable losses and damage is done to Soviet
science by preventing Soviet doctors and scientist to
take part in international scientific meetings. Donne's
metaphor 'No man is an island entire of itself' can be
improved on by saying that no man is more than a few
hours journey from all other men. In the western world
millions of people choose to migrate from one country
to another each year, but in the 'most advanced' state,
which claims to be the embodiment of freedom of the
nations, no citizen of one particular state can go to
another without a special passport, issued after long
delays and troubles by the bureaucracy. Can there be
something more obsolete than internal passports in
the SU? Particulars about these internal passports
restricting the mobility of Soviet citizens, one can
learn from Solzhenitsyn's novel 'Cancer Ward' and
from quite recent news reports about prison sentences
imposed on a group of Georgian Jews who dared to
go demonstrating to the central Telegraph Office of
Leningrad without having proper internal passports!
These are the sordid marginalia written on the bragging
manifestos of fighting imperialism! If you ask me
whether there is any future [for] this sort of socialism,

---

[249] See p.406 and note 100, p.187.

I shall decisively say 'No'. All these states are passing through a series of ultimately self-defeating cycles, each perhaps more complex than the last, but heralding doom in the end. The simple reason is inadmissible interference with cultural evolution. If you prevent nations from learning, inventing, borrowing, storing and transmitting information no increased utilization of material energy can prevent decay. In societies in which cultural evolution is prevented, the most important resource of energy remains forever untapped, the creative potentials of homo sapiens. In one of your last letters you said yourself that to overcome difficulties you have to inspire people to reach out for the stars, to seek what seems beyond attainment. But we are doing only what we are told to do, not a bit more – and otherwise we are dozing away our days. The heat is closing in on me and my neck is getting very stiff. I badly need recharging of my batteries on the sunny beaches of the Mediterranean.

Cheers to you all!
Yours

Paul

94

Woodthorpe, York, England
9 August 1971.

My dear Paul

For four years I was taught Church History by a gent
of 60 summers named Father Herbert Kelly.[250] He
ranged over every conceivable area which legitimately
or illegitimately could be called history. He covered
so much ground that on looking back I wonder how
I managed to learn anything in particular. But l did
learn one or two things. First the ramifications of
History. Secondly that history is always on the move,
willy nilly, men and women. He was in fact a sort of
Hegelian, a sort of Platonist, a sceptic of moralists
and historians. His weakness was when he turned
up his eyes to heaven at some problem and said we
should know all about it in the good bye and by as we
were nice little boys. He was very antagonistic to me
when I regarded this view of men versus the Mysteries
of God with grave suspicion and often antagonism.
I maintained that men should strive to solve all
problems that could in large measure be delineated.

The problem that stuck in the minds of many
students was the problem of hurt and pain caused by
circumstances that no amount of original sin could

---

[250] Herbert Hamilton Kelly (1860–1950), Anglican priest, founding
father of the Society of the Sacred Mission (1892) and the associated
theological college which moved to Kelham in 1903. See Introduction,
p.25.

be called upon to excuse. The Old Man[251] agreed, but
seeing the enormous antagonism between the idea of
a beneficent Creator and pain and hurt he refused to
commit himself.

INTERRUPTION – where was I?

The Old Man could take up this obscurantist attitude
despite his efforts to convince us that Mens' Minds
always work to a Unity and All Life is One. Had he looked
a little closer into his constant pursuer St Augustine of
Hippo, he would have found that St A. believed that all
life is one and adjusted his idea of God and Man and
original sin.

How shocking my typing is this a.m.

All of which leaves me firmly in the belief that we
must work against those who fragment life for their own
conceits, personal aggrandisement or merely because
they have been taught to. Men will never get the best
out of Man until each Man is convinced that what he is
doing is the best for himself and the majority of others.
Then you may well call [it] homo sapiens. The human
race is still striving through the mud and slime of pre-
history. That pre-history weighs [men] down with its
constant lessons which they cannot learn and its brutal
inability to see en masse the way to human fulfilment.
In capitalism when they are not brutalising [the] many
they are tribalising the others. You may get gleanings
from the Telegraph about the lack of science in the
bragging [socialist] countries but if the Telegraph could
have its way it would lead us into the eternal come and
go, the un-merrygoround [sic] of constant frustration in

---

[251] Father Kelly, no longer the Director of the Society, was indeed
called 'the Old Man' by the students.

poverty, unemployment, means tests, slimy politics and the sensationalism of the gutter press. Wherever we are we have to be constantly on guard to keep intact the good and the vision and aspiration that are within us. I am not too good at this myself. I become irresponsible, nagging, stupid and moaning, to the detriment of one and all.

While we have to guard against the big' uns in every profession that wish to use [them] for their own ends we have the horrible business of guarding all and sundry against the myriads of little men who inhabit the dark interstices of soviet [society]. 1968 left these flunkies, these ignoble deserters from the cause of humanity, these liars and pirates of men and women, these adulterers of the truth, those weeviling [sic] conspirators to fester in the darknesses and come forth like a fearful flight of termites and locusts to destroy the new foundations. Maurice, not the one who visited Usti, has written to me. He says he thinks we have been guilty of petit bourgeois idealism or p.b. liberalism. What matter so long as you have a stone to hide in from where you cannot see the sun or any horizon? So long as you have a name for it. An enemy of the people, a revisionist, a slanderer of the State, a bourgeois this or a p.b. that? Any port where the head may be bowed and the eyes closed against realities may do in a storm. Or worse still, in an imagined storm. The important thing is not to think, is not to discuss, not to analyse.

A living machine is a dreadful invention. It has every cause to perpetuate itself. Its destruction, which must surely come, will come with much dislocation and pain. But that pain will never be so much deserved as the pain it has already created. Nevertheless, despite the extraordinary morasses that have been created, I firmly believe that the communist countries are not going through infinite circles of decreasing circles. I meant

to say – an almost infinite series of decreasing circles.
Although the absence of exploitation has produced an
infinity of stupidities that must cost lives and produce
infinite pain, the absence of exploitation is the first
necessary step to the eventual freedom of man that he
may move towards sapiens. That there will always be
struggle goes without any fear of contradiction and, alas
for those who wish to eliminate struggle, criticism [and]
analysis, in their own provinces. This is the great sin
– the attempt to limit men's minds. There is no chance
whatever of this is being done; partly because men
cannot [stop thinking] once they have been called upon
to use their minds in whatever lowly social capacity and
partly because of the necessities of the State itself. You
cannot go to the moon and remain ignorant of the rest or
the world. You cannot embark on a history of the world
without becoming aware of your own history. You cannot
demand to know how to make this and that or how
to live without blowing each other up without people
becoming curious, then desirous of building anew. Men
are not lost yet. The necessities of life will demand a new
way of living.

If the gents of the Labour Party and those of
Threadneedle Street and those of the Conservative
Association could take away any part of potential or
actual freedom that comes from the fundamental fact of
non-economic-exploitation, they would rejoice and be
exceeding glad for that is the lump that sticks in their
craws. They just cannot swallow it.

We are sorry that you have become a slave to smoking
under tension although I realise that your work is almost
never-ending. Enid says she is particularly sorry for
Bohumila. And I must say that her burden is doubly
heavy. I hope you have recovered and attained a serenity
that a monk of the purest heavenly aspirations might

envy. How she would like you to come over here for a few weeks. You could attack the permissiveness of our hospitals. You could listen to Bach in the Minister. You could drink a small amount of whisky because it is very dear here. You could assure me that you refuse to die of a lung cancer like my friend recently because I simply could not stand two friends dying of lung cancer now. You could dig in the garden, which could stand it. You could sit on our new piece of concrete while I hammered out the wrong ideas on the wrong keys. You could complain about the weather – too hot or too cold or too miserable – and you could tell my daughter not to drink alcoholic liquors because they are bad for the baby. You could mow the grass. And sleep. And sometimes eat. Perhaps it would be better if we came to see you?

We have now got most of our books housed. We need only six feet of additional spacing to enable us to get the remainder out of sight, even out of my sight.

I saw a new eye-man on the 6th. He was very charming and said HE thought I had a thin retina which had lacked proper blood for some time. He thought he could not do anything for me but said he would like to see me again in six months time. I immediately sent this news to my osteopath and I am waiting to see what he says. Thank you for mentioning this to your specialist whose name l cannot recall without calling in Enid from her work. The York man said that they were now not much in favour of the laser beam because it was 'too strong' and difficult to control. I think he said they preferred diathermy, but I am not sure.

My hiatus hernia is not now showing signs of violently objecting to food. I put this down to (a) change of water (b) change of linen (c) change of heart on the part of the hernia (dfgh) anything else. But generally speaking I can eat almost anything now including plum pie. But too

much whisky don't care for me. I really must go now.
I hope you get this.

My Russian transistor radio is rather poor. That don't
cheer me up.

Yours affectionately

95

Usti nad Labem, Czechoslovakia
10th August 1971.

My dear Leslie and Enid,

In my extreme solitude I am measuring the intensity of
friendliness by the number of letters I am receiving from
abroad. According [to] this scale you are my best friend
and quite low down is my brother and sister-in-law in
England. At the end of June I received a publication of
the University of Keele, informing me that Jitka Zalud,
their daughter, received the BA in chemistry with second
class honours. Not a line included. They have, however,
bought a new car and are proud as punch of it. Even
according [to] Czechoslovak standards it is by no means
a mark of distinction to have a car. It seems to me that
cars are easier to get than a real Gillette razor blade,
special air mail notepaper or an insecticide-spray against
mosquitoes which are at Usti just as bloodthirsty as they
are at York. There was perfect harmony at our home
before David left with his parents for 2 weeks holiday in
Moravia. David was having a grand time. He went to a
swimming pool in the mornings with his father and in
the afternoon he splashed about in his plastic basin in
the garden. Full of beans he was, running and rushing

about naked in the house and in the garden, getting suntanned. Now our house is quiet and desolate with only the grandparents in it, seeking protection from the heat. The latest news about David is that he is making progress in 'swimming'. As I am listening twice daily to the BBC, in Czech and in English, I am well informed about the first, second, third etc. circle of hell in the Commons, about the real inferno in Belfast and Londonderry, about the state of emergency and internment camps. The events of the Upper Clyde are also well known to me.[252] I also noted that the Soviet government has declared the British Navy attaché a persona non grata as he took advantage of the official permit, granted by the Soviet authorities, to exceed the 40 miles limit to which all foreign diplomats accredited to the Kremlin are subject. Another 'nice' incident took place at that capital city when several men began to smash up an American car, marked with the letters CD – corps diplomatique. The Comecon has just ended a conference at Bucharest, imitating the integration of European countries in the EEC which not only shows lack of imagination but also confirms, by the way, the convergence theory of Andrej Sacharov (sic!).[253] One cannot fail to note how the countries of the Warsaw Pact are enjoying to display their military might at the manoeuvres near the frontiers of Romania and Yugoslavia. The Americans have withdrawn some forces from S. Vietnam and are deeply worried about inflation, the balance of payments, the value of the dollar and the shame of their cities. I have not the slightest doubt that the majority of American taxpayers – and who is not a taxpayer? – are tired and fed up with the role of the US

[252] See note 243, p.357.

[253] See pp.245–6 and note 133.

as a superpower which implies, of course, policing Asia and Europe and keeping most expensive contingents of forces and troops there. While the US is paying Japan, Western Germany and the Benelux countries are doing very well under the atomic umbrella of the US. Any government which can be voted out of power is always more concerned with creating wealth and economic welfare. Any government which can be changed only through bloodshed is always giving the highest priority to building up its military might. This is borne out by numerous examples and is a quasi-law of common sense.

Well, if all goes well, I shall go to the cinema tonight and see an Italian film with all the monsters of charm they usually show. This will be the first visit to a cinema after 3 years while the TV is still permanently off. I traced my allergic ailments to be due to Doriden, a sleeping tablet I have been using for some time. Unfortunately I have to drug myself to get some sleep at night. I have been reading the life story of Hemingway and I see myself to be the Old Man who has to get his fish, only to be robbed of it by the sharks. As in that famous story there is, of course, the boy Manolo. For months I have received only medical journals and no other printed matter. But tourists are sometimes leaving a book behind which they have been reading during their voyage. The minute English-speaking community in this town is, of course, also helpful in fighting off boredom. Train and car crashes which are each year recurring during the summer are keeping us quite busy at the hospital. Your letters are, indeed, a tremendous source of entertainment for me. So please, keep on writing and winning over all your shameful foes!

Cordially Yours,

Paul

96

Woodthorpe, York, England
17th August 1971.

My dear Paul,

I rejoice in your letter. It came as bonus when my letter
box brought nothing else. But I do regret that you should
be so depressed. I do not know what sort of drug you
are patronising to get you off to sleep, but I do hope it is
not one of the barbiturates. These are much more gently
used in this country than they used to be. One doctor
on the radio even went so far as to conclude that they
failed to make people sleep but never failed to make them
depressed. Our doctors are much more inclined to use

Long interruption:

The sun shone and we had lettuce and mass-produced
anaemic ham and whisky and Liebfraumilch and more
sun with Maurice the Mathematician and not M. the
economist and here I am back at the grindstone to ask
you to stick to tranquillisers and get a holiday if you can
because it sounds as though you need both for about
a month. We long to see you although now we have no
sea to offer you. We do have tea and r blades and Rhine
wines and pop music from next door's when one of the
lovely Williams girls gets home and finds sunshine and a
place to lie on the lawn.

Last night we had a meeting of three intelligent
communists and we intend to discuss a lot of things
pertaining to a lot of things. Among them I wish to
answer the question regarding 1968, 'We do not know
much about what happened'. I am afraid I kept no diary

of the events because l was too much concerned about
the whole affair. If you are able to clarify some of the
protagonists' contentions I should, though the matter
might well be painful, be much obliged. Had not [my]
eyesight become withered I should long ago have a
long thesis on the causes and the effects. I believe with
Garaudy[254] that these things must be brought to the
light of day though they may bring light to the eyes of
our enemies. These at least do little better in way of lies
though their days of invasion and desertion petered out
at Suez and will peter out sooner or later in Vietnam.

My book talking machine persuaded itself to recount
Antony Nutting's book on Suez and his perfidious
friend Antony Eden. Eden took an almost pathological
dislike that amounted to an obsession of [with] Nasser
and determined to regain the Suez canal. The French
and the Israelites presented him with a plan by which
they would persuade the world that a fight between the
Egyptians and Israelites should be made the excuse
for invading E. in order ostensibly to separate the
combatants and thus secure both ends of the Canal. All
the peoples of these countries and the govt of USA were
kept in the dark. Lies innumerable were told. The most
disconcerting plans were concerted and failed miserably.
Everyone was annoyed including the French and partic.
the US. Nine airfields were destroyed together with all
the air force of Nasser and the British after having killed
1000 or more civilians were compelled by world opinion
to withdraw. There is one lesson here we cannot afford
to ignore – I do wish I could see the damned type – and
that lesson is that we all without any exception in any
country...

---

[254] See note 59, p.130.

M. the maths man has at last gone. Very nice chap who despairs of mankind making anything but an eternal mess of everything. Reads a fair amount, works quite hard at times, is always good company but proclaims this pessimism whenever there is nothing much to do.

I do not think that the convergence theory has anything to recommend it save the rather tenuous theory that technological gadgets are the prime moving force of any economy. A gent called Lyn White, I think that is how he spelled his name, propounded this theory in a review of the 9th C.[255] Charles Martel was king emperor and what not,[256] and White said that the that the principal cause of the development of the economy was the discovery of the stirrup. This enabled ironclad knights to stand in their stirrups and unhorse their less stabilised opponents. This ignores the prime necessity and determination of Martell and Co to expand their realm, the development of war tactics and the economy that made possible the improvements in weaponry. The dynamic of the whole development was the necessity of continuing in the face of opposition – competition they call it. This is not to contend that development of technology is not a factor in the development of an economy and the success of its proponents, but the prime cause of success lies deeper than the mere invention of gadgets be they stirrups, trip hammers or calculators. Technological developments could never by itself unite two economies so different in aim and fundamental ownership as that of the USSR and USA. Of course there is always the possibility that certain men of low mind might try to assert their personal

---

[255] This is a reference to Lynn White, *Medieval Technology and Social Change*, published in 1962.

[256] Charles Martel was the ruler of the Franks from 718 until his death in 741.

rule over certain sections of the socialist economy and thus produce or try to produce first a hybrid kind of capitalism and then a new kind. There is no sign as yet that the USA is moving in any way to the common ownership of the means of production and exchange save the very tenuous one that the Senate has agreed to 'save' an aeroplane frame company. In my own country the Tories and many Labour men are determined to undo the nationalisation of certain industries so that private ownership may flourish the better. It may be that common ownership in some socialist countries is attended with certain caste prejudices and an arrogant bureaucracy and a certain horrible manner of increasing private bank balances, but the whole world including the Tory world looks askance at this sort of corruption. If it were more than personal corruption of the lowest kind then we should have to tremble for the existence of what I call primitive communism. I have as you know no use for certain ways of government primarily because they often in certain sections bring the growth of socialism to a grinding indecision and sometimes a halt.

Whatever the shortcomings of the socialist countries you should be convinced by now that the ruthless treatment of Vietnam and the never-ending slights and insults that are indulged in by even our best newspapers and the highly respected BBC are not because the gents who run these establishments are themselves highly moral and therefore object to the immoralities of the Leadership, but because they cannot reconcile themselves to any economy that is not based on the private ownership of the means of production and exchange. They might and do fight like cats and dogs among themselves (as they are now doing over the dollar), but they will willingly always join together to turn to rend the dragon that is now something more than the ghost that Marx said in 1848 was haunting Europe. The USA has, apart from some of the old colonial countries the very worst poverty ever seen, yet they with loud morality spend 10,000,000,000 dollars every year blasting the people and the land of Vietnam with high explosives, bacteria and chemicals that will take a century to obliviate [*sic*]. We all know about the waste and silliness of the NKVD, but that is child's play to the CIA all over the world plus the FBI and several other specialised units in the USA.

Every excess of the French in Vietnam and in Algeria, and perhaps nothing was more bloody, hardly received a mention even in our newspapers which purport to report facts and worthwhile news. In a sense these people here rejoice in the indignities and superfluous legal monstrosities and the shooting of workers in Poland. But when we have something quite as bad as this in Northern Ireland they try to smooth it all out. Who except the knowledgeable few knew that for nearly 50 years in Northern Ireland there was the Special Powers Act by which anyone could be imprisoned without trial 'on suspicion'?[257] Very few knew that. Thousands of comparatively innocent people had previously been interned in NI before they began to discuss the ethics of the present interment. Here we have an utterly immoveable government setting itself up as prosecutor, judge, jury often giving a blind eye to an indictment that is nothing less than a lie. A government that has connived for fifty years to maintain its ascendency by bribing its own quite respectable working class by dishing out to them jobs and houses to the detriment of the thousands

---

[257] The Civil Authorities (Special Powers) Act (Northern Ireland) 1922, passed by the Parliament of Northern Ireland, was repealed in 1973 on the imposition of direct rule.

of colonialised RCs. Criticism of one section of the
world's govt must not allow us to blind ourselves to
the monstrosities of another section. Up to the time of
asking 16 million pounds sterling has been paid out
in compensation for damage wrought in the present
uprising. There would have been no uprising had those
16 million been spent on houses and factories. Before
this affair is over 100 million pounds sterling will not
cover the cost, and all the money in Threadneedle Street
will not suffice to heal the wounds of the deprived.

I am not very much surprised that even your brother –
and I have a very high regard for your integrity – should
be corrupted by the dross of the motorcar and the gadget
owning society. They pay their willing servants and
morality, except that which you hang on [to] for dear
life, [goes] easily out of the door. A bit in the bank, a
high mortgage, living among 'nice people', never thinking
beyond what the Daily Mirror or the Daily Express,
each [with] 7 million readers, tell them and hoping the
sherry won't run out and the weekend will be fine, 20
deaths a day on the road and heaven knows how many
in hospital and a nice wife in bed or some other's wife in
a plushier bed and the bloody awful rat race at the office
and a thrombosis which allows another man to step into
your shoes. In the middle incomes there are a million
corrupted by this and they call it life. We spend almost
as much on betting as we do on education and nearly
as much on alcohol, and all the time the great colossi of
industry bite and scramble and claw each other to bits
and revel in cannibalism that is taken for granted as an
expression of industry which is unavoidable. If you wish
your brother to regain his morality then let him take
part in a social struggle and risk his precious neck and
lovely income. But no immigrant in any of the European
countries dares to do this save a few thousand coloured

and black immigrants and Irish, and they are of the working class. Once you get the Hollywood treatment then you are ready to turn out the Hollywood muck not merely in pictures, bombs, stunted children, lousy houses but ready to acquiesce in every rotten development and furthermore defend it with the trite phrases of the Sunday papers and the most cynical dailies printed anywhere in the world. Fleet Street is filled with liars and those who spew the filth from their bellies as they tuck up their pay packets and hurry off to the radical and 'underground' periodicals in order to tell the truth for once in a while as a sop to their miserable consciences.

For the Lord and the people's sake, do not despair. We have new worlds to conquer before we die. Life is comical; life is bloody; life is lovely; life is all.

Love

Leslie

97

Usti nad Labem, Czechoslovakia
21st August 1971.

My dear Leslie and Enid,

For months I have been longing that the postwoman will bring me a parcel with the books my friends abroad have promised to send me. But all I received last week were 4 copies of medical journals. I know that at least one book, a free copy of **DAVIES: SOCIAL MOBILITY AND POLITICAL CHANGE** was already sent off in May by J. P. Murphy, MacMillan Services Ltd, Brunel Rd.,

Basingstoke, Hampshire, England. It ought to be in my
hands by now unless the censor is reading it in order
to judge whether it is the right stuff for me or a kind
of ideological diversion. It would be very interesting to
know whether this – my – copy was duly returned to
the above mentioned booksellers or otherwise disposed
of. Far from being satisfied with all the marvels of
modern medicine, I turned to reread your last letter
of August 9th. It starts off with a discourse on history
and religion, with Father Kelly in short. My attitude to
religion is somewhat similar to yours. I simply cannot
accept that there is a supernatural power which knows
better than we know what is really good for us and to
which I could ascribe my personal responsibility for
all the adversity which has spoiled my life so far. But I
like, admire and esteem people with faith and I would
never dream of persuading anyone to cancel such a
rare gift as religious faith and thus perhaps inducing
him to worship men or the status quo instead of God.
Asking myself why I feel attracted to your letters and
through them to you both, I have to conclude that there
is a good deal of religious faith blended with what you
call communist ideology which makes you both dear
to me. From where stems e.g. the faith that there is a
way through history to human fulfilment, a necessity
demanding a new way of living without exploitation?
While I share with you both that men ought to aspire
to create better conditions of life and to use all the
resources of reason and moral dedication, I never
could see that there are iron laws of history which
allow forecasting that the desirable state of society
or mankind must necessarily become a reality. It is
our duty or obligation to work for a just, democratic
and egalitarian society, but to prove it necessary,
independent of our efforts, is to me to prove too

much. There is nowhere an inevitableness of the end of capitalism, of the arrival or the doom of communist societies, in short of the course of history. Inevitable course can never be proved nor refuted, and therefore the belief in historical necessity is very similar to the religious belief that the universe is from the beginning guided by some immanent purpose. It is very edifying to believe historical necessity is on our side, but all we can say with Marx and Engels [is] 'We make our own history'. Our discussion surges along like between deaf people. All these states are passing through a series of ultimately self-defeating cycles, each perhaps more complex than the last, but heralding doom in the end.

You are realizing that we are far from this happy state of affairs, but you still maintain that through a change in property relations the SU and the other socialist states have gained a momentous leverage point which puts them in a moral rank order highly above all western industrial countries. To think so is a very big error and contrary to all known facts. Between 1945 and 1960 the former colonial powers of Europe have given independence to almost a fourth of the human race. How many nations and nationalities are subjugated and exploited by the Russian oligarchy you must ask chairman Mao. Why are they exploited and what are my reasons for such an heretical view? The millions of workers, collective farmers and other people – all property of the state – have not the slightest say how the GNP is to be divided. How much should be invested, how much freed for consumption and how much should go for defence. Not even the members of the CP or the members of the Central Committee have any say in this matter. These vital decisions are made by a small body of elder statesmen, militaries [*sic*] and experts in the Kremlin. All delegates and representatives are just permitted to rubber stamp, approve and applaud these decisions. Now it is obviously true that through fixing wages, prices, the amount and the kind of consumer goods available on the market, are many faced by means of exploitation. By preventing nations to run their own trade and dictating what to produce and to whom to sell their products and at what prices another subtle form of exploitation is available. To enforce consumption of certain goods of usually low quality and refusal of others, enforced savings is also a form of exploitation. It is a fact that workers, collective farmers and all the rest of the serfs of the state are not in the slightest interested in fictitious property relations. All they are interested in is the amount and kind of goods they are able to buy for their wages or salaries. To say that the men who are making the decisions are representatives of the interests of the millions is one of the biggest jokes in history. It is inconceivable that men who have worked their way up to the top of the hierarchy under Stalin and are holding life-long offices know and represent the interests and the will of the masses. The formulas with which they are justifying that they are the only and final arbiters of truth, not only in economic and social affairs but also in science (Lysenkoism) and in the arts and in literature contradict the rational foundations of Marxism. The reality and practice refute the ideas on which the system actually is supposed to rest. In this country communism is a symbolic expression of a certain nationalism and most people regard it as a honorary code by which the members of the hierarchy identify themselves. They are regarded by the majority as the very men and women who displayed the strongest will and ability to secure for themselves the maximum of material advantages and power. After Lenin had built up a conspiratory [*sic*] party of professional revolutionaries

and was faced with the problem of seizing power in
the most despotic and backward country of Europe
he forged the formula of the identity of working class,
CP and the state. This formula represents a method
to enforce industrialisation by authoritarian means
in underdeveloped countries. The irony of history is
that this formula perpetrates the oriental tyrannies
which Lenin wished so passionately to destroy. The
identity of class, party and the state has in this part of
the world as much credence (credibility) as the holy
trinity of father, son and the holy spirit. Marx spoke
of the dictatorship of the proletarians as a transitional
stage to a classless society and to the fading away of
the state as an instrument of oppression. Those who
have monopolized some bits and pieces of the ideology
have after 50 years socialism completely abandoned the
provisional character of one party rule, of dictatorship
of a few, and are now trying to convince us that the
monopoly of unitary power in the hands of a few men
is the very essence and the forever-lasting fundaments
of what was once regarded as a half way house. At this
point the Russian doll comes to my mind. Have you ever
seen a Russian doll? A small doll fits into a larger [one]
of exactly the same colour and shape and that one fits
into a still larger one and so on. You get a whole series
of exactly the same dolls of different dimensions. And
so we are suffering in serfdom and captivity in spite of
the good intentions of Lenin from a monstrous oriental
despotism, the largest edition of the former Tsarism.
[sic] That's why I am smoking 30–40 cigarettes daily
and consciously fostering my lung cancer or myocardial
infarction preferably. I am often thinking of suicide by
taking an overdose. There is so little joy and beauty in
our life – I mean the life of an aged intellectual – that
death appears as a welcome redemption from eternal

want, monotony, drudgery, boredom and sordidness. I
wish I could share your faith!

Yours cordially

Paul

PS. I have just finished with the last sheet of air mail
paper which is not available in this country. Do you
think you could send me a block of it? I have plenty of
envelopes.

98

Woodthorpe, York England
8th September 1971.

My dear Paul,

My English friends tell me that my typing is appalling
but they can decipher it if they are aware of the
keyboard. It would seem that I shall have to send you a
typewriter so that my letters become clarity its very self.
    We were glad to receive your cards. Enid has a
childish delight in picture post cards. They are all lined
up over the gas fire which has a long mantel in what
we variously call the living room or the sitting room or
the lounge or even sometimes, when we are on our best
bourgeois behaviour, the withdrawing room though Enid
says the kitchen fits the last description rather better.
    We have just had a week of sunshine and been
gadding about with David and Margaret and infant
Laura. Before that we had five people and now all is
quiet. Even the vacuum carpet cleaner is stilled. All is

quiet save for the heavy thunder of this machine. I'm sure as you are much the stronger man you should have it to thunder defiance in the dead of night and through the autumn stillness. I suppose you use a Czech machine – are the letters the same and can you use a German one with equal facility? Mysteries to me.

The question of faith is very ad rem. Belief in a Godhead implies that all is well or bad with the world though the world may not be all well or bad with you. Christ once [and] for all offered salvation or hell, rather predetermined. You have only to sit tight and hope and pray and believe because fundamentally you can do nothing else. Even when l was a Christian I was not so placid in the face of evil. Social evil attracts my attention much more than individual sins. I was neither Pelagian nor Augustinian. In the end the atrophied Church doing nothing about social evils dragged me away. But I do not believe as the liberals of the last century [did] that we are inevitably on the way to progress and that by ignoring the problems of the world we shall or our children will find that they have disintegrated. Men achieve through struggle personally and much more through cooperative struggle. This struggle in different times takes somewhat different forms, but in the exploiting societies these forms are more or less paralleled. We now have a chance through the increase in science, technology and education and intelligence to found a more equitable society. But the existence of those things and qualities does not inevitably bring about the qualitative change that is necessary – to wit, the handing of all controls to a generally progressive democracy. The last enemy to be destroyed in our times is capitalism, which with its political circumscription of the human and technical potential abundance can and does bring misery to the masses. The social force opposed to the capitalist force is the working class in all its varied sections – from manual to technological and scientific. Either this class is forced to rouse itself by some crisis or other or it will as it did in Germany become the dead slaves of the system. This is a necessity with them, for them if they wish to be emancipated. People like you and us are partially emancipated. That is in capitalist society. It is this partial emancipation that made all the educated people flee from C-S to capitalist countries. But they cannot find consolation for their children there.

The revolution is no ABSOLUTE NECESSITY. Attempts at it might well fail for a variety of reasons – Ghana, Guatemala, Mexico and sometimes being partial are worse than the previous state. The necessity lies in there being only [one] way for England and France and Italy – through the working class. There is no absolute necessity that they should take advantage of the 'right' crisis or even if they do that it should be successful. When the organised masses come largely to believe that something has to be done, that a fundamental change is absolutely necessary then if they are organised enough they will succeed. I do not adore every working man or Marx or Lenin, but I have a respect for them when they are devoted to throwing off this utterly beastly low lot.

I should not expect the withering away of the state while imperialism [exists] with all its hatred for any new society based on something better than it itself provides. Nor should I expect any withering away in the sense that the people must be given more and more responsibility while this crowd are in power. They really do believe they are the True Sons of Correctitude. They [offer] new Papal Infallibilities – they proclaim the Russian model as the eternal and ONLY model of socialism, they proclaim that directives are the sole source of what is right in every sphere. They are not only taking the steam out of every cultural development in some parts of their demesne, but by their stupid lust for power they are delaying and frustrating the very developments that some of them quite sincerely hope for.

No country run on the constant surveillance of the security police, informers, and so forth can flourish democratically.

Yes, it is quite true that Lenin and I think Marx too, made the State and the Proletariat and the Party synonymous. Lenin in his last two years or maybe three was realising that something had gone wrong with this equation in practice. While he was lying utterly frustrated by being able only to dictate for 5 minutes every twelve hours and the great thinkers Kamenev, Rykov, Bucharin[258] etc were concocting plans for the future of the USSR etc., Stalin, about whom they laughed in their beards and whom they twitted when he suggested some theoretical proposition, was forcefully gathering round him the nucleus of a power loving government. The completely devastated country made this possible. Because of the necessity of instant decisions which could be made in the military field and then in the economic and agricultural area Stalin was able, as soon as Lenin was dead, to build as he wanted, as best as he was able. And he wanted very much and he was very able. Once Trotsky – a very able man with the help of Lenin but rather given to being [...] in far away places – was got rid of then his way was clear and the trials of the thirties were believed by most.

Men when they want to better the condition of

---

[258] Nikola Lev Borisovich Kamenev (1883–1936), Alexei Ivanovich Rykov (1881–1938) and Ivanovich Bukharin (1888–1938) were leading Bolsheviks. All were executed on the orders of Stalin. Only Bukharin could claim to be a significant thinker and author.

mankind are often quite credulous. Besides those left alive wished to feed.

[Whilst] Yagoda, Yezhov[259] and Beria[260] have gone with most of their extremes, the core of the system remains.

C-S is the worst treated of the 'colonies'. But if Moscow could bring Y-slavia and Romania to heel C-S would have some relief. At the present time not only are the intellectuals pressing for greater freedom of expression, an enlightened all Russian science, and not merely of those areas in which truth is absolutely essential, [for] greater respect for truth in history, for greater freedom of social expression in literature and plays, but an increasing section of the people [are also] generally growing restive about the immense expenditure in arms and armies and concomitants. Outside Russia there is a great reluctance of the fraternal parties to openly inveigh against SU govt, but the necessity of their having a decent appeal to the people [sentence unfinished]

Even the Jews were able to demonstrate in the hall of the minister of the interior for two or three days and were not imprisoned. Some years ago Mrs Daniel was given two years for demonstrating on the street against the seven years her husband had got.[261] There is among some economists a demand for greater control of many important factories. Some work like my transistor set is

---

[259] Genrikh Grigoryevich Yagoda (1891–1938), born Yenokh Gershevich Iyeguda, and Nikolai Ivanovich Yezhov, or Ezhov (1895–1940), served under Stalin as Directors of the NKVD – the Soviet Union's security and intelligence agency. They oversaw the trials of the old Bolsheviks. Both in turn became victims of the great purge and were executed.

[260] See note 189, p.307.

[261] See letters 62 and 64, notes 134 and 140, where the details are more accurate – though there is no record of the two-year sentence to which Leslie refers more than once.

somewhat shoddy, absenteeism is considerable, petty pilfering from state shops not unknown and among Party bureaucrats some material corruption. All the world knows that in the SU there is a very wide distribution of a periodical which gives all sorts of information about the general set up, the treatment of prisoners, [and which] produces novels and plays that are not acceptable to that body of corruption, the Writer's Guild.

There are all sorts of other indications in East G., Hungary and some sections in Poland of a move towards what is generally called liberalising the effect of this stupid government.

1 am not surprised that your govt refers everything of importance to Moscow. In the first place they are largely the same bad lot that D. got rid of save Husak and they did so badly before that they must be shockingly aware that will do badly again. Besides 'doing well', or more correctly 'doing correctly', can only be judged by the Muscovites.

I do NOT think either morally or governmentally the present S. govt. is an equivalent of the tsarist govt. I do think this is impossible because the condition of the govt in all and every respect is different – and immensely better. I am inclined to think that C-S is being robbed in a new colonial way. Not of its raw materials as the caps did in the old time, but of their consumption goods.

I detest the fact of the immoveable govt and also that it allows the people no say in what happens to the GNP, but much more than that I detest the refusal of the govt to ask the people what quality and sort and diversity of GNP they wish to produce.

And above all I completely blame and detest the govt for turning out a man and woman not accustomed to thinking for itself. The new man is there, he is not the capitalist old man but he is by no means the new man that continually develops, redevelops, creates and recreates himself as he sets his body and his intelligence to the tasks necessary in building the New Society. But I am quite sure the new man as he is will begin to demand the opportunity for his children that this new society, however imperfect and unsatisfactory, makes possible.

The men hurling bombs in Northern Ireland sense the possibility and they hurl them at the old society; the men gathering at their work in the first ever effort of worker's control in Britain sense and many know what they are doing – they are shaking the old. The harder you have to shake and the more despicable and implacable their opponents are, the lower down the ladder will our new society start. Men do not make glorious things out of economic ruin. They are not wholly free of the corruption that clings to them. We are all weighed down by our bloody history.

You possess one of the most vigorous minds and one of the most articulate it has been my happiness to meet. I cannot let you become a psychopath. Destruction is nonsense, sheer depravity. We see endless destruction all around us. We need every loving soul, every active body, every issuing mind in our struggle for the future of humanity and in their midst the future of our own children. I am literally appalled that you should be so at the mercy of your enemies that you have allowed them to condition you to regard self-destruction as your only possible relief. It is monstrous. We, people you have never seen, depend upon you and your own family depend upon you for comfort and intellectual encouragement and moral support. You simply must not do [it]. Only very recently a friend of forty years has just died from lung cancer. Can you deliberately, quite deliberately visit this upon me again in my old age? Can you leave your wife uncomforted? Your grandchild appalled for the rest of his life? The conditioning has been allowed to go on too long. Even the lowest of the proletarians lying in a Spanish or a Greek jail, even those being tortured to the very end throughout the world for their views do not subside and collapse. No Stalinist and no bloody minded capitalist would cause me to think that the best thing to do with my life is exactly what they want me to do. Throw your drugs away. Rejoice in your poverty in your freedom of mind and throw your cigarettes away too.

I am writing about the book.

Speaking of books, I understood from you that it was useless our trying to send you any. Is this still so???????

Some young people have been into York and procured some airmail paper which I am sending you. They had only paper with lines, but you can ignore them. Airmail paper is not much used in this country. I can send you any amount of the kind of paper which I am now typing on. It is rather cheaper than air mail. Would it be of any use? I could also send some thicker as enclosed and upon which I often write to you any good?????

Could we come to see you? Could you possibly put up with a three-quarters blind man? Where could I, I mean where could WE stay in Usti?? Would it help?

We think of you all with deep affection.

99

Woodthorpe, York, England
18 September 1971.

My dear Paul

I have a pile of unanswered letters on my desk, but
more often than not when I think of writing letters I
almost always think of you. This tendency, however, will
not necessarily make a good letter writer. I am a feeble
indisposed carcase, too idle to rise and to slow to work.
There is a lot, a lot to write about. The aristocrats of the
newspapers, the compositors etc are thinking of saving
the population from the trivialities of the English press
by going on strike because their differential in wages
is not different enough from the lower breed who do
something else. Twice the anti-miracle has occurred
which means that our Times was actually thee hours late.
In addition to this national calamity we have Mr Heath
declaring to all those on the face of Europe that the hour
is near, that there is no time to be lost, and that the basis
of our European unity is of course Defence. After Mr
Healey,[262] now silent but wandering here and there like
the ghost of Iago – saying that he could puff the Soviet
fleet off the waves of the Mediterranean – we may well
count our future hard.

I am happy to say that they are now miserably
contemplating the tariff wall that their dear friends in
the USA, one 'tricky Nicky', has erected for the benefit
of the USA. This has put all the financiers of Europe in
a flutter. While they all obviously intended sooner or

---

[262] Denis Winston Healey, Baron Healey (1917– 2015), Secretary of
State for Defence 1964–70 and Chancellor of the Exchequer (1974–79).

later to declare a sort of tariff war on the USA when they had got their European house in order, they were not expecting their dear friend to do the dirty on them so quickly.[263]

The Tory's life like that of the policeman is not a happy one. No sooner than they settle one contumelious swagger of the miserable never satisfied workers they take over the shipyards or force them to nationalise something else. And on the same day [?],000 steel workers get the sack, making us nearer to the million unemployed in this land of fair does and dear beer.[264] Meanwhile the nightmare of Northern Ireland shows itself farther from settlement. They have let out 100 from their internment camp but refuse to let out any more, though at least half of the rest are about 60 or over. On the other hand the democratic forces are a little splayed out. The Republicans do not agree with the Labour Party and Social Democrats do not agree with either of those, and none of these are in love with the shooting and bombing that goes on endlessly with more than bloody success to the bombers and shooters. All the working class democrats including the CP are doing their nut because of the shooting and blaming both Govts for doing nothing more than exacerbate the whole bloody and miserable condition. The whole thing

---

[263] On 15 August President Nixon, in what was effectively a devaluation of the dollar, suddenly suspended the right of foreign countries to convert dollars into gold and imposed a 10 per cent surcharge on imports. This led to the emergency closure of the foreign exchange markets in London.

[264] The official jobless total on 23 July 1971 was 829,181, but *The Times* reported that with 400,000 young people about to leave school the effective total would soon be more than one million. The figure given for the redundancies among steel workers is unfortunately not clear in the original typescript, making it difficult to establish to whom Leslie refers.

is a disgrace that has been created by fifty years
of misrule.

Meanwhile we have a statement from the CP and
Govt or Poland that reads rather like [a] Bill of Rights[265]
and the like, which if it has substance seems a fairish start
to a new era. It is a shocking thing that the old brigade
have to indulge in blood letting before their atavistic
minds work at all. This development is a nice little bright
star the which I almost pray will be magnified by the
new freedom of criticism and suggestion that the people
of Poland have been offered. Actually, really actually
the people have been asked to say what they want,
what they expect. They are asked [to] believe that their
creative energies as [are?] necessary to the increase of the
standard of living including thank heaven more protein.
Our beloved Muscovites will think about this. In reply we
can only say that even Poles have to be fed and clothed if
they are to make ships at a cheap price and submarines at
any price. I do really look forward to seeing what happens.

You will probably learn that in the Times today there
is a Q. and Answer interview between the Italian Vie
Nueve and Comrade Smrkovsky on the present condition
of C-S.[266] It is very honest and very revealing and pretty
well depicts what I would expect. The harrowing, utterly
imbecile condition to which the top party people have

---

[265] On 6 September the Polish Communist Party published for general
discussion a draft programme of radical reforms designed to meet
most of the demands made in the wake of the previous year's riots.
These included constitutional changes to give greater power to the
Government, parliament and local assemblies, and continued efforts
to normalise relations with the Catholic Church.

[266] A shortened version of the interview was actually in the previous
day's edition of *The Times*. Josef Smrkovsky (1911–74), elected
Chairman of the Czech National Assembly in 1968, was one of
the most popular of the reform leaders. He was expelled from the
Communist Party in 1970.

been reduced and the utter waste of many specialists cannot be condemned too much. The utterly spurious cry of this fatherland or that motherland is in danger from the class enemy has not only resulted in the reduction of science and democratic government but will retard the advancement of the economy in the same way that Russia has been retarded. It could now be conclusively proved that the economy is nothing like what it would have been had the people been allowed to work with a sense of dedicated purpose, freely giving their inexhaustible energies. And of course we have been reading Medvedev whose description of the circumscribing of science and scientists and their relative backwardness makes a good honest comrade grind his teeth. So while Med certainly embellishes the imperialist scientists with far too much altruism, forgetting that science is not 'free', particularly in the USA, [not] to take advantage of what the 'other' scientists offer is too stupid for words. The isolation of science from the immediate welfare of the people in capitalist countries is wicked enough ... but it is at least to be expected; but to find that in the USSR the quality of scientific achievement is often, though not always, dictated by people who have long since forgotten what active research is like and by bureaucrats who foreshorten the areas of science and scientists is utterly stupid and very disadvantageous to the people. Over and over again scientists who are quite incapable of writing an advanced paper are preferred for international meetings and conferences while the internationally known and internationally invited scientists are refused [permission to travel] on some paltry peccadillo. When permission is refused the scientists in question are asked to write themselves that they are too busy. Paltry, deceitful and utterly non-socialist. Enemies of the people, that's what they are.

The next day all bright and sunny.

The Soviet Weekly made no mention of Khrushchev's benefits either to the Top Lot in Stalin's time or to his Secret Speech,[267] which disentangled a few misconceptions in a few minds about a certain murderous autocracy. Though l might say some thousands even in England regard [it] as a great disloyalty to a Party that must never be criticised, at least honestly, by those not in the Party. They may of course criticise dishonestly, which they often do. That can be battled with, but that the real morality of socialism should show through the bloody hotchpotch which is regarded as a moral sort of government is not to be regarded as anything less than damnable, anti this and anti that. Poor old Nikita, the tool of Stalin, laughed at and insulted by Brown[268] and Eisenhower, scoffed at by the Chinese and hated by the Old Gang who shall sing what praise the remnants of thy self respect demands? Perhaps those poor wretches that streamed from twenty or more concentration camps and eventually when they did not die found a little foothold in a society that even then only half understood what had happened. And also perhaps a few lovers of truth, a few historians and those very few that can forgive everything however black it may be.

Did you get the airmail paper? I hope you did because it cost twice as much to send as to buy. Our new currency is the very devil and is a savage means

---

[267] At the Twentieth Congress of the CPSU on 24–25 February 1956 Khrushchev delivered a report in which he denounced Stalin's crimes and the 'cult of personality' surrounding Stalin.

[268] George Alfred Brown, Baron George Brown (1914–85), formerly Foreign Secretary and Deputy Leader of the Labour Party until the 1970 General Election.

of depriving us of a definite part of or our livelihood. A telephone call which used to cost only 3d is now 2 new pence which equals 5d old rate. Peaches now 4 new pence equals 9 and a half old pence were once 5 old pence etc. etc. Greengrocers who were once satisfied with 33% profit now make 100%. Despite nearly 900,000 out of work, profits for the last financial year have sent the City rejoicing to all their suburban wives and concubines. Lower salaries are depressed whilst workers have to fight for every penny they can get and also for many of their jobs. Everywhere everybody has to watch the gross politicians – there is no other salvation.

Oh yes. Please ask David's mamma if she would like us to get anything for David as the winter approaches and please be sure to tell us his height and his chest measurement. Last time you absolutely refused to do this so that we never knew that his underwear fitted or not.

Enid sends her love to one and all and I send my respectful salutations to all those who need them.

100

Woodthorpe, York, England
28th September 1971.

My dear Paul,

Every day for too long a time we have said to each other no letter from Paul. To our relief we find that you have been immersed in the waters of Bulgarian Lethe and in methods of administering Lethe to those who lie trustingly in your antediluvian operating theatre. We rejoice and are exceedingly glad that your soul requires no more propellent to the point of Salvation than a consistent nagging about too many cigarettes per diem than that of any other rather stupid healer who cannot be bothered to heal himself. We, ourselves no longer a prey to this abysmal habit and therefore full of virtue, will consider it our parts and duties to nag you for all we are worth – providing of course that we remember. Meanwhile we must assure you that we have the pleasure of your friendship for so much longer the longer you do not smoke. For the moment a little thought – most of us are well concerned with the integrity of our minds, but we give little thought to the integrity of our bodies until the so and so things go wrong. On the relation of body and mind see my next effusion.

You never answer my questions. Therefore I am sending in this letter five pounds sterling for David and David's beautiful Mamma and also his lovely Father for Christmas. You think this is early for Xmas. It is never too early to save. I hope as life goes on he will be able to raise his voice strong and clear and call Attention, Attention, a seat for every man and woman in the whole wide world. I shall feel comforted if you will oblige me by depositing a gentle grandfatherly kiss on his noble brow. I am very conscious that you are deprived of modern English books. I regret this almost daily, but unless the KGB raises its utterly fatuous embargo on the most innocent literature we are at present completely at a loss what to do. Of course we have not been told that there is any embargo for these clots work in their own gutter-based ways. Our own reading is somewhat circumscribed by my inability to read and Enid's inability to read aloud for the long stretches that we once enjoyed. This is largely due to the inroads of emphysema about which no-one seems to be able to do anything. I am largely confined to my book talking machine whereon I perforce have to place those books provided for one.

My machine has gone wrong again. I shall have to send you the carbon copy. Never mind so long as you can read it.

On October 6th we go for ten months to Shrewsbury where I am to undergo a course of treatment at the hands of an osteopath to persuade my retina to burgeon and flower as alas it has never burgeoned and flowered in its whole lifetime. People with the intention of making me feel sorry for not being a policemen or a day labourer with pick and shovel are now telling me that I have read too much in times past. How I now regret that I have not in times past read seventy times seven more than I have. It is ridiculous to only discover your potential at the age of 70. It also makes one very impatient.

Where were we? Oh yes the Osteopath. All my orthodox med friends say what a waste of money of the which I have actually very little. But as I go blinder and blinder I must try something. This osteopath chap is very impressive but not in a bogus way and he has been successful with some and promises me next to nothing. All in the game of deception you say. Perhaps. We'll see.

My address from October 6th will be Abbey Gardens Hotel, SHREWSBURY and I hope I have spelled that correctly.

I went to a Party meeting last night, the first for over two years. The Party Lambs somehow got separated from the Ultra Left Wolves consisting of some Maoists, some International Socialists and International Marxist Group and a one time member of the CP, all of whom told us how wrong we were. Apart from the ultra dirt of these ladies and gents I was struck by their parrot sort of knowledge that was fairly common in Party circles in the UK before the War and until 1956 when a number had to begin to think. The speaker was the Organiser of

the Party, a Scotsman, who displayed some flexibility
in dealing with the Wolves but who to my mind was
perhaps a little, perhaps forgivably, superficial.[269] He
must have been very tired because the anti-Tory feeling
among many millions in this country together with
the Upper Clyde and Northern Ireland crises sent our
speakers scurrying up and down as fast as British Rail
can carry them.

Interruption. No idea where we are.

I have a mind now like an ancient sieve which
suddenly gives way letting everything drain away.
I am probably no longer capable of a new idea or
assimilating one. That I suppose is why I am more
interested in Life on a Mediaeval Manor than in life
in a modern igloo. You must provide me with a new
thought some day.

Yes, I should like to come and rescue you and
I think it had better be in September 1972, which
is Sept next. Then I should leave this godforsaken
typewriter behind. I might even be able to make out
your features if that Theosophist answers the right
conundrums. Oh yes. If you prefer reading English I
suggest that you read some of our greatest novelists:
Jane Austen, upper class 18th to early 19th C writer,
George Eliot 19th C. Titles Adam Bede, Felix Holt. On
and off we are reading Thackeray circa 1870. Or I can
offer you the best of Engels?? Do you know the short
stories and the Barrack Room Ballads of Rudyard
Kipling? The hardest thinking modern (contemporary)
novelist I know is Graeme Green [sic]. I have just read

---

[269] Gordon McLennan, later General Secretary of the Communist Party
of Great Britain.

The Power and the Glory for the second time. For the upper class in an entirely different light Evelyn Waugh, another TC. I am waiting rather impatiently to renew my acquaintance with Descartes. We have been invited to a conference of Med Practitioners in York and now we cannot go.

101

Usti nad Labem, Czechoslovakia
4th October 1971.

My dear Leslie and Enid,

Thank you very much for your letter of 18.9. You are always one letter ahead of me because I am able to take to letter writing only on weekends. I am always looking forward to this hour of stock-taking and talking to you. While you have again and again such a lot to write about I have nothing special to report. We are, after all, a special sort of information processing system and if input is lacking you can hardly expect any output.

I am very glad that you took notice of the interview Joseph Smrkovsky gave to the Vie Nuove and that someone spoke up for us and had to say the truth. I am afraid the bulk of the people around me, doctors, sisters and orderlies, are virtually bereft of all political interest and drowned in a deep and merciful torpor. They mostly failed to notice this event. I on my part didn't know about the statement of CP and the government of Poland, which according to you reads like a bill of rights. Our CP and the government is also soliciting participation of those who have hitherto been passed over in silence in view of the elections

in November. Anaesthetically speaking a sudden
emergence from a deep coma, after the patient has
been heavily drugged, is most unlikely. Congratulatory
and complacent orations are the least suitable means
to exercise the ghost of actively stirring millions of
workers and students. No one, however, doubts that the
only list of candidates will receive 99.9 % of all votes
in the November elections – as everything is precisely
as it has always been. Moreover, the image of pre-
established harmony, the price extorted in 1968 and
1969 for appeasement, has become a vested interest
of nearly all of us. So there will be no backsliding into
pandemonium.

The recent utterances of Leonid Brezhnev in
Yugoslavia could drive half barmy those who still expect
principles of marxism-leninism when there are none. I
have never been able to understand how so contradictory
policies can be deduced from the very same principles.
When the armed forces of 5 socialist states entered the
territory of another socialist state without the consent
of the party and the government of that state, everyone
who dared to use his intelligence without external
guidance saw in this act an infringement of the principle
of national independence and non-interference. It is
difficult to quote from memory, but I remember clearly
that the gist of the many fine speeches delivered and
the statements made in cold print in justification of
that act was that national sovereignty had to give way
[when] the common interest of the other socialist states
and of socialism itself is at stake. Now it has been said
at Belgrade that this overriding principle has never
been invoked. There was and still is only one road to
Socialism for C-S. But His Lordship is now granting
to the nations of Yugoslavia the right to travel by a
different road to the same goal, provided the painful

and thorny question of C-S is not being considered any longer.[270] I am weary of all these questions of principles and of all the diabolical complexity involved. It is very easy to enunciate principles, but to live up to one's cherished principles and observe them in the daily piling up of sorrows and anxieties is, indeed, the most difficult task we have to face as individuals. It would be ludicrous to demand consistency of politicians, but how much consistency, integrity and resilience ought to be demanded of individuals whose livelihood depends on being a part of the hierarchical power structure? I am at the moment much more concerned with the sovereign responsibility of the individual than with political sovereignty. The regime is tightening up enforcement of old regulations and is making new regulations for committing everyone to serve its aspirations. As head of a department I am holding a certain rank, and I am now being compelled to file a political profile of every member of my department together with an efficiency report. No medical seminar must be held without a political review. I am very worried about these new regulations as I don't want to lend myself to advertising or to the perversion of truth.

I had now several letters from you and I got the air-mail paper alright. I am very sorry for having caused you unnecessary expenses as I only now found out that the postal rate for air-mail letters to European countries

---

[270] President Brezhnev arrived in Belgrade on 22 September 1971. The next day he delivered a speech to factory workers in which he basically said that while the present organisation of social life in Yugoslavia did not meet with the approval of Soviet communists, he was against someone imposing their own methods on others, and that the doctrine of limited sovereignty which had been used to justify the invasion of Czechoslovakia was a myth. See *The Times*, 24 September 1971, p.6.

is the same as for ordinary mail. In view of all the kind services you have rendered us already I hesitate to send you the measurements of David. We are happy with your letters which bring us hope and comfort, humour and courage, of which we are in great need!

With love and best wishes to you all
Yours sincerely

Paul

PS. Apart from a postcard from Germany I have no news from my brother in England.

102

Usti nad Labem, Czechoslovakia
12th October 1971.

My dear Leslie and Enid,

I feel very mean for keeping you waiting again for my reply to your remarkable letter of 28.9 containing a special note. We were as astonished as embarrassed by the benefits received. I have to thank you on behalf of Ian, Zdena and David. You are very hard hit with your near-blindness, and in spite of the expenses involved in the treatment of it you are attending to our worries and to our David. This is to me an astonishing and unique example of kind-heartedness and generosity. Now I am blaming myself for having confessed to you my occasional depressions and provoked you thus to the notion that you have to send some provisions to these poor beggars. For nearly a week I have been attempting

to compose a letter which would meet yours squarely
in fluency and richness of metaphors and delicate wit.
I failed utterly and I declare myself defeated. The more
things are going out of focus for your sight, the wider
and more sparkling is the spectrum which your inner
eye is encompassing. My walk of daily avocations is stale
and desolate. My life is devoid of books and pictures,
let alone stimulating social contacts. My resources are
drying up. My intellectual wardrobe consists chiefly of
plagiarisms from the few English and American writers
whose books found their way into my library. Although
there are still some untouched paperbacks such as, for
example, Adam Smith, The Wealth of Nations, gathered
in 1968, I have to conclude that you have assimilated
them all and it will serve no useful purpose to unpack
them. Of the books you mentioned in your last letter I
think, I should like only Graham Green's The Power and
the Glory. There is no reason why it should not pass the
embargo. As my mind is blank I shall confine myself to
a few news and sentiments and desist for the time being
from commenting [on] the very interesting developments
in the Morning Star and the coming congress of the CP of
your country. I am going to a town in southern Bohemia
tomorrow to attend the annual scientific meeting of the
Czech Society of Anaesthetists. I have prepared a paper
which my assistant is going to read there. Two of our
four 'antediluvian' operating theatres – how appropriately
you can put it! – have to be closed for most urgent repair.
It was not the danger of flooding and inundation of
the floor space this time which made closure imperative.
The defective pipes for autoclaving and sterilization
by steam caused the breakdown. As a result we have
to introduce day and night shifts for completing the
ordinary operating lists. My 3 new doctors, among them
a very handsome lady doctor, are already hard on the job

of giving anaesthetics under supervision. Whether they
will all stick to the tedious drudgery and stay on with my
department is not quite certain yet. Without any personal
pretensions, I think, they are liking me as their chief and
teacher. I am entering the premises of the hospital with
fear and misgivings as there is the place where pressure
is aggravating daily. Hardly a day without some sort of
admonitions, directives and/or meetings with compulsory
attendance. It is very difficult under these circumstances
to keep one's backbone straight. With a sigh of relief I am
leaving the place of my work to return to my home where
David is usually greeting me with shining eyes and a lot
of fanciful chit and chat. Although it seems odd to me
that you should undergo treatment with your osteopath
I wish nothing more than his success and betterment of
your condition. There are no osteopaths any more in this
country. Unless I finish this letter now I shall probably
miss my train in the morning!

With love and once more many thanks

Paul and Family

103

The Abbey Gardens Hotel, Shrewsbury, Salop, England
19th October 1971.

My dear Paul
At last I have excavated the typewriter, but what the
result will be will only be revealed in signs, if not in
sense, to you. You will probably be complaining that I
have sent you a series of senseless words. But I will do
my best while Enid takes the sun and a Graham Greene

novel JOURNEY WIHTHOUT MAPS to the post office. We are sorry that the best bookshop in S. had not the Power and the Glory. I think of our own copy residing somewhere in the interstices of our bookcases at home. YOU MUST SAY WHAT BOOKS YOU THINK we might have the pleasure of sending you.

We are grateful for the letters from you, October 3 and 12, and also for three picture cards received rapturously this morning. Enid is now back with the glad news that the postage for paperbacks is cheap. So there.

I am sorry that you have no osteopath in CS. The competent ones do pretty good work in England and the very competent ones do very good work. The orthodox medics do not despise them nor rage against them so much as they used to before the war. Of course like orthodox medics there are comparatively useless extra-orthodox people, particularly I think in some parts of America. My chap has a full waiting room each day, charges very reasonable or low fees and is regarded with some approval by the Town. I will let you know what improvement if any that he makes in my eyesight which this last year has been deteriorating quite a lot. I go three times a week and have my sutures manipulated, my eyeballs manipulated and a little cheerful conversation.

This is a homely sort of hotel that is very busy in spasms. The food range is somewhat narrow but good, with plenty of salads and strong coffee and a drop of whisky in a cupboard in our room. I wish you were here. You could drink my whisky, listen to Medvedev and enjoy the sort of non-conversation that freeborn Britishers indulge themselves in. The weather, generally whether it is wet, too wet, very wet, awfully wet or damn wet. As Lenin said 'The Reason why Englishmen discuss the weather so much is that the weather is the only thing they have in common'.

Mr Kosygin has been pushed down in Canada and that liberal bombast, Trudeau, has proclaimed that Canada is humiliated.[271] I wish it had been Stalin. On my book talker I have just finished listening to Svetlana's 20 letters, now published everywhere, about her life in Russia particularly her first twenty [years].[272] A very emotional woman this, who rather thinks that Stalin got himself wrapped up with GPU[273] et Cie as did also other members of the govt. The A. service gradually got rid of all the old Stalin staff who had been there for years and years, and even tried to get rid of Svetlana's nanny though they did not succeed. But they did succeed in putting the domestic staff on the wages list of the NKVD so that the nanny or child nurse became under Sergeant X. Did you ever? It was interesting to note that Stalin scarcely ever removed his body from [his] room for 20 years. He ate in it, slept in it, had committees in it and shouted at people in it. If he wanted a change he had four other rooms of exactly the same size furnished largely in the same way. He could be very crude and rude to people and was so to his wife, who committed suicide because of the increasing Beria murders. In fact Beria got rid of half Stalin's own family and lots of the old Bolsheviks whom he had round him for a score of years or even two score. Yet S was deeply attached

---

[271] The Soviet Prime Minister was attacked and pushed to the ground by a Hungarian protester on 18 October 1971 as he and the Canadian Prime Minister, Pierre Trudeau, were leaving the Parliament buildings in Ottawa.

[272] Stalin's daughter Svetlana Iosifovna Alliluyeva (1926–2011), later known as Lana Peters, defected to the United States in 1967. She published *Twenty Letters to a Friend* the same year and *Only One Year* in 1969.

[273] Soviet Secret Police 1922–3, succeeded by OGPU, 1923–34 and NKVD, 1934–41.

to both Svetlana and her mother, who was his second wife. Svetlana, now married to a New York tycoon, is an extraordinarily sensitive, deeply emotional lover of nature, believer in God, passionate sort of person. She has been divorced twice, widowed once and married four times and left her children in the USSR. Yet despite all she was TOUGH. As tough as old boots, as we say. But I think a good woman, who made her way through infinitudes of corruption more or less unsmirched though not heroically. Medvedev on the other hand is concerned with the international relationships of scientists, and is particularly determined to prove that the very great restrictions on Soviet scientists is very bad for the USSR financially and technologically. The book is long and is at present dealing with the immense difficulties of anyone not morally pure and politically pure and bureaucratically acceptable to get out of the USSR whatever his scientific rank and standing. In order to get a passport for any sort of visit, however personal or however scientifically important, your application must be started months before the time of departure and must go through laboratory heads, local party, regional party, provincial party and right through a labyrinth in Moscow until it reaches the Exit Department of the Polit B. Even there it can be sunk. In order to ensure that [a] limited number is chosen more are started off, and even at the top elimination may only be by a throw of a coin or some other occult device. More often than not a scientist only gets the GO 24 hours before the plane takes off. BUT he can be stopped at the moment he begins to climb into the plane. Inter alia it is not too good even now for a Mendelian. Poor old Mendel.[274] Oh, that

---

[274] Gregor Johann Mendel (1822–84) was a Moravian scientist and Augustinian friar regarded as the founder of modern genetics. He established many of the rules of heredity.

he had been a Russian. Many Russian papers have to be read at foreign conferences by others than the writers and listened to I fancy by some Russian geneticists that pray for the return of Archangel Lyscnko.[275] One of these second raters was reproached in the report for finding the shops of Chicago rather more attractive than the Conference itself. I well remember reading a half crown Party pamphlet in 1949 about the glories of Lysenko making nineteen to grow where only one grew before and having to resurrect what I knew of Mendel from what is taught to an enquiring theological student and writing to a biologist on the Party hierarchy in London and saying that L. was rubbish and having in reply a letter written sotto voce that of course it would be better to accept it for political reasons. Meanwhile J. S Haldane, one of the foremost geneticists of the day and quite a genius, had to withdraw from the Party.[276] Had I been anything but the modest thing I am and certainly had I been a scientist I should have been compelled to pursue the matter further. I might even have isolated the gene for Comrade Dutt[277] and Comrade Lysenko and got shot in Trafalgar Square on Labour Day.

And now my typing and energy has fled. Thank you for finding time to correspond with me. Your letters are a great blessing to me in particular and my wife in general. Give David and the sax player our love and our affectionate greetings to you both.

---

[275] See note 99, p.187.

[276] J. B. S. Haldane, born John Burdon Sanderson Haldane, Fellow of the Royal Society (1892–1964), joined the British Communist Party in 1942 and left in 1950.

[277] See note 31, p.44.

104

Usti nad Labem, Czechoslovakia
28th October 1971.

My dear Leslie and Enid,

In reply to your letter of 19 October from Shrewsbury
I again address this note to your home address at York
as I assume you are back from your stay for treatment
at Shrewsbury. Before this letter will reach England the
month of your being away from home should be over.
Your letter was by no means senseless to me, but as
always highly amusing, cheering and welcome. Do you
suggest that the honourable MPs in the Commons and
in the Lords are debating the weather tonight? The only
thing they have in common, according to a witticism
allegedly of Lenin. The whole world is awaiting with
immense curiosity with how large a majority [the]
government will lead the UK into the EEC. Here the
drab slogan 'United we work and united we shall vote'
is pasted all over the country. If there must be an all
pervasive unity why vote at all? We have, on the contrary
to the British, everything in common – our weather,
our loyalty to party and government, our goose skin[278]
and miseries. There are no divisions and no waverings.
I am calling this the intimidating internecine unity
mentality. No, Enid and Leslie, I would not mind to be
greeted by someone 'Nice morning, doctor, isn't it?' on
my daily walk to the hospital in the foggiest October
mornings. And in the best English tradition I wish to
let you know that as soon as the fog is clearing we are

[278] A reference to President Husak. See letter 9, pp.68–9.

having two hours sunshine and then clouds of smoke from numerous bonfires in the gardens spreading the penetrating, not disagreeable smell throughout the residential quarter. Sky and air are clear and frosty by night while I am sitting in my study, dressed in my slacks, reinforced by a thick dressing gown for the pressure in the central heating is giving just too little warmth to make you feel comfortable. Of everything too little! I am, however, fairly contented, having done my honest best throughout the week, including last Sunday. Now we have three whole days off duty as today is the foundation day of the Czechoslovak republic, called now the day of nationalization. I am free to ponder about the consequences of the admission of mainland China to the UN and particularly about how long it will take before Taiwan will suffer the same fate as Czechoslovakia.[279] But to pass on to your considerations of Mendelian genetics, of the 'Rise and Pall of Lysenko' and the fate meted out to the late JBS Haldane, I should like to mention that I am fascinated by molecular biology without having the necessary knowledge of biochemistry to follow recent research in depth. Strange to think that what we are, we are by a throw of a coin through which our genes have been selected from the pool of our forebears. One of the most exciting books I have read is the book THE DOUBLE HELIX by James D. Watson, published by Weidenfeld and Nicholson in 1969. I understand that Watson has written an enlarged second edition of this book, perhaps under a different title, in the USA which I am eager to read too. Another very attractive book appears to be "FACING REALITY" by Sir John Eccles (Springer, New York, 1970). There must be hundreds of

---

[279] On 15 October 1971 The People's Republic of China was admitted to the United Nations, while Taiwan was expelled.

interesting and good books published each month in the UK of which I have no knowledge. The book reviews on the BBC are lately very poor and deal with fiction only, as against the critical reviews of political books which the Deutschlandfung is transmitting every Sunday for 15 minutes. The price of the above mentioned books is forbidding and I beg you not to spend any more money on our behalf as you have done for me and my family more than any of my close relatives to whom I ought to turn in the first place. We are already too much indebted to you! Anyhow the cheap paperbacks I would select might not pass the 'embargo'. David is suffering from a bout of bronchitis with very troublesome spells of coughing. I feel sorry for the little fellow, but I don't want to feed him with antibiotics for fear to induce drug resistant strains of bacteriae.

I just heard on the news that Britain entered the EEC with a majority of 112 votes.[280] Being loaded down with heavy sorrows and walled off from the world I am neither rejoicing nor unduly depressed by this historic decision. Not a day passing without one or two men shot dead in Northern Ireland makes me thoroughly sick with disgust.

I hope you will move into your home refreshed and with your sight improved!

We are thinking of you both with affection and love
Yours

Paul

---

[280] This is a reference to the House of Commons vote on 28 October 1971 to enter the Common Market. The Treaty of Accession was not signed until 22 January 1972, and that came into effect only on 1 January 1973.

105

Usti nad Labem, Czechoslovakia
29th October 1971.

My dear Leslie and Enid,

I wrote a letter to you yesterday, but got up too late to
post it. In the meantime my wife reminded me to let
you know that the cardigan from the red wool you sent
us one year ago turned out very nicely. Bohumila looks
very smart in it and, what is perhaps the best proof of
a complete success, other ladies in our street are full of
admiration and envy. As I have plenty of time to converse
with you I wish to recapitulate briefly what happened
in October 1913 in Bohemia, Moravia and Silesia which
were then part of the Hapsburg Austrian-Hungarian
monarchy. After the Hungarian regiments left the Italian
front line to defend their own soil, Czech soldiers and
sailors who have hitherto been the most gallant and loyal
defenders of the monarchy became restless and started
to desert either to the enemy or home. The Czech social
democratic party called for a general strike to begin on
October 14th 1918 and for a mass rally on the square
in front of the Old Town Hall at Prague (see coloured
postcards) at which the declaration of independence
was planned to be made public. A proclamation was
widely circulated in all factories and I am going to
translate some salient points from it for you: 'We, the
Socialist Council of the Czech working people, protest
against the export of any further articles of food and
coal from Bohemian lands, against the devastation of
our country and against the slaughtering of our people
at the front... Four years of terrible suffering are ending
now! Our negotiations with men who were instated by

the Imperial ruling power have come to an end. It would be humiliating to continue negotiating with authorities which are not responsible to the people. With one hand they dealt out promises of autonomy, with the other they robbed us ... the hour of independence has arrived. Our will to be sovereign citizens of a free Czechoslovak republic has been recognized and sanctioned by the whole democratic world. (Note: this is obviously an allusion of the fact that Professor Thomas Carrigue Masaryk and the formal head of the Czech government in exile at Paris Doctor Benes had achieved recognition of an independent Czechoslovak state with President Wilson.[281]) Our defence against hunger and death is being supported by the German working people.' (After a warning against the use of force the proclamation continues) 'We can no longer be deprived of our right to live in freedom! Woe to those who would be as foolish to attempt to crush our striving towards a glorious future!'

On October 14th 1918 there were indeed mass demonstrations in most major towns, red-white-blue flags were displayed and the hated eagles and pictures of Emperor Franz Joseph were destroyed and removed from most official buildings. The security forces went into action and managed to prevent masses of demonstrators to reach the square of the Old Town at Prague. However 35,000 workers actually followed the call for a general strike. On that day the MP Sveceny managed to call out [declare?] the independence of the Czechoslovak republic in the suburb Zizkov of Prague. A garrison near Usti mutinied against their Austrian officers and 35 were shot. On October 14th the governor Count Coudenhove

---

[281] President Wilson is still revered for his role in supporting Czechoslovakian independence. There is a statue of him outside Prague's main railways station, which was renamed after him in 1919.

went to the Viennese Court to seek advice. He was told that the policy of the Emperor does not wish a bloody escalation but favours 'autonomous national states under the auspices and conservation of the monarchy as the supreme power'. You must remember that at the time negotiations for an armistice were already well on the way. The Czech Socialist MP Tuszér refused to go to the front lines to persuade the Czech regiments and divisions to hold on and refrain from mutinies and desertions. He, however, accepted the post as ambassador of the Czech autonomous state to the Imperial court! The chairman of the Czech National Council Doctor Rasin made good use of the absence of the governor and demanded the unconditional surrender of Austria-Hungary, working in secret conspiracy with Masaryk and Benes. Most of the other bourgeois leaders of the official Czech opposition were safely staying in neutral Switzerland to await the outcome of the negotiations conducted by professor Masaryk and Benes with the allied leaders and president Wilson. The Czech National Democratic leader Kramar stayed at the 'Hotel de France' at Vienna and was also, so it is reported, on his way to Switzerland! It remained to Doctor Hasin at Prague to constitute a provisional government during the stay of the almighty governor at Vienna. His deputy, a Czech general, agreed to subordinate all security forces to the command of the officials of the strongly nationalistic physical training organization 'Sokol' (Falcon). The resistance movement was concentrated in the National 'Sokol' and all security forces obeyed their commands – this is the best joke of history! In the meantime a member of the provisional government at Prague isolated Bohemia and Moravia effectively from Vienna by stopping trains at the frontiers. The governor Count Coudenhove, however, was permitted to return from Vienna to his office at Prague.

He was arrested on leaving his train at the railway station by members of the stately 'Sokol'. What followed the triumphant return of Masaryk and Benes and others was more or less ceremonial celebrations and manifestations. Here and there the Sudeten Germans caused some trouble, but the birth of the republic proceeded with very few shots fired and only a few victims. Far more bloody was the anabasis of the foreign legion of Czechs fighting their way through Russia to Vladivostok for returning home. They were under constant attacks by Trotsky's Red Army! This is the story of the birth of the Czechoslovak republic on the 28th of October 1918 as my mother told it to me! Affectionate greetings

Paul

[Here Paul inserted some lengthy 'Points from a memoir of Professor Thomas G. Masaryk to Sir Edward Grey delivered in April 1915']

PS: The lesson I am drawing from this excursion into history is that to be in harmony with any power of one's age is politics and politics is noise making and hand clapping and evil. I don't want to belong to any party and don't want to raise my hand for or against anyone. My occupation for the rest of my life will be the humble one of remaining an individual.

Our love and best wishes to you

Paul, Bohumila & David

106

Usti nad Labem,Czechoslovakia
December 6th 1971.

Dear Leslie and Enid,

Ever since the flow of letters from Leslie stopped
I could not help speculating upon the reasons. I
anticipated trouble; and it is very painful to me and
Bohumila to have our worst fears confirmed. However,
Enid's letter of November 29th, speaking of recovery
and fighting off the aggressor once more, makes us feel
easier and is offering hope and consolation. Anyhow
Leslie's condition needs very close watching for some
time to come. We are delighted to hear that you have a
fine grandson! May luck be with you both so that you
can observe a replication of the Parker family genome
growing and developing.

On the day you wrote your letter to us I left
home for Prague for one week of instruction in the
implementation of the far reaching legislation, giving
anaesthesia and resuscitation a far higher status in
our health service system. I stayed with my sister-
in law. Starting at 8am we had lectures, very lively
discussions and demonstrations of audio-visual aids
and programmed examinations every day until 4
o'clock at the Institute of Postgraduate Education at
Prague. During lunchtime I looked at an old copy of
the Morning Star in the common room. There was a
comment on Genet's play 'The Balcony' and a short
notice that no alcoholic beverages are being sold
during the two election days on the 26th and the 27th
of November. But the 27th is Ian's birthday – his 28th
year – and Zdena managed somehow to get hold of

a bottle of champagne. We voted for champagne and 'many happy returns' after having discharged our civil duty of putting a list of candidates into the voting box, standing freely exposed, in the room next to that of the election commissioners. The fellow who sat behind the desk and showed us into the room was well known to me to and to my wife. In 1945 he had to make out an inventory of property left behind by the Germans in our house for nationalizing it. We soon found out that he procured a good many items of the German property for his own private use. But let us forgive and forget his past history. He should be delivered from all his sins, as far as I am concerned.

Nothing was more cheering to me than to meet old comrades – the senior consultant anaesthetists of this country who have grown old in doing something which has never been done before in this country – although it has been a 100 year old tradition in British medicine, namely to upgrade anaesthesia to a professional task for a medical specialist. Although creeping and itching over my whole body is coming each night, I did not mind the spots and marks from scratching on my skin. I rendered my share in making this gathering of leading anaesthetists a memorable success. Coming home and turning on the radio to which I had no access during my stay at Prague, I learn that a state of war exists between India and Pakistan.[282] Are we going to light our candles in two weeks time from now for Christ or for millions of annihilated Indians and Pakistanis? Why, for Christ's sake, must we start down that road again?

---

[282] Pakistan launched pre-emptive air strikes on 11 Indian airbases on 3 December 1971, leading to India's entry into the Bangladesh Liberation War on the side of Bangladeshi nationalist forces. Pakistan surrendered on 16 December.

I wish you a speedy recovery from all the ills and ailments troubling you at present. In due time you will receive our traditional Christmas greetings.

With all the affection and love we are sending you both the best wishes and greetings

Yours

Paul and Bohumilia

PS Many thanks for the beautiful postcards.

1972

EPILOGUE: JANUARY

107

Usti nad Labem, Czechoslovakia
10th January 1972.

David, my dear Enid

I was very pleased and greatly relieved to receive your
letter because the death of your father had cast a shadow
over our holidays. As soon as I received the wire with
the sad news on the evening of Friday, December 10th I
posted an airmail letter to you all but, I am afraid, I sent
it to the house at York and it apparently has not reached
you. I read the funeral oration with tears in my eyes
which proved the cogency and felicity with which you
composed it. In similar vein I attempted to praise Leslie's
unique personality in my letter to York. I confess willingly
that I derived not only amusement from the constant
intercourse with your father but his way of thinking
moulded my thoughts and on many occasions his letters
dragged my spirits up, as did your excellent obituary. No,
Leslie will never be forgotten and his memory will live on
in this country so distant from England.

On the 14th of December I had to be hospitalised for
the first time in my life at the dermatological department.
On admission the lady doctor diagnosed my condition
correctly as lichen ruber planus, later confirmed by
biopsy. The hospital routine – no smoking except in the
WC, regular meals, enforced leisure – did me a lot of
good. They treated me with aureomycin, antihistamines
and twice daily I had to strip off my pyjamas and
a nurse painted my whole body with lotions and
ointments of many colours. Everyone was very kind and
accommodating to me and on the 23rd I was discharged,
greatly improved.

We had a quiet and peaceful Christmas and New Year. David was nearly out of his mind when he saw the German-made scooter and model railway – made in the GDR – under the Christmas tree. We received about 40 Christmas cards from Germany, England, Canada, Sweden, USA and even one from Australia and one from South Africa. It was nice to feel ourselves not abandoned by our friends abroad. New Year's Eve we stayed at home in a small family party, with David refusing to go to sleep as he wanted to see the fireworks usually displayed to greet the New Year. My son, Ian, was however playing in a cafe till 7 o'clock in the morning to earn a little extra money for himself. Since January 4th I am again working. The year is still young but the old tedium and misery has started once more and wiped away all traces of the holidays. A young lady doctor is leaving my department after her short stay with us, naturally, to join her husband, having failed to secure a flat and a job for him at Usti. A new play by the Swiss writer Durrenmatt, dispatched from Dusseldorf already in November 1971, has not yet arrived and I am giving up hope that it will get through. With no prospects to go to the West in summer, they destroy even the liberty to choose the books I like to read in my spare time. It is hardly endurable to travel on the long blind road and gazing at the same landscape all the time.

Looking forward to hearing from you from time to time and kind regards to Laura and your wife.

Yours sincerely

Paul

SOME REFLECTIONS

Within two years of Paul's death, the communist regime in Czechoslovakia was no more. Its end became as inevitable as it had been unforeseen once the Soviet Union, itself in the midst of political and economic reforms partly inspired by the Prague Spring, made clear that it would not intervene to protect communist governments elsewhere. In August 1989 a non-communist government had come to power in Poland as the result of partly free elections, and in September Hungary opened its borders to the West. On 9 November the East German government yielded to immense popular pressure as crowds swarmed across the Berlin Wall, and the process of demolishing it started. The political revolution in Czechoslovakia began with student protests on 16 and 17 November; it was effectively over by 29 November, when the Federal Assembly deleted the provision in the constitution referring to the 'leading role' of the Communist Party, thus paving the way for its predictable defeat in subsequent elections.

Initiated by students, taken up by theatre employees and actors, members of literary and artistic associations, followed by television employees and finally by the staff of Slovak newspapers (including those of *Pravda*, the Slovak Communist Party's newspaper), Czechoslovakia's revolution was in the first instance the work of the intelligentsia to whose steadfastness Paul had paid tribute. Three-quarters of the population – the silent majority whom at one moment he feared had settled for a certain degree of prosperity – then responded to the call for strike action and the government capitulated. Decades of censorship came to an end and the dissident playwright Vaclav Havel was appointed President of the

Republic by the Federal Assembly, symbolising and confirming the leading role played by intellectuals and cultural workers in toppling the communist regime.

This was a revolution made in Paul's spirit. Had he lived to see it, his joy at no longer being a 'disposable intellectual', a 'displaced person' in his own country, would have known no bounds.[283] It is difficult not to conclude that his death was actually hastened by the debilitating loss of his intellectual independence and the ability to engage freely with colleagues and friends in those Western countries whose history and culture he so admired. Without this, he wrote after Leslie's death, it was 'hardly endurable to travel on the long blind road and gazing at the same landscape all the time'.[284] What Paul experienced as a personal necessity he also articulated as a social imperative. By obstructing 'cultural evolution' the socialist countries, he declared, had no future: 'if you prevent nations from learning, inventing, borrowing, storing and transmitting information no increased utilization of material energy can prevent decay'.[285] For Paul intellectual freedom was a – if not the – *sine qua non* of human progress. 'It can easily be proved,' he told Leslie, 'that 50–90% of all really revolutionary discoveries in science and particularly in the social sciences during the last 20 years originated in the democratic societies of Europe, the English speaking overseas countries and in the USA.'[286]

Leslie observed, somewhat gently, that the elite and some intellectuals tended to equate their cause with

[283] Letter 85, p.328.

[284] Letter 107, p.422.

[285] Letter 93, p.363.

[286] Letter 85, p.327.

the 'WHOLE cause of freedom'.[287] Unsurprisingly he also offered a more qualified view of science in the capitalist countries, noting its 'isolation from the immediate needs of the people'. He was, nonetheless, clear that inexpert bureaucratic control of scientific research in the Soviet Union was 'utterly stupid', damaging rather than sustaining the communist cause. 'The production of a docile people is bound to weaken patriotism, socialist loyalty and retard economic progress and that area of science which the top lot think it is not profitable to pursue.' But unlike Paul, who believed that the communist states were 'passing through a series of ultimately self-defeating cycles ... heralding doom in the end',[288] Leslie maintained that they would eventually recognise the need to open up. 'The top lot,' he wrote, 'may strut for a short moment parading their policemen and their silly soldiers and adorning their feeble minded magistrates with falsities but they cannot in the end withstand the continual needs of a vital part of society which is included in those two neutral words, Culture and Science.'[289] As a member of Amnesty International, he went out of his way to be informed about the treatment of dissidents in Eastern Europe and took heart from the sometimes successful struggles in the Soviet Union for their release.[290] In the last weeks of his life he was hopeful too about apparent indications in East Germany, Hungary and Poland of a move towards 'liberalisation'.[291] Relaying the news of the

[287] Letter 64, p.257.

[288] Letter 97, p.380.

[289] Letter 64, p.258.

[290] Letter 64, p.255.

[291] Letter 98, p.388.

Polish Communist Party's proposals for political reform to Paul, he said that they 'read rather like a bill of rights ... which if it has substance seems a fairish start to a new era'.[292] With the benefit of hindsight we know that, far from being the beginning of a new era for the communist regimes, it was the start of a process leading to their dissolution. In a way both men were right. The Soviet leadership under Mikhail Gorbachev did eventually grasp what was necessary, but about 20 years too late.

How would Leslie have reacted to the outcome? Despite his hopes for the struggle of those who fought to democratise the communist regimes, he would probably have not been surprised. A constant theme of his letters was the folly of trying to build socialism without a democratic and humanist quality. In the lengthy exposition of his political *raison d'être* of 27 January 1969, mutilated by the Czechoslovakian censors, he declared that the two 'gravest problems of communism' were firstly to 'keep alive under pressure from the West' and secondly to address the question of democratic government.[293] Expressing himself more freely in a letter to me about the news from Czechoslovakia in August 1970, he declared that 'It is most revolting to know that the Party in C-S would not stand for a day if it were not bolstered by secret police and the army'. The events of 1989 proved him right on all counts, and no doubt he would have felt that the Stalinist politicians for whom he had the deepest contempt deserved to be kicked out.

Yet there is equally little doubt that, in the larger historical perspective which underpinned Leslie's views, he would have seen the events of 1989 as a profound

---

[292] Letter 99, p.393.

[293] Letter 6, p.60.

setback. Throughout his exchanges with Paul he stuck to the view that the prerequisite for human progress was the ending of capitalist exploitation. The communist regimes which he described as 'primitive', despite all, had accomplished the essential first step.[294] 'Although,' he said, 'the absence of exploitation has produced an infinity of stupidities that must cost lives and produce infinite pain, the absence of exploitation is the first necessary step to the eventual freedom of man that he may move towards sapiens.'[295] It was at this juncture in Leslie's thinking that the two friends, philosophically speaking, parted company. Paul acknowledged their shared and 'deep-rooted common bias', only to continue by saying that this made it easy to 'forgive you that you prefer to express your thoughts and feelings in the idiom of a doctrine which on account of first-hand experience with socialism I regard as a little bit antiquated'.[296] This difference of perspective expressed itself most sharply in their disagreement over Cuba. Leslie reproached Paul for going off 'like a whirlwind' with a catalogue of the sins of a regime born out of the mess created by capitalism and which was endeavouring to sustain a revolution against American pressure.[297] Paul gave some ground, accepting that his criticisms of Fidel Castro were not fully informed, but still insisted that the Cuban regime was 'yet another application of a holistic theory of social experiments which are impossible without suppressing public criticism,

---

[294] Letter 96, p.375.

[295] Letter 94, p.367.

[296] Letter 31, p.137.

[297] Letter 59, pp.234-5.

without destroying knowledge'.[298] A year later Paul amplified his critique of what he perceived to be Leslie's almost religious faith that 'there is a way through history to human fulfilment, a necessity demanding a new way of living without exploitation'. 'There is nowhere,' he continued, 'an inevitableness of the end of capitalism, of the arrival or the doom of communist societies, in short of the course of history ... the belief in historical necessity is very similar to the religious belief that the universe is from the beginning guided by some immanent purpose.' In reply Leslie offered a distinction between necessity and inevitability. While it was indeed necessary for the working class, defined in the broadest possible way, to be emancipated if they were not to become slaves of the capitalist system, nothing was inevitable as revolutions could fail for many different reasons.[299]

Readers of their letters may conclude that in the end the differences between the two men were not unbridgeable, or at least were of little importance. They were at one in their view of the disastrous destruction of freedom in Czechoslovakia, railing together against the humiliation of Alexander Dubcek whom they both admired and trusted. It is entirely possible that had the Prague Spring turned into a socialist summer, they would both have settled for the result. Rarely can such a deep personal friendship have been bonded through intellectual engagement by two people so committed to the greater good. Paul, who could have had a highly successful career and a happier life in the West, chose otherwise. He scorned those former colleagues who had fled and 'turned within the span of one year from

---

[298] Letter 60, p.239.

[299] Letters 97, p.380 and 98, p.385.

Socialists into money grabbing egoists' who had 'lost all interests and connections with their homeland'. Nor was he much impressed by his exiled brother's preoccupation with material possessions.[300] Leslie, for his part, invested a large amount of his diminishing supplies of energy and some of his modest income into sustaining the morale and well-being of Paul and his family. His determination to do so accorded as well with the famous declaration of Paul the Apostle that knowledge and understanding without love is deficient as it did with the in-vogue aphorism of the late 1960s that 'the personal is political'. For Leslie his engagement with Paul was at one and the same time a moral, a personal and a political obligation.

Nothing better exemplifies the inseparability of the personal and the political than the letters themselves. This is most obvious in Paul's graphic descriptions of the impact of normalisation on him, his family and his country. They provide an incomparable insight into the processes whereby an entire country was disciplined. Leslie shared in the experience thanks to Paul's letters; for a veteran communist, albeit a highly independent one, absorbing and acting on its implications was far from easy. 'I think sometimes,' he remonstrated with Paul, 'that you appear to think that because I remain in the CPGB that I approve of the things that many in the C countries are learning to abhor ... You are not aware of the sweat, emotional upset and intellectual shocks we have given ourselves while we have been appraising the situation by seeking knowledge and talking and writing to those people whom we can influence. We have not hesitated to make

---

[300] Letters 16, p.97 and 74, p.291.

our opinion known wherever it has been possible to make them known.'[301] It would certainly have been imprudent of Leslie to have apprised Paul of the characteristically forthright letters which he dispatched to the Soviet Ambassador in London, to the editor of *Pravda* in Moscow and to Palme Dutt, the leading British apologist for the Soviet Union – as well as to the more receptive leaders of the British Communist Party.[302] To its General Secretary went a suitably anonymised extract from Paul's letter of 5 December 1968 (letter 3).[303]

Despite the intensely personal nature of their exchanges and their disagreements, the two men were able to stand back sufficiently to create a perceptive and coherent dialogue which illuminated the hopes and travails of the world which they surveyed. While the reflections of two intellectuals cannot encompass the whole truth, the epistolary journey undertaken by Paul and Leslie offers a unique means of approaching the great issues of their time. An understanding of the past requires an understanding of what made people tick, though this is often beyond reach; with Paul and Leslie we can be in no doubt. That their thoughts have been left to us in letter form is of course the result of circumstances which made no other possible; but they are also the legacy of an age when letters were still valued as a medium of communication and were part of a tradition of crafted dialogue. Both men had an instinctive flair for juxtaposing the personal and the

---

[301] Letter 59, pp.230-1.

[302] Letters to these recipients of 23 July 1968, 30 July 1968 and 21 October 1968..

[303] Letter to John Gollan, 8 December 1968.

political, blending the mundane and the philosophical. They also knew how to challenge each other without ever descending into the facile or nasty repartee that Twitterdom appears to encourage.

The circumstances that gave rise to their letters will never be replicated. Yet in a globalised world in which power and wealth have become ever more concentrated in the hands of the few, the need for greater democracy and social justice has never been more obvious. Leslie's polemics, directed at offensive and disastrous levels of social inequality, at untrustworthy journalists and incompetent politicians would undoubtedly resonate today with many who would not share his politics. Social democracy is in crisis across Europe. Loss of confidence in its ability to protect people from the impact of market forces, while encouraging some unpleasant right-wing parties, has opened up the way for reinvigorated anti-capitalist and socialist movements. The fall of the communist regimes certainly did not herald 'The End of History'.[304] Despite the flood of intellectuals who renounced Marxism in the aftermath of 1989, it is premature to dismiss Leslie's view that Marxism in some form 'would fashion the minds and perceptions of men and women … as long as the Great Corruption weighs them down'.[305] One of the world's wealthiest men, Warren Buffet, has no compunction about acknowledging the reality of class warfare which he says his side, the rich, are winning. Everything is stacked in their favour, as millions of

---

[304] Yoshiro Francis Fukuyama, *The End of History and the Last Man* (1992). In this work Fukuyama argues that the end of the Cold War signalled the 'end point of mankind's ideological evolution and the universalization of Western liberal democracy as the final form of human government'.

[305] Letter 59, p.233.

people well understand.[306] Yet the people do have at their disposition what Leslie called the 'normal political organisations, like local councils and Parliament, that the great majority, despite their fierce criticisms, regard as essentially theirs'.[307] Although he declared himself a believer 'in the councils of the people – on every level from the Army to Refuse collectors from Nurses to teachers and factory girls and boys and students', he could not 'see Communist democracy developing in my own country from anything but capitalist democracy'.[308] He would have been fascinated by the way the resurgence of the socialist left in Britain, unlike continental Europe, is taking place within rather than outside its social democratic party. His faith, as Paul called it, in a better future in which the people would come into their own would surely have been undimmed.

---

[306] *The New York Times*, 26 November 2006, http://www.nytimes. com/2006/11/26/business/yourmoney/26every.html?_r=1.

[307] Letter 32, pp.140–1.

[308] Letter 6, p.61.

INDEX OF LETTERS

LETTER NUMBER	LESLIE TO PAUL	PAUL TO LESLIE	PAGE
1970			
24	7 January		115
25	Undated [*c.*15 January]		117
26		19 January	118
27	24 January		122
28	31 January		125
29	Undated [*c.*7 February]		130
30	14 February		133
31		15 February	137
32	25 February		139
33		2 April	146
34	21 April		149
35	25 April		152
36	2 May		155
37		9 May	158
38	11 May		161
39	17 May		163
40		20 May	167
41	24 May		169
42	*c.*2 June		171
43		5 June	174
44	9 June		176
45		16 June	179
46	16 June		184
47	19 June		186
48	22 June		189
49	23 June		192
50		27 June	194
51	5 July		197
52		15 July	202
53	15 July		207
54	21 July		211
55	23 July		216